Mourning the
Unborn Dead

Mourning the Unborn Dead

A Buddhist Ritual Comes to America

JEFF WILSON

OXFORD

UNIVERSITY PRESS

2009

OXFORD
UNIVERSITY PRESS

Oxford University Press, Inc., publishes works that further
Oxford University's objective of excellence
in research, scholarship, and education.

Oxford   New York
Auckland   Cape Town   Dar es Salaam   Hong Kong   Karachi
Kuala Lumpur   Madrid   Melbourne   Mexico City   Nairobi
New Delhi   Shanghai   Taipei   Toronto

With offices in
Argentina   Austria   Brazil   Chile   Czech Republic   France   Greece
Guatemala   Hungary   Italy   Japan   Poland   Portugal   Singapore
South Korea   Switzerland   Thailand   Turkey   Ukraine   Vietnam

Published by Oxford University Press, Inc.
198 Madison Avenue, New York, New York 10016

www.oup.com

Oxford is a registered trademark of Oxford University Press

Library of Congress Cataloging-in-Publication Data
Wilson, Jeff, 1975–
Mourning the unborn dead : a Buddhist ritual
comes to America / by Jeff Wilson.
    p. cm.
Includes bibliographical references and index.
ISBN 978–0–19–537193–2
1. Fetal propitiatory rites—Buddhism. 2. Fetal propitiatory rites—United States.
3. Abortion—Religious aspects—Buddhism. 4. Buddhism—Social aspects—United
States. I. Title.
BQ5030.F47W55 2008
294.3'4388—dc22   2008017072

9 8 7 6 5 4 3 2 1
Printed in the United States of America
on acid-free paper

This book is dedicated to the many consultants, in both the United States and Japan, who so generously shared with me their time and insights; and to all those, wherever they may be, who have suffered the loss of a pregnancy.

Acknowledgments

It is impossible to list all of the assistance that contingently produces a work such as this one. Most especially I wish to thank the consultants whose generosity made this work possible. Among the many people who assisted me in this capacity I would particularly like to thank Amala Wrightson, Jan Chozen Bays, and Kojima Shūmyō for their assistance over several years of this project.

This book developed from my Ph.D. work at the University of North Carolina at Chapel Hill. The members of my dissertation committee helped me in many ways, large and small. I am especially grateful to Thomas Tweed and Richard Jaffe for many years of support, advice, and critique. I am very fortunate to have had such good advisors. Graduate student colleagues and other members of Tweed's "Living Room Group" were subjected to various early incarnations of this work and their feedback was valuable. Likewise, comments from the Zen Buddhism Seminar at the American Academy of Religion helped me to hone my arguments.

My research was assisted by a Numata grant administered by the Ryūkoku International Center at Ryūkoku University, allowing me to do three months of fieldwork in Japan, for which I am truly thankful. I wish to thank the staff of the Hongwanji International Center for their help and hospitality. Also deserving of thanks are Professor Ikoma Kōshō and the other professors of Japanese religion who took the time to discuss their findings and opinions about *mizuko kuyō*. In particular I want to express my deep gratitude to Professor Tatsuguchi Myōsei of Ryūkoku University, who proved to be both a mentor and a friend.

I thank Oxford University Press and my editors for their hard work, as well as two anonymous reviewers who provided insightful criticisms that have improved this book. I would also like to acknowledge the many ways that my parents and other family members supported me in the process of writing this book. My wife, Kristen, has had to suffer through the process of being a "dissertation widow" to a degree even beyond that of most spouses in this unenviable position. I thank her for her proofreading skills, her patience, and, most of all, her constant love and support.

Contents

Introduction: "Different Meanings, Different Ends," 3

1. "Carried with Jizō Bosatsu": *Mizuko Kuyō*
   in Japanese-American Communities, 19
2. "A Shadow in the Heart": *Mizuko Kuyō*
   in Convert American Zen, 55
3. "We Need to Free Ourselves": Adaptations
   of Convert *Mizuko Kuyō*, 79
4. "Branching Streams Flow On in the Dark": Rethinking
   American Buddhism in Light of *Mizuko Kuyō*, 107
5. "Without Biblical Revelation": Rhetorical
   Appropriations of *Mizuko Kuyō* by Christians
   and Other Non-Buddhist Americans, 129
6. "Thank You Getupgrrl for Giving Me My Mizuko":
   Therapeutic Appropriations of *Mizuko Kuyō*
   by Non-Buddhist Americans, 163

Postscript: "Where Is Buddhism?" 193

Appendix: Convert Zen Centers Performing *Mizuko Kuyō*, 199
Notes, 201
References, 237
Index, 255

Mourning the Unborn Dead

Introduction

"Different Meanings, Different Ends"

Since rituals are actions that lack intrinsic meanings, in terms of both what they intend and what they accomplish, they open the floodgates to an indefinite flow of possible interpretations or symbolic motivations.
—Harvey Whitehouse, *Modes of Religiosity*

The original conception of this book occurred to me around Mother's Day in 2002 during a research visit at the Rochester Zen Center, where I was gathering information on the temple's large and beautiful Japanese-inspired garden.[1] Combing through the temple's archives in their library, I wondered absentmindedly about some small statues arranged on a nearby table. They were figures of Jizō, the "patron saint" of travelers and children, each wearing a little red hat, bib, or cloak. I asked a female priest about them, and thus discovered that the temple had just held a "water baby ceremony," their rather literal term for the ritual called *mizuko kuyō*. I was surprised by this revelation. The historiography on American Zen I had read presented it as a rather unritualistic spin on the Asian tradition, and Rochester Zen Center in particular has always been fiercely proud of its emphasis on strenuous meditation practice and powerful personal breakthrough to enlightened mental states, largely without the "trappings" of Japanese Zen. Hitting the books, I could find no works about the presence of *mizuko kuyō* in convert Buddhism; in fact, precious little seemed to have been said about ritualism in general among this rapidly growing population. The incongruity of those little statues was still nagging at me when I matriculated as a doctoral student in religious studies at the University of North Carolina that fall, and though I didn't know it then, Jizō was going to lead me on a journey around the country and all the way to Japan in search of answers.

Historian of American religion Robert Orsi has noted that "it is one of the peculiarities of an international and transhistorical system of signs such as Catholicism that signifiers rooted in one place and time may detach from the specific historical and cultural ground on which they arose and circulate freely, becoming available in very different cultural environments, sometimes acquiring different meanings in the process of translation, sometimes acquiring different ends."[2] I believe that Orsi's statement applies just as fully to Buddhism as to Catholicism, and that Buddhism's movement into the United States is an excellent contemporary example of this phenomenon. More to the point, I argue in this book that the process and impact of the Americanization of Buddhism is a more complex phenomenon than has generally been described. The story of Buddhism's adaptation in the United States requires simultaneous attention to multiple communities, including differing groups of Buddhists, people marginally involved in Buddhism, and others who are (at least usually) opposed to Buddhism. This complexity can be seen clearly by investigating the way various Buddhists and non-Buddhists use rhetoric, ritual performance, and material and visual culture derived from *mizuko kuyō*, a Buddhist post-pregnancy loss ritual.[3]

A common ritual in Japan, *mizuko kuyō* has gradually come to the United States over the past four decades. In the process, it has acquired some very different meanings and been put to use for ends that readers may find quite unexpected. I examine how and why Americans of different backgrounds—Buddhist and otherwise—have brought knowledge and performance of this popular Japanese ceremony to the United States. In following the American journeys of the bodhisattva Jizō, chief figure of the *mizuko kuyō* ritual, I seek to provide a new window into the life of religious groups ranging from Japanese-American Buddhists to European-American evangelicals. Particular attention will be focused on obscured pathways of emotions, artifacts, and rituals in this transpacific story of international networks and adaptive processes. My hopes for this book, like the cultures it spans, are broad; I hope that it can contribute not only to the fields of Buddhist studies and American religious history, but also to women's studies, ritual studies, and the study of Christian practice in an increasingly pluralistic American society.

A Brief Overview

The exploration of *mizuko kuyō* in America begins in chapter 1 with Japanese-American temples, particularly those of the adjacent Little Tokyo and Boyle Heights neighborhoods of Los Angeles, one of the richest historical sites for Buddhism in North America. Chapter 1 describes the *mizuko kuyō* practices of these temples, focusing especially on the Sōtō Zen, Nichiren Shū, Jōdo Shū, Shingon Shū, and Risshō Kōsei-kai denominations, with some additional information about the Jōdo Shinshū, Sōka Gakkai, and Nichiren Shōshū traditions. I consider the doctrinal positions, immigration patterns, economic forces, generational divides, and other factors that help shape the frequency and manner in which these rituals are conducted. I also consider whether the narrative of Japanese acculturation to American religious patterns is altered by attention to rites such as *mizuko kuyō*.

Chapter 2 moves from the Japanese-American Buddhist community to that of European-American converts to Zen. Despite their popular depiction as unritualistic, these new Buddhist groups have increasingly taken up *mizuko kuyō* as a practice to help women and their partners deal with pregnancy losses, in some cases losses that occurred thirty or more years earlier. In chapter 2, I explore the channels that have brought information about *mizuko kuyō* to these converts, paying particular attention to the female priests and laywomen who have pioneered the practice.

Chapter 3 opens with a description of a *mizuko kuyō* performed at a Zen monastery in Oregon, setting the stage for a detailed analysis of how and why American Zen converts have produced *mizuko kuyō* in ways that differ from the ritual's typical practice in Japan.

Chapter 4 offers a reconsideration of themes in the study of American Buddhism in light of *mizuko kuyō*. A major concern of this chapter is accounting for the lack of attention to ritual in previous accounts of American Zen and for the increasing willingness of this religious subculture to incorporate new ceremonial forms. Places, artifacts, bodies, and emotions are suggested as particularly productive sites of investigation for *mizuko kuyō* and convert Zen Buddhism, and the convert and Japanese-American rituals are examined in a comparative manner.

From Buddhist communities I move in chapter 5 to the wider American culture to examine how and why right-wing Christians, left-wing feminists, and others have appropriated discussion of *mizuko kuyō* to suit their political and religious agendas. How do non-Buddhists learn about Buddhist practices and in what forums do they rhetorically apply this knowledge? What strategic ammunition do abortion opponents, women's rights advocates, bioethicists, and others believe *mizuko kuyō* provides them in America's culture wars? And how do these appropriations change our understandings of both Buddhism and larger American religious and cultural groups?

Chapter 6 examines the surprising phenomenon of non-Buddhist Americans seeking cultural and personal healing related to pregnancy loss through the imaginative and actual uses of *mizuko kuyō*. I consider how foreign practices are used to critique American society, why Americans might turn to unfamiliar religions to address such intimate pains, and how this unexpected strategy may hold implications for the development of new trends in American religious pluralism. In the postscript, I reconsider the lessons learned from these various wanderings and propose new directions for writing the history of American religion, especially American Buddhism.

Japanese Background of *Mizuko Kuyō*

This section provides a brief background on *mizuko kuyō* in Japan for readers unfamiliar with the subject. Since this book focuses on the acculturation of Buddhism in America, it is not my intention to give a comprehensive description and analysis of Japanese *mizuko kuyō*. Readers who wish to explore *mizuko kuyō* in greater depth may avail themselves of two excellent English-language monographs that approach the subject from different angles: William LaFleur's *Liquid Life* and Helen Hardacre's *Marketing the Menacing Fetus in Japan*.[4]

Mizuko kuyō is a practice primarily devoted to the bodhisattva (a type of spiritual being nearly as advanced as a Buddha) known in Japan as Jizō.[5] Never a particularly popular figure in India, his status increased in China, where through his role as a patron of travelers he became associated with the journeys taken through the afterlife.[6] In *The Sutra of the Past Vows of Earth Store Bodhisattva*, a Chinese text from the Tang Period (618–907 CE), he acquires a new role as the savior who ventures into the Buddhist hells to rescue beings trapped there by evil karma.[7] After Jizō was introduced to Japan from China in the Heian Era (794–1185 CE), he acquired a reputation as the guardian of children and childbirth. As all of these various ideas gradually coalesced, Jizō finally took on a distinctly Japanese form as the bodhisattva who watches over children, especially those who die young, ensuring that they will be freed from a suffering rebirth and led to a better place in the afterlife.[8] It is from this role that he was marshaled to preside over *mizuko kuyō* in the latter half of the twentieth century.

In the post-WWII era, Japan underwent massive social and political changes. Among them was a tremendous increase in abortion rates, resulting from a number of factors. Japan faced a sudden population boom as defeated soldiers and colonialists throughout Asia were forcibly repatriated; this was conjoined with a baby boom brought on by the end of the war. Contraception was generally unavailable, unreliable, or expensive, a problem compounded by Japanese society's unwillingness to induce men to take responsibility for their role in conception. The result was a huge increase in unwanted pregnancies at a time when Japan faced food shortages and a decimated economy. The wartime Shōwa regime had been aggressively pro-natalist, but now abortion was decriminalized, and it rapidly became the most common form of "birth control."[9]

With the dramatic rise in abortions eventually came the creation of *mizuko kuyō*. *Mizuko* (literally "water baby/child") is an alternate term for a fetus, though it has largely taken on the meaning of a fetus lost through miscarriage, stillbirth, or, especially, abortion. *Kuyō* is a memorial rite, derived from the verb "to offer," as in to offer prayers and apologies. There are countless varieties of *kuyō* in Japanese Buddhism, and they are among the most common religious practices—everything from ancestors to sushi to broken sewing needles receive *kuyō* rites. The actual procedural details of *mizuko kuyō* differ according to the particular person or group performing the rite, but they fall into several general patterns. Typically a woman approaches a Buddhist priest and requests the service. The ceremony is held in the main worship hall of the temple or a special shrine specifically for *mizuko kuyō* (a *mizuko jizōdō*), where the priest chants sutras, expresses the wish that the *mizuko* will become a Buddha, and prompts the layperson to make offerings of incense, toys, and food (fig. I.1). Often the woman purchases a small, childlike statue of Jizō, dresses it with bibs and knitted hats, and prays to it for forgiveness; in some temples, a memorial plaque (*ihai*), normally used to enshrine ancestors, takes the place of the statue. Alternately, she may place bibs or other objects associated with infancy on a larger temple statue of *mizuko* Jizō (or in some cases *mizuko* Kannon, a female bodhisattva), depicted holding a baby and with children plaintively clutching at his robes (fig. I.2). This latter activity may or may not take place after a full *kuyō* has been performed by a priest, and it represents a more informal, personal approach to *mizuko kuyō* on the part of the laity. Another way in which laypeople ritualize pregnancy losses that is partially outside the aegis of priests is by purchasing votive tablets (*ema*) and writing messages to the spirits or Jizō (fig. I.3). Money may be exchanged at many points in these practices, such as to induce the priest to pray for the *mizuko*, to buy offerings to present to Jizō, or to purchase statues (one per abortion). Many temples post set fees for *mizuko kuyō*, whereas others merely rely on the common Japanese practice of slipping some money to the priest in an envelope (fig. I.4).

Researchers have suggested multiple reasons for why women and their family members practice *mizuko kuyō*. Meredith Underwood has argued that that it offers women a way to represent themselves as caring mothers, and Elizabeth Harrison speculates that *mizuko kuyō* enables people to reestablish family ties with beings now in the spirit world.[10] Both of these impulses remain within the normal religious attitudes of Japanese Buddhists: displaying

FIGURE I.1. *Mizuko kuyō* at Enmanin in Ōtsu. Note the use of chairs for the elderly in this relatively new worship space.

that their abortions are not a rejection of their ordained role as mothers is a "strategy of survival" for women in patriarchal Japan, and re-forming family bonds with the dead is a basic part of Japanese religion, which imagines the dead as departed yet close by, actively shaping the lives of the living and in some sense dependent upon the prayers and ritual activities of their descendants.

A chief concern of *mizuko kuyō*, one represented in both the primary sources and much scholarly work on the ritual, is to prevent spirit attacks (*tatari*). According to many proponents of *mizuko kuyō*, an aborted fetus doesn't just cease to exist—it passes into a sort of nether existence as a ghost and may cause harm to the living, especially its mother or her family. The logic of *mizuko* is explained in a brochure produced by a temple specializing in these rites:

> The *mizuko* resulting from a terminated pregnancy is a child exist-
> ing in the realm of darkness. The principal things that have to be
> done for its sake are the making of a full apology and the making of
> amends to such a child.
>
> In contrast to the child in darkness because of an ordinary mis-
> carriage or by natural death after being born, the child here discussed

FIGURE I.2. *Mizuko* Jizō at Chingodō in Tokyo.

is in its present location because its parents took active steps to prevent it from being born alive in our world. If the parents merely carry out ordinary memorial rites but fail to make a full apology to their child, their *mizuko* will never be able to accept their act.[11]

FIGURE I.3. *Mizuko* votive tablet at Daishōin in Miyajima.

Common alleged symptoms of *mizuko tatari* are sickness, accidents, loss of a spouse's affections, decline in sexual appetite, disobedience by one's children, loss of business, and mysterious pains. Over time, this symptomology has expanded to encompass virtually any and every misfortune— even a person who had never had an abortion could be haunted by random *mizuko* generated by the millions of abortions in Japan's postwar era.[12] No matter what problems one experiences, it might be suggested that they resulted from *tatari*, necessitating *mizuko kuyō* to correct the situation. Siblings of a *mizuko* are particularly singled out as vulnerable to distraught or angry spirits:

> It often happens that the living children of persons who have repeatedly had abortions will in the middle of the night cry out "Father, help!" or "Help me, Mommy!" because of nightmares. Uncontrollable weeping or cries of "I'm scared! I'm scared!" on the part of children are really caused by dreams through which their aborted siblings deep in the realm of darkness give expression to their own distress and anger.[13]

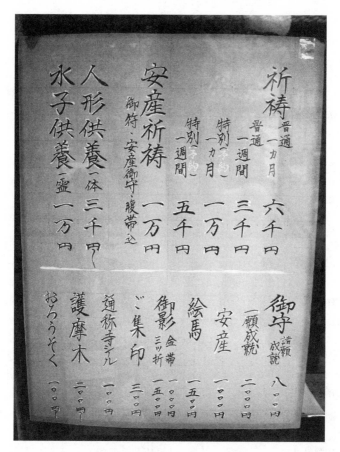

FIGURE 1.4. Schedule of service prices at Sōtōkuji in Kyoto, including *mizuko kuyō* (10,000 yen per *mizuko*, about $100).

Contrary to the marketing rhetoric of priests and other promoters of *mizuko kuyō*, the practice in its current form appears to be of very recent origin. No direct precedent exists in Japanese Buddhism; prior to the twentieth century, there are few records of memorial rites of any kind conducted for aborted fetuses, even though abortions certainly occurred.[14] Not surprisingly, *mizuko kuyō* shares many similarities with the so-called New Religions of Japan, such as a concern with spirits, this-worldly benefits, and rapid spread based on active proselytization.[15] Furthermore, the atmosphere of the *mizuko kuyō* frequently has a judgmental tone absent from premodern Jizō-related motifs: Jizō in premodern Japan was the caring protector who sprung people from hell and healed their illnesses without comment on possibly karmic causes for their suffering. Helen Hardacre has shown that *mizuko kuyō* was disseminated to the masses via lurid articles in tabloids from the 1970s. Partnered with the tabloids were spiritual entrepreneurs, temple priests, or sometimes independent faith healers who proclaimed that virtually any problem in one's life was likely due to angry *mizuko* exacting revenge. The targets for this rhetoric were mainly young women, who were characterized as immoral, sexually depraved, and immature, bringing about trouble not only for themselves but others through the consequences of their selfish, thoughtless actions (especially sexual ones).[16] As Hardacre points out:

> *Mizuko kuyō*, especially in its tabloid advertising campaigns, regularly invokes fetocentric rhetoric, framing abortion as a moral violation of the fetus's personhood and predicting that the wronged fetus will exact revenge on the mother.... It seeks to motivate young, unmarried women to pay for rituals to appease wrathful fetuses.[17]

The creation of *mizuko* rhetoric was made possible in part by the introduction of new medical technologies that allowed pictures to be taken of the fetus in the womb. Suddenly, the woman dropped out of the picture, and the fetus could be portrayed as a viable, independent being, implicitly a fully autonomous person. Tabloids took up these evocative new images, publishing doctored pictures of young women cowering under the sheets as disembodied fetuses floated threatening above the bed—these pictures appeared alongside stories about the spirit attacks resulting from young women's selfish sexual actions and abortions, often with directions on how to reach people and temples providing *mizuko kuyō* and with sample prices.[18]

Often the staunchest advocates of the need for *mizuko kuyō* were right-wing thinkers and politicians, some of whom formed ties with new temples established solely to perform *mizuko kuyō*. All of this flowed from a general ideology that was reactionary toward the modern Japanese state; it viewed the present day as spiritually corrupt, overly influenced by foreign (mainly American) culture, and estranged from the purity and strength of Japan's ancient allegiance to the emperor and to strict social mores. Japan's soaring abortion rate was seen by such people as the clearest sign of this alleged moral rot, and women were blamed as the downfall of Japanese virility, independence, and social values. Deeply guilty for their sexual profligacy, their murderous abortions, their implied rejection of their naturally ordained status as mothers, and the damage all of this would surely do to the family—the bedrock of Japanese society—women were seen by these social commentators as hopelessly sinful, in dire need of atonement through *mizuko kuyō*, which humbled them and put them back into the proper position of submission.[19]

One final note on the Japanese background of the ritual: despite the sometimes rancorous rhetoric of *mizuko kuyō* proponents, no strong push has been made to outlaw abortion. Japanese society seems to have accepted the need for access to abortion, resorting to ritual rather than legal avenues for managing the procedure's potentially corrosive effects. This contrasts with the highly politicized situation in the United States, where abortion is among the most contentious modern social issues—a strong stimulus for interest in *mizuko kuyō* among Americans, as chapters 5 and 6 will demonstrate.

Religion and Abortion in America

A second topic requiring a brief overview is the relation of religion to abortion in U.S. history. As in Japan, abortion did not emerge as a religious issue of major importance until the twentieth century, especially in the last quarter of the century. Since the introduction of European colonies in North America, abortion was widely available via traditional practices of herbology. Abortion took place at home and was presided over by the woman herself or a female midwife. The practice was private, outside of the legal system, and was rarely discussed by religious writers.

Beginning in the mid-nineteenth century, there was a push to criminalize abortion. However, it took place almost entirely within the purview of the emergent professional medical establishment, rather than being a religious concern. Ostensibly, the issue was not the humanity of the fetus but rather the health of the mother—herbs and primitive surgeries were widely considered dangerous to women, and unlicensed medical practitioners were the target of the antiabortion movement. On another level, this was really a front in the battle against quacks and midwives by doctors, who sought to rationalize, professionalize, and centralize medical techniques (and, not incidentally, to become the sole legitimate providers of medical care).[20] In an era of growing Catholic power and great Protestant crusades on public issues, the religious establishment was nearly silent on abortion. Working with the states, doctors gradually managed to criminalize abortion throughout the United States before the end of the century. To the extent that religion entered into these debates, it was typically the scientific community railing against the intrusion of "fringe" religionists, such as Christian Scientists or other New Thought communities, who sought to offer alternative (untested and unsafe, to the minds of the doctors) approaches to healthcare. It also played a somewhat subliminal role because one of the arguments was that abortion reduced the number of native-born American births, especially among wealthy, educated, white Protestants (and this during a time of tremendous immigration from mostly Catholic countries).

For the first five decades of the twentieth century, abortion remained a very minor issue in American religion.[21] When it appeared, it was typically on stereotyped lists of various "crimes" of sexuality railed against by Catholic priests and Protestant ministers. In the meantime, generations grew up for the first time in a new America where abortion had always been criminalized.

The change began in the 1960s. A new generation of progressive Protestant ministers were visited by frightened pregnant women—some married, some not, some very young, and including members of their own congregations. In previous decades, such women were usually met with stern lectures. But as ministers in the liberal and mainline denominations began to feel the influence of the growing women's movement and the cultural push of liberation movements more broadly, they reacted in new ways to the situation. Some clergy obtained the names of doctors who were willing to provide secret abortions and passed them on to women in need; others sent women to Japan or England, where abortion procedures were legal. Many ministers were influenced by studies showing that making abortion illegal merely drove women to unlicensed abortionists, in whose hands some women died. Abortion emerged as an issue of medical responsibility and women's rights, and progressive Protestant clergy helped to argue cases that led to the relaxation of abortion restrictions in many states. The groundwork was laid for the 1973 Supreme Court decisions (especially *Roe v. Wade*) that decisively legalized abortion throughout the country; clergy alliances were an instrumental part of bringing these cases to trial.[22]

The seemingly sudden reversal of American abortion policy shocked conservative American Christians. Previously, they had been nearly uninvolved in the building debate over legalized abortion, which was seen as a peripheral issue unlikely to become a reality. Along with the profound shock came almost instantaneous and even greater anger. Conservative Christians rightly saw abortion as the newest battleground over the role and privileges of women in American culture. Within days of the *Roe* decision, Protestant and Catholic leaders petitioned Congress to recriminalize abortion, calling it murder of unborn babies. These leaders represented their religions as always having been vigorously opposed to abortion, declared that abortion was against fundamental American values, criticized the procedure as unsafe for women and degrading of their natural role as mothers, and suggested it was something more fit for communist and atheist Russia or China than for godly America.[23]

What had changed between 1900 and 1973? One factor already mentioned—that generations of Americans had come to see abortion as naturally illicit and historically illegal—should not be dismissed. But more important are certain religious shifts that occurred over those decades. The twentieth century saw impressive gains by women: suffrage, the birth control pill, greater access to education and employment, liberalized divorce laws, the ascendance of female clergy in many denominations, and other developments that left American women in a far stronger position than they enjoyed at the century's inception. Many of these gains had been made by activists who identified religion, especially Christianity, as one of the main causes of women's oppression in America. Conservative Christians, both Catholic and Protestant alike, often saw these gains by women as directly deleterious to American culture (virtually a sacred entity in itself) and to churches that thrived on male authority on the one hand and massive lay (and in the case of Catholics, religious) female participation on the other. Conservative Christianity tended to idealize a sort of Victorian model of American religion and culture, where women were meekly and happily subservient to husband (and minister) and saw their own main role as raising future generations of Christians in the home and nurturing Christian institutions and movements in the public sphere. This conservative Christianity was itself a product of the acrimonious debates over modernism that occurred within American Christianity during the two or three decades on either side of the turn of the century, and which produced fundamentalists in the 1910s and '20s and neoevangelicals in the 1940s and '50s. Especially in its neoevangelical form, this new old-time Christianity was aggressive, reactionary, well-organized, and prepared to exert political and social power to contain the liberation movements, growing religious diversity, and liberal Christianities that so disturbed it in the 1960s and '70s.[24] Thus just as abortion was legalized in America, an American Christianity had developed that was naturally predisposed to oppose it and efficient enough to do so on a large scale.

Antiabortion groups quickly appeared in the mid-1970s, most having some religious connection. When it became clear that the Supreme Court was unwilling for the time being to rescind its legalization of abortion, these groups developed a three-pronged strategy. First, they worked to restrict abortion on the state level, pushing local authorities to introduce strict controls over how, when, and by whom an abortion could be procured. Second, they promoted antiabortion political candidates at all levels of government, but especially for the presidency in an eventual bid to change the tone of the Supreme Court and rescind *Roe v. Wade*. Third, they sought to directly prevent abortions by blocking access to clinics and intimidating doctors and clinicians into finding another line of work.[25]

Religion was almost always explicitly at the heart of these newly organized movements to restrict abortion. The American Catholic hierarchy demanded that every Catholic church in the United States host a chapter of an antiabortion organization, and many priests emphasized the evils of abortion in their sermons. Catholics were the first to organize clinic-blocking operations, often drawing on their experience with the Civil Rights movement and couching their new struggle as one for the rights of unborn children and women forced into abortion.[26] Early Catholic participation was soon overshadowed by neo-evangelical Christian movements such as Operation Rescue, which took an even more militant (and often less female-positive) stance, regarding women who had abortions as heinously sinful wretches. For such groups, opposition to abortion became the defining characteristic of a righteous Christian, and the further one went in preventing abortion, the more righteous one was. Such attitudes eventually led to acts of violence, at first of actions meant to terrorize clinic personnel and damage clinic facilities, and by the early 1990s actual murders of clinic doctors, security guards, and receptionists. Such attacks can be seen not only as resulting from the increasing vehemence of antiabortion rhetoric but also as a response to the perception that actual results were slow in arriving. To Christians opposed to abortion, it was self-evidently evil, and they thought that God would not allow such a practice to continue. With God's Providence slow to manifest itself and other Americans slow to wake up to the horror of abortion, conservative Christians involved in the anti-abortion movement grew both more frustrated, and more fearful that divine judgment might burst in to ravage America as a whole.

Yet their side was making progress, primarily because of the remarkable network of antiabortion groups that had been created. Like neoevangelicalism itself, these networks tended to be para-church operations, which defied strict denominational boundaries and drew on sophisticated use of various media (especially antiabortion journals in the earlier phases and religious antiabortion Web sites since the mid-1990s). The antiabortion movement was at once part of the rising conservative Christian tide and partially responsible for it: it benefited from other gains made by the expanding evangelical Protestantism and anti-Vatican II Catholicism, and at the same time gave conservative Christians a common, visceral core issue to organize around.

Liberal religionists, meanwhile, largely lost ground to their conservative counterparts on abortion. While many mainline denominations officially proclaimed that individual women must make their own choices on abortion, or even came out in explicit support of abortion rights, the public sphere was increasingly polarized along lines of "values" versus "rights," and prochoice Christians remain largely caught on the horns of this dilemma, wanting to affirm both but often unable to do so in a concise way.

For the purposes of this book, one of the most important aspects of the abortion phenomenon in America is that historically abortion has not been an object of ritualized religious recognition, neither during the long early period when it was legal but unacknowledged, nor during the shorter period when it was illegal yet often secretly available. It did not receive recognition in Christian ritual until the 1980s, and much of its early ritual treatment seemed aimed as much at political as religious ends. Thus there have been in some places mass Christian memorial services for "all the victims of abortion in America" and abortion memorials erected as monuments akin to Holocaust memorials.[27] Prayer vigils outside abortion clinics were common in the 1980s and 1990s, but they decreased with George W. Bush's election, perhaps in response to perceived progress in political circles on the antiabortion issue. And some new organizations established in the wake of the *Roe* decision, such as Rachel's Vineyard (founded in 1993), seek to provide a degree of counseling or prayer for people who feel wounded by abortion.[28] Overall, however, as will become especially clear in chapters 5 and 6, many Americans feel religiously left out in dealing with their pregnancy losses, either because they do not have access to such services or find them inadequate for their needs.

A Note about Sources and Approach

A principal source for this book is a series of telephone and face-to-face interviews conducted with more than forty priests and laywomen who have participated in American *mizuko kuyō* rites.[29] These were supplemented with published accounts of *mizuko kuyō* by Americans and on-site research at more than two dozen American Buddhist temples, especially Rochester Zen Center, the Zen Center of Los Angeles, Zenshuji Soto Mission, and Great Vow Monastery in Clatskanie, Oregon, where I collected orders of service, newsletters, minutes, memorial books, intertemple correspondence, photographs, and other archival sources that related to the ritual. Great Vow in particular proved to be a rich source of data, and it was there that I was allowed to directly participate in two *mizuko kuyō*-derived ceremonies and question other participants afterward. For my research on *mizuko kuyō* among non-Buddhists, I identified well over a hundred written works that discussed the ritual in some fashion, from articles in major pro-life magazines to online forums devoted to pregnancy loss. The sheer abundance of these materials came as a surprise and required considerable time to work through and understand. I also spent three months in Japan studying *mizuko kuyō* in its native land, talking in English and Japanese with numerous priests and scholars alike about the ritual, observing its practice by priests and laypeople at many sites, collecting primary sources on the ritual, and learning the intricacies of *mizuko kuyō* performance, material culture, and economic situation. Although direct reference to that Japanese fieldwork is sparse in this book dedicated to tracing the ritual in America, it was influential in shaping my understanding of how *mizuko kuyō* operates on both sides of the Pacific. And of course I draw explicitly and implicitly on the work of scholars of Japanese religion, particularly those who have written about *mizuko kuyō*, historians of American religion and culture (such as Orsi and others), and ritual theorists.

As public advocates of *mizuko kuyō*, the names of priests interviewed for this project are provided in the text. Lay Buddhist consultants, on the other hand, have been given pseudonyms. Japanese names are written family name first, and Japanese terms have been given macrons to indicate a long "o" or "u." I have not elected to use diacritics for the much smaller number of Sanskrit and Chinese terms that appear here. A concerted effort has been made to keep foreign terms to a minimum; on those rare occasions where a non-English term is employed and not immediately defined in the text, please consult the endnotes for an explanation.

I

"Carried with Jizō Bosatsu"

Mizuko Kuyō in Japanese-American Communities

From its beginnings in India to its varied cultural and regional forms throughout Asia, Buddhism has been and continues to be a religion concerned with death and with the dead.

—Bryan Cuevas and Jacqueline Stone,
The Buddhist Dead

The Reverend Kanai Shokai, the head priest at Los Angeles Nichiren Buddhist Temple, was almost never born. His mother was in poor health, and the doctor gave her a stark choice: she could terminate the pregnancy, or she could deliver and die, leaving the newborn and her other two children motherless. She put his life before her own and passed away a few days after his birth, unsure of what the future held for him.

As it turned out, the motherless baby followed in the path of the Buddha, who lost his own mother when he was just seven days old. Rev. Kanai's parents had lived in a Japan at war with the United States, but he grew up to become one of the few Nichiren Shū Buddhist priests to spend his life ministering to Americans. As we sat in the pews of his temple in Boyle Heights, beneath a vibrantly colored stained-glass window portraying the Japanese saint Nichiren, I thought of all the turns that a life takes from conception to death. Among his many duties as a messenger of the dharma (the Buddhist teachings), Rev. Kanai now finds himself called upon by women to help them deal with the aftermath of abortions that, unlike his mother, they have elected to receive.[1]

With the late winter's light filling the worship hall, we discussed the rituals he conducts for these women. At a certain point in each ceremony, he gives a short talk. "I also encourage them to understand what a *mizuko* is," he said. I glanced at my recorder to make sure it was still taping. "How do you explain *mizuko* to them?" I asked. He paused, and his eyes unfocused a bit as he looked through me toward a memory from many years ago:

> I had an experience, a very, very strange experience. One day a person I knew called me, actually this is from Japan. This was the mother of a teenager. She had only one daughter. One day the daughter asked the mother, "Is there any sister? My sister? Elder sister?" And the mother was shocked and asked why. According to her daughter, she dreamed that one day she passed through a temple gate and there was a girl walking toward the temple ahead of her. Suddenly the girl turned back and saw her face to face. And in the dream, that girl in front of her said, "I am your sister." So that's why the daughter asked her mother if there was a sister. Of course, the mother said, "No, that's a dream." But actually, she had an abortion when she was in high school. The mother called me and asked if she should tell her the reality or not. But I told her that she had better tell her daughter the reality of what she did when she was high school age.... The husband knew the incident, but it was with a different man—the father of the abortion was a different boy. The husband said "Don't tell."

He shook his head slightly, with the hint of a frown. Then he took a deeper breath and continued:

> Anyway, I believe it is very important to realize even a baby, an aborted baby—you should treat it right, do the memorial service, and appreciate it. The husband and mother or whoever, because of financial reasons or whatever the reason for abortion, she or the husband are still alive because of that abortion. Therefore they must appreciate that. A memorial service means attending the spirits of the Buddha Land, and also appreciating what I am now. If the baby was supposed to be born when [the mother] was high school age, she would have had lots of turmoil going to school and getting a job, but by doing abortion she was able to finish school and get a job. So what she is now is because of her abortion. Therefore, she must appreciate [the aborted baby] by offering so many memorial services again and again. The spirit of the aborted baby will help and support its sibling. That's what I explain.[2]

Mizuko kuyō, the Japanese practice of offering special memorial services for abortions and other pregnancy losses, has come to America. Our journey through the landscape touched by this popular ritual begins in the most logical place, with the Japanese-American temples that have nurtured Buddhism in the United States for more than a century. In particular, this chapter describes *mizuko kuyō* practices among the Japanese-American Buddhist temples of Los Angeles. That city offers one of the largest and oldest populations of Japanese-Americans in the United States, with temples representing a wide range of Japanese Buddhist denominations. Observation of the differing Japanese-American approaches to *mizuko kuyō* reveals variety in the Americanization process and, most important, demonstrates that acculturation is not a straightforward progression toward a future of fully integrated American Buddhism no longer subject to influence from overseas trends. Examining these communities also allows a baseline to be set for the discussion of *mizuko kuyō* in convert Zen temples that occupies the following three chapters.

Mizuko Kuyō Opponents in America

My choice of starting points for discussion may seem a bit unusual, but it is important to acknowledge from the start that *mizuko kuyō* is not an uncontested ritual in Japanese-American Buddhism, and the forces constraining *mizuko kuyō* are as much a part of the story as those promoting it.

Despite its popularity in Japan, *mizuko kuyō* is not as common in Japanese-American Buddhist temples as it might be. A primary reason for this is that two of the largest representatives of Japanese-based Buddhism in America—Jōdo Shinshū and Sōka Gakkai—are opposed to observance of *mizuko kuyō*. Jōdo Shinshū (also known as Shin Buddhism) is by far the largest school of Buddhism in Japan and has been institutionally present in America since the 1880s. It is a type of Pure Land Buddhism, which is distinguished by a particular emphasis on the mythic Buddha of Boundless Light and Life ("Amida" in Japanese), and is perhaps the most common form of Buddhism today. Jōdo Shinshū is mainly represented in the United States by two organizations affiliated with the Nishi Honganji (Honganji-ha) branch of Shin: the Buddhist Churches of America and the Honpa Hongwanji Mission of Hawaii. The membership of these organizations is heavily—though by no means exclusively—Japanese-American.

If people come to a BCA or Hongwanji Mission temple asking for *mizuko kuyō*, they are typically told that Shin considers such rituals superstitious and does not perform them. When there is a temple nearby that performs *mizuko kuyō*, such as Koyasan Buddhist Temple (a Shingon temple near the Los Angeles Hompa Hongwanji Buddhist Temple), then ministers will sometimes refer the seeker there. People who are insistent that they are Jōdo Shinshū members and want a service done for their aborted or miscarried fetus do sometimes receive additional help.[3] In such uncommon cases, the ministers explain that they do not believe in *mizuko kuyō* but are willing to do a regular memorial service for a pregnancy loss. They then use this as an opportunity to teach orthodox Jōdo Shinshū Buddhism and stress that they do not believe in spirits or bad luck. These services are basically identical to those performed for children or adults who have died; it is worth noting that in the orthodox Shin perspective, funeral and memorial rituals are performed for the benefit of the living as a way to expose them to the Buddhist teaching, rather than for the benefit of the dead as in most other Japanese Buddhist traditions.[4] This approach—official dis-avowal, but willingness to strategically perform a normal funeral if insistently demanded—is also maintained by the small number of American temples of the Higashi Honganji (Otani-ha) branch of Jōdo Shinshū.[5] Shin Buddhism in Japan displays the same attitude: doctrinal opposition to *mizuko kuyō*, but a degree of flexibility toward memorials for pregnancy losses as a way to minister to and instruct those who are unsatisfied with the official policy.[6]

Sōka Gakkai, a large Buddhist new religious movement with roots in the Nichiren Shōshū sect, disclaims *mizuko kuyō* as well. It is not performed in Japan, where followers see the practice as overly exploitative of vulner-able women and basically a moneymaking scheme by priests.[7] In America, Japanese-Americans make up only about 22 percent of Sōka Gakkai practition-ers.[8] As in Japan, *mizuko kuyō* is not practiced by Sōka Gakkai in America.[9] Sōka Gakkai, an entirely lay-led organization, has no special memorial services for pregnancy losses or the deaths of children or adults. If someone wishes to remember a deceased person, she may gather a group of friends and relatives, but the actual practice will be identical to that of a normal daily service: chant-ing the title of the *Lotus Sutra* (a major Buddhist scripture), reciting chapters two and sixteen of the *Lotus Sutra,* and saying silent prayers. No wooden tablets or memorial plaques (common Japanese mortuary items) are used by Sōka Gakkai in Japan or the United States, since they are seen as little more than de-vices for Japanese priests to squeeze money from lay believers. Given that Sōka Gakkai endured a rancorous split from the priestly Nichiren Shōshū tradition in 1991, this anticlerical attitude is perhaps less than surprising.

Mizuko Kuyō in Japanese-American Zen

Jōdo Shinshū and Sōka Gakkai are not the only Japanese Buddhisms oper-ating in America, however. Another important one is Zen, a school of Bud-dhism distinguished by its devotion to a semi-legendary lineage of masters and a rhetorical emphasis on the practice of meditation. Studies of Buddhism in America often stress a split between practitioners with a cultural connection to Buddhism—often labeled "ethnic" Buddhists—and those who have converted to Buddhism.[10] In other places I have argued that this distinction can obscure as much it reveals and tends to eclipse Asian-American Buddhism (by far the numerically larger side of American Buddhism) in favor of the stories of Euro-American pioneers in Buddhism.[11] In examining the practice of *mizuko kuyō*, however, Zen Buddhism in America does seem to differ substantially along these lines. Therefore, this chapter includes an examination of *mizuko kuyō* at a Zen temple founded to minister to the Japanese-American population, whereas chapters 2, 3, and 4 look at *mizuko kuyō*-derived rituals in convert Zen temples with few Japanese-American members.

Japanese-American Zen finds itself the ironic victim of a double eclipse. On the one hand, a disproportionate amount of scholarly and popular media attention is given to white converts to Buddhism in America, among whom Zen is the most popular tradition. This tends to obscure not only the practices and perspectives but even the very presence of nonwhite cultural Buddhists. On the other hand, when attention is directed away from converts toward Buddhists of Japanese descent, the large majority of investigators focus on Jōdo Shinshū Buddhism, which is the preferred denomination of most Japanese-American Buddhists.[12] Studies of Shin Buddhism far outnumber those of any other type of "ethnic" Buddhism, making Jōdo Shinshū into the paradigm for the Japanese-American Buddhist experience and thereby further obscuring the presence of Japanese-American Zen.

I have attempted to counter this phenomenon by providing attention to *mizuko kuyō* at one of the few Zen temples in America that is not oriented toward the convert community: Zenshuji Soto Mission, in downtown Los Angeles.[13] Founded in 1922, Zenshuji is the North American headquarters for the Sōtō Shū sect, the largest Japanese Zen denomination. It is one of the pillars of a Southern California network of Japanese-American Buddhism that dates back to the first half of the twentieth century, which also includes nearby Jōdo Shinshū, Jōdo Shū, Shingon Shū, and Nichiren Shū temples. Zenshuji primarily draws Japanese-Americans or Japanese citizens living or working in Los Angeles, although a smaller number of people from non-Japanese backgrounds also attend, and the temple has recently acquired a European-American priest to assist the two Japanese priests.

Whereas the nearby Jōdo Shinshū temples actively try to dissuade Buddhists from seeking *mizuko kuyō*, Zenshuji, like many Sōtō Zen temples in Japan, is willing to perform the ceremony upon request. The primary priest who performs such services is the Reverend Kojima Shūmyō, a Japanese immigrant who has served at Zenshuji since 1995. He holds *mizuko kuyō* on average four or five times a year upon request from laypersons. A full description of the actual process of performing *mizuko kuyō* at Zenshuji will help illuminate important aspects of the ritual, as well as aid the analysis of convert Zen *mizuko kuyō* in later chapters.

Mizuko kuyō at Zenshuji begins with the arrival of those requesting the ritual—in most cases, a young Japanese couple—at the temple, where they are met by Rev. Kojima. He leads them into the main worship hall (*hondō*). This space is separated into two areas: the pews, where laypeople sit, and the stage, an altar area that includes holy images and seats for the priests. The arrangement of the room is a mix of traditional Japanese and American sacred spaces. The pew area, by far the larger space, is identical to most mainline Protestant churches' seating arrangements. Entering the main worship hall by the double doors in the back (along one of the short sides) of the hall, one finds a long space that slopes slightly down toward the altar (fig. 1.1). An aisle separates thirteen rows of wooden pews, with service books containing chants and hymns tucked into shelves along their backs. This contrasts with traditional Zen and other temples in Japan, which utilize no seats for laypeople, who sit on a level,

FIGURE 1.1. Main worship hall of Zenshuji Soto Mission.

not sloped, floor. Another Americanization is the placement of the altar area along one of the short ends of the hall; in a traditional Japanese temple the altar would be along a long side of the room.

The stage, on the other hand, is closer to being an import directly from a Japanese Buddhist temple. This raised area has a large central altar with offerings and many hanging golden adornments that symbolize the heavenly realms (this area is known as the *naijin*). A statue of Shaka Nyorai (Shakyamuni Buddha) is seated in the center, flanked by images of the bodhisattvas Monju (Manjushri) and Fugen (Samantabhadra)—these are the historical Buddha and two important helpers. On either side sit a row of low chairs for priests, facing inward toward the Buddha image, at a 90-degree angle to the congregation—and secondary altars, one with a statue of Dōgen and one with Keizan, the two revered founders of Sōtō Zen. Bells of various sizes and drums to accompany the rituals are also scattered about the stage. However, while more similar to a Japanese temple than the space for pews, this area has also been adapted to American realities. A typical Japanese Zen temple would have a larger altar area divided into *naijin* (main altar), *daima* (ritual space in front of the *naijin* for priests), *seijo* and *tōjo* (seating areas flanking the *daima*), and *nishi* and *higashi shicchu* (subsidiary altars flanking the *naijin*). Zenshuji lacks the sort of space available to Japanese temples of comparable status and thus has squeezed these elements together, eliminating some outright, with implications for the performance of rituals that will be explored below.

The bifurcation between the sacred space of the stage and the profane area of the pews is slightly mediated by incense burners, lanterns, and two lecterns, one on the stage and one to the side at ground level. But the separation is nonetheless absolute: laypeople cannot enter the stage, and no one is allowed to wear shoes into the altar area. Therefore, those who attend a *mizuko kuyō* ritual are directed to a pew while the priest goes onto the stage to prepare the altar. The priest intentionally takes his time lighting the candles, preparing the incense offering, and so on, to give those assembled some time to quietly reflect as they sit in the "spiritually peaceful place" of the worship hall. Rev. Kojima explicitly stated that this is not *zazen* (formal seated meditation); rather, it is simply ten minutes or so of consideration of the actions that led to the ceremony and preparation for saying goodbye to the being who was never born.[14]

Before the couple arrived, the priest will have already made some preparations. He folds a piece of paper into an origami representation of a baby, since there are no physical remains available from abortion. He also makes a wooden memorial plaque, inscribing it with the name "*mizuko no rei*"—"mizuko spirit" (fig. 1.2). This is a rough plaque; if the couple wishes to have a more permanent black lacquer one made for enshrining in the home altar, the priest will order it

FIGURE 1.2. Kojima Shūmyō fills out a *mizuko* memorial plaque at Zenshuji Soto Mission.

from a Buddhist supply service in Torrance, California. As the couple waits, the priest places the plaque before the statue of the Buddha (fig. 1.3).

The ritual begins when the priest strikes a bell and strides onto the stage to make an offering of incense to the Buddha, followed by three bows. Another incense offering is made, and then the priest takes his seat near the main altar to begin the sutra chanting.[15] First, he chants the *Sankiraimon* (Three Refuges Prayer), declaring his faith in the Buddha, the teachings, and the community. Next, he chants the *Heart Sutra*, followed by a dedication of the merit of the sutra chanting. This three-part set of the refuge chant, *Heart Sutra*, and dedication forms the opening of many Sōtō rituals and is not unique to the *mizuko kuyō* or memorial services in general. As Rev. Kojima explained, it serves as "a kind of greeting to Shakyamuni Buddha" before the main service gets under way.[16]

The specifically *mizuko*-oriented portion of the service begins with another chant by the priest. Usually it is the *Daihishin Darani*, a mantric text that embodies the compassion of Kannon bodhisattva.[17] Less often, the priest selects a portion of the *Jizō Bosatsu Hongan Kyō* (*Sutra of the Bodhisattva Jizō's Vows*), which provides a longer ritual experience. During the chanting, the priest will

FIGURE 1.3. *Mizuko* memorial plaque and origami "baby" made by Kojima Shūmyō.

indicate that the people who requested the ritual should approach and make a quick incense offering in the large burner set before the stage. At the same time, he will set the origami baby alight with one of the altar candles, reducing it to ash. After the sutra, the priest chants the Jizō mantra, which is performed twenty-seven times: "Om Ka Ka Ka Bi San Ma E Soha Ka." This is followed by a dedication of the sutra-chanting merit and a more general dedication. The priest makes three bows and finishes the formal portion of the service by reciting the four bodhisattva vows.[18]

The total length for all the chanting is approximately twenty-five minutes. It is important to note that the priest is the only participant who chants and performs the ritual actions—the lay person or people who initiated the *mizuko kuyō* watch passively from their seat in the pews as the action of the ceremony takes place on the stage. All chants are done in Japanese or Sino-Japanese, and because of the technical language or unfamiliar pronunciations, many are incomprehensible even to native Japanese speakers.

After chanting, the priest will deliver a short sermon. These talks tend to focus on Jizō's role in taking care of the unborn spirit and the universality of loss, as Rev. Kojima explained to me in his office at Zenshuji:

KOJIMA SHŪMYŌ   Even if we just see the faces of the people in our company or the market, even those people, many people have lost a child, not only you. Jizō Bosatsu is the guardian of babies who passed away, so we visit and offer the incense to O-Jizō-san for taking care of the child. That's why we have to offer the incense.

AUTHOR   So that's what you explain to the people?

KOJIMA   Yes.

AUTHOR   It's interesting when you say that many other people have experienced it. I assume you are doing that so they will realize it is not just them, but others also experience loss. It is part of human life. Is that why you explain that?

KOJIMA   Yes. Not simple, but each time I pick up some stories. I did this many times. One of the fathers, he was really in pain and could not forget. So he made an angel figure, like a pin. And always he put it here [gestures to his lapel] to keep remembering the baby. Because of his work, he met many people. And many people ask him, "Oh, what is that cute angel?" And each time he explained, "It is because my baby died." So to keep reminding him. Then many people responded, "Oh, really? Me, too." So then he made the same pin and gave it to [them]. Then he calculated so many pins he made to share. And at the next memorial service, he took off the pin and put it with the ashes. "I realized it was not only me. I could share the pain with so many people. [Speaking to the spirit of the baby:] 'I am lucky that I could meet you. Even without this pin, I will always be with you. You are always part of my family.'" So he would not need the pin. "'I cannot be with you right now because I have many things to do before I die. The next generation, your brother, and my wife. So instead of me, I put this pin with you. You are with me, my baby. But now I am with you.'" So he put the pin with the dead ashes.

AUTHOR   He didn't need it as a symbol anymore.

KOJIM   Yes. He can feel the baby always.

AUTHOR   Is this a story that you might tell after *mizuko kuyō*?

KOJIMA   Yes, that is one of the sample stories. So I believe that to talk to them, to share this experience with others, that is part of the ceremony.[19]

The final part of the ritual involves making incense offerings to all of the Jizō figures in the temple. First, the priest and the mourners enter the columbarium

FIGURE 1.4. Columbarium with Jizō at Zenshuji Soto Mission.

(nōkotsudō) off of the worship hall, where an image of Jizō is enshrined among many boxes containing the ashes of past parishioners (fig. 1.4). The priest offers incense, passes some to the participants to offer, and recites the Jizō mantra. Next, they go into the hall by the front door, where a small Jizō stands atop a table in the reception area, in front of a plaque with donors' names. Again the priest offers incense, invites the people to offer incense, and chants. Finally, they walk outside, where six large Jizō statues stand in a covered shelter by the parking lot (fig. 1.5).[20] Once again incense is offered by priest and laypeople, and the Jizō mantra chanted. The priest then scatters the ashes of the origami baby in the wind. If he senses that a mourner is feeling sad and needs to remain a little longer at the temple, he will offer her tea inside and perhaps chat with her for a few minutes. Most people, however, leave immediately after the ceremony ends. In total, the *mizuko kuyō* takes about forty minutes at Zenshuji.

Mizuko Kuyō at Nichiren Temples in America

While Japanese-American Zen temples tend to be partially obscured by convert Zen on the one hand and Japanese-American Jōdo Shinshū on the other, additional Japanese forms of Buddhism in the United States are more or less completely

FIGURE 1.5. Roku Jizō at Zenshuji Soto Mission.

invisible to both the scholarly and popular media communities. There are almost no studies of American Shingon, Jōdo Shū, Nichiren Shū, or temple-based Nichiren Shōshū (as opposed to Sōka Gakkai) Buddhist institutions, despite the presence of some of these organizations in major metropolitan areas for close to a century. Even survey works on American Buddhism rarely discuss these schools. For instance, Richard Seager's *Buddhism in America* contains no information about Shingon, Jōdo Shū, or Nichiren Shū Buddhism in either Asia or America. Likewise, Tendai and Risshō Kōsei-kai, two other forms of Buddhism that receive some mention in this book, are nowhere discussed in *Buddhism in America*. Nichiren Shōshū appears more or less only as a foil for Sōka Gakkai. Japanese-American Zen receives almost no attention except when it briefly interacts with convert Zen. For instance, not a single Japanese-American temple is considered worthy of Seager's term "Zen Flagship Institutions." The Zen Center of Los Angeles, which has perhaps one-tenth as many members as Zenshuji, does receive inclusion in this group; Zenshuji, meanwhile, appears only as one line in a profile of the Zen Center's founder. And yet, compared to many other studies in the field, Seager's work is one of the most admirably comprehensive of its kind. It seems that new approaches to the study of Buddhism in the United States are needed that allow these smaller but historically significant communities to be included in the realm of acceptable subject material. Projects that track a particular ritual across denominational and racial lines are one possible answer to this tendency to overlook certain forms of Buddhism in America.

Among these other schools, a variety of *mizuko kuyō* practices can be found. The first to consider is *mizuko kuyō* in Nichirenist temples. These temples follow the teachings of the thirteenth-century monk Nichiren, who advocated special devotion to the *Lotus Sutra* and chanting its title as a practice suitable for all people. Though Sōka Gakkai does not perform *mizuko kuyō*, Nichiren Shōshū, the temple tradition that Sōka Gakkai separated from, includes a very basic form of *mizuko kuyō* within its repertoire of rituals. The sect has six temples in the United States that together serve the entire country, which is divided into six large geographic parishes. The Nichiren Shoshu Myohoji Temple of Los Angeles, located in West Hollywood, just below Sunset Boulevard, is the head temple for Nichiren Shōshū in America. Myohoji's parish has four hundred to five hundred regional members from a wide variety of racial and ethnic backgrounds; the largest group, however, are Japanese or Japanese-Americans.[21] It was founded in San Bernardino County well to the east of Los Angeles in 1967 and moved to its more central location in West Hollywood in 1996.[22]

Myohoji includes a rite that it calls *mizuko kuyō*, which is done in the same manner as at Nichiren Shōshū temples in Japan.[23] However, this *mizuko kuyō* is essentially subsumed into regular memorial rites and does not carry a special character as a separate ceremony. It is a frequently requested service by members of all racial backgrounds.[24] However, only Japanese members use the term *mizuko*, so it seems likely that the Americans are simply asking for memorial rites for their abortions and other pregnancy losses without necessarily being aware of their precedent in Japanese Buddhism.

The process of *mizuko kuyō* at Myohoji is quite simple. The layperson requests that her *mizuko* be remembered during the regular evening service (*gongyō*). A priest prepares a thin tablet (*tōba*) with the shape of a Buddhist monument (stupa) on top.[25] These tablets are one of the most common pieces of Buddhist material culture in Japan, where they are typically made from sheets of wood and have the names of the dead written on them with a brush.[26] A $10 donation is requested to cover the cost of the *tōba*.

The *tōba* is then put on a rack in the main worship hall next to the altar area. The worship hall itself is divided into altar and seating areas like the sanctuary of Zenshuji, though it is significantly larger and has a stadium-style sloped audience area that boasts seats rather than pews. After chanting the evening service, the head priest addresses the calligraphic mandala that serves as the central object of devotion in Nichiren Shōshū, reading aloud a list of names of people to be remembered, including any *mizuko* who have been requested. This is the extent of the *mizuko kuyō*. During the service, laypeople and priests do all of the chants together, although the head priest is the only one who addresses the mandala with the list of names. The entire service takes about thirty minutes.[27]

Nichiren Shōshū performs only a nominal *mizuko kuyō,* but Nichiren Shū temples offer a much more complete and specific service for pregnancy losses. Nichiren Shū, while not as well known in the United States as Nichiren Shōshū, is by far the larger branch of Nichiren Buddhism in Japan, and has significant differences in doctrine and practice. It has also been in the United States for more than twice as long as Nichiren Shōshū or Sōka Gakkai—the first temple was founded in Hawaii in 1901—but the high visibility of these other groups, attributable to their active proselytization efforts, have tended to overshadow Nichiren Shū.

The Los Angeles Nichiren Buddhist Temple, founded in 1912, was the first Nichiren Shū institution in North America. The temple is two miles east of Zenshuji in Boyle Heights, a neighborhood adjacent to Little Tokyo that was once heavily Japanese-American but is now 95 percent Latino. The L.A. temple has performed *mizuko kuyō* since the 1960s and does about four such ceremonies per year on request from laypeople. Often these are newcomers to the temple, usually of Nichiren Shū background, though members too may memorialize new *mizuko* or remember older ones. The resident priest, the Reverend Kanai Shokai, whose reflections opened this chapter, encourages people to perform yearly *mizuko kuyō* around the anniversary of their abortion or miscarriage. At a minimum, he hopes that women and their husbands will honor the Japanese Buddhist tradition of rites for the deceased on the first, third, seventh, and thirteenth anniversaries of the death.[28]

Participants in the *mizuko kuyō* ceremonies at the L.A. temple are requested to arrive with flowers, milk, baby food, and perhaps toys. Rev. Kanai takes these and leads the mourners into the main worship hall, which, like other local temples, is divided into a sitting area (with pews) and a large stage area housing the main altar and many large hanging golden adornments (fig. 1.6). The main altar has a calligraphic mandala like the one at Myohoji, but also includes a statue of Shakyamuni Buddha and one of Nichiren, all placed in a line moving away from the viewer. The offerings are placed before the main altar while the layperson sits in a pew. A wooden tablet with the words *"mizuko no rei"* (*mizuko* spirit) is placed before the main altar.[29]

The first chant is *Kanjo,* an invocation of Buddhas, bodhisattvas, and deities honored in the Nichiren tradition. The priest announces that the service is for a *mizuko* who died on such and such a date and his or her parents. Then the priest and mourners chant extracts from the *Lotus Sutra.*[30] Sutra chanting is followed

FIGURE 1.6. Main worship hall of Los Angeles Nichiren Buddhist Temple.

by extended chanting of "Namu Myōhō Renge Kyō" ("Adoration to the *Lotus Sutra*"), during which the layperson(s) approach and offer incense.[31] After the chanting there is a dedication of merit. Then the participants recite two American Buddhist compositions. First is *Lord Buddha's Children*, which begins:

> Lord Buddha is our infinite Father.
> We are His children.
> Let us love one another as Buddha's children.
> We are all endowed with Buddha Nature.
> Let us pay homage to everyone's Buddha Nature.

Next is *Golden Chain:*

> I am a link in Buddha's golden chain of love that stretches
> around the world.
> I will keep my link bright and strong.
> I will be kind and gentle to every living thing and protect all
> who are weaker than myself.
> I will think pure and beautiful thoughts, say pure and beautiful words,
> and do pure and beautiful deeds.

May every link in Buddha's golden chain of love be bright and strong,
and may we all attain perfect peace.

The service wraps up with a short talk by the priest, typically about ten minutes in length. During this time the priest takes the opportunity to speak more
about the nature of *mizuko* and why *mizuko kuyō* is important, as explained in
the introduction to this chapter.

When the sermon is complete, Rev. Kanai removes the offerings and hands
them back to the attendees. He asks them to drink a little of the milk, and then
to pour the remaining milk down the drain. This is done to help them realize
that the mizuko is essentially water and to let it go.

Mizuko Kuyō at Jōdo Shū Temples in America

Just as a variety of approaches to *mizuko kuyō* can be seen in differing
Nichiren schools in America, so too Pure Land Buddhists of separate denominations hold different opinions on the ritual's value. As discussed
above, Jōdo Shinshū does not perform *mizuko kuyō*. However the Jōdo Shū
branch of Japanese Pure Land Buddhism, which sprang from the same historical roots as Shin and is the second largest Buddhist denomination in
Japan (after Jōdo Shinshū), does permit the practice. Jōdo Shū enjoys much
less prominence in the United States than Jōdo Shinshū, especially on the
mainland: all but two of Jōdo Shū's sixteen American temples are in Hawaii.
One of these is Jodo Shu North America Buddhist Mission, a few blocks
from Zenshuji and across the street from Higashi Honganji Buddhist Temple in Little Tokyo. Just as the larger numbers and more active outreach of
Sōka Gakkai causes Nichiren Shū to be hidden from view by Americans, Jōdo
Shū's unique doctrines and practices are overshadowed by Jōdo Shinshū in
the United States.

Once or twice a year the Reverend Tanaka Kōdō of the Jodo Shu North
America Buddhist Mission receives a call requesting *mizuko kuyō*. Rev. Tanaka's first response is to inquire whether the caller is affiliated with a particular
Buddhist denomination other than Jōdo Shū. If she is, he encourages her to
ask a priest in her own tradition to perform the ceremony—Jōdo Shū is not an
aggressively proselytizing sect, and his preference is for Buddhists to deepen
their ties to their own denominations, reserving his missionary work for Jōdo
Shū members or those who are unaffiliated.[32] If the petitioner is a Jōdo Shū
member or has no specific Buddhist connections, an appointment is set up
for the *kuyō*, and participants are asked to arrive with flowers, toys, food, and
similar items to offer to the *mizuko*.

Mizuko kuyō mourners are met at the temple door and ushered into the main worship hall. As at many of the other temples discussed in this chapter, Jodo Shu North America Buddhist Mission's worship hall is divided into a pew area and a stage with main altar, subaltars, and places for ritual leaders to sit. The offerings, along with a wooden tablet, are taken onto the stage and arranged by the priest.[33]

The *mizuko kuyō* begins when the priest tolls a bell and offers incense to the Buddha. If there are two priests available, one acts as the officiant while the other handles the bells and drums. Next, the officiant chants *Sanbujō*, calling upon Amida, Shakyamuni, and all the Buddhas of the ten directions to enter the sacred space. This is followed by a repentance verse and ten recitations of *nembutsu* ("Namu Amida Butsu"—"Homage to Amida Buddha"). This is the first ritual element that the laypeople participate in, and the priest typically indicates that they are to recite along with him. Next the officiant moves onto a high box-shaped seat (*kōza*) directly before the Amida statue to lead the chanting of a sutra, often *Shiseige*, an extract from the *Larger Pure Land Sutra*.[34]

During the sutra chanting, the mourners are motioned to come forward and offer incense. Then the officiant dedicates the merit of the sutra and *nembutsu* to the *mizuko*, followed by several minutes of communal *nembutsu*. The priest makes another dedication and asks for Amida Buddha to help relieve the parents' suffering. The service closes with ten more *nembutsu* and *Sobutsuge*, the returning of the Buddhas who oversaw the ritual. The officiant then delivers a short sermon, typically three to five minutes in length. The total ceremony lasts about forty-five minutes, but is also often followed by about ten minutes of chatting over coffee so that the priest can be sure the mourners' minds have been put at ease. Laypeople depart with the toys that the mourners brought, and food items are kept to be shared with members of the temple.

Mizuko Kuyō at Tantric Japanese-American Temples in America

There are two more types of Japanese-American Buddhism that need to be discussed: tantric Buddhism and Buddhist new religious movements. The prime example of the first is Shingon Shū, which is important to this study because it is the most common purveyor of *mizuko kuyō* in Japan, and, not surprisingly, the Shingon temple in Los Angeles performs more *mizuko kuyō* than any other Buddhist group in the United States: an average of at least fifty each year. Tantric Buddhism such as Shingon Shū is distinguished by adherence to esoteric texts called "tantras" and special emphasis put on symbolic hand gestures, powerful words (mantras), and geometric deity images known as mandalas. The Koyasan Buddhist Temple, a few blocks from Zenshuji in the Little Tokyo section of Los Angeles, was founded in 1912 and was the first Shingon Shū temple established in North America.

The format at Koyasan is somewhat similar to *mizuko kuyō* at Zenshuji. A person calls and asks for the service, and an appointment is set up with one of the priests. When the mourner arrives on the day of the *mizuko kuyō*, the priest prepares a wooden tablet.[35] As at Zenshuji, the ceremony takes place inside the main worship hall, which at Koyasan is divided into a large auditorium space with chairs in rows and a stage area. Koyasan's stage has a main altar and many subsidiary altars, images, and mandalas (fig. 1.7). The main object of devotion is Dainichi Nyorai, the Great Sun Buddha, who represents the awakened nature of ultimate reality.

The priest places the wooden tablet in front of an incense burner and begins the service by chanting sutras. The first text is the *Hannya Rishu Kyō*, a main sutra of Shingon Buddhism. This is followed by the *Heart Sutra*. Next the priest chants a series of mantras, repeating each three times.[36] The service concludes with a dedication of merit. Throughout the ceremony, the layper-

FIGURE 1.7. Main worship hall of Koyasan Buddhist Temple.

son or people who requested *mizuko kuyō* remain seated in the audience area, rising only one time to make a short incense offering during the first chant. Laypeople are given a service book to use if they wish to chant or follow along, but in actual practice few participate beyond holding the book and watching the priest's activities on stage.

When the chanting is finished, the priest delivers a short (three- to six-minute) sermon to the mourners, as Bishop Miyata Taisen explained:

AUTHOR   What is the kind of thing you would say?

MIYATA TAISEN   In case of a sermon for a miscarried baby, that talk is to console the mind of each woman and attendant. *Mizuko* is not a different kind of life—your life and the *mizuko* life are the same, same nature. You must care and respect your body and mind and Buddha-nature. In the case of unborn babies, *kuyō* sends him or her to perfect peace, nirvana. Carried with Jizō Bosatsu, to maybe cross over the river.

AUTHOR   Sai no Kawara [the mythical Japanese river of the dead].

MIYATA   Right, Sai no Kawara.

AUTHOR   So the *mizuko* goes to the Pure Land?

MIYATA   Yes. Taking a peaceful journey to be born as a universal being, to be born as Buddha-nature, we are wishing that for them.[37]

After the talk is done, the ceremony is complete, and the laypeople leave. In total, it takes approximately forty minutes from the time the mourners arrive to when they leave, with the chanting occupying about twenty-five to thirty minutes. The introduction of chairs into the worship hall is the only real change related to how Koyasan performs *mizuko kuyō*, which is otherwise "exactly the same" as how the ritual is carried out in Japan.[38]

After the laypeople leave, the wooden tablet is collected and kept in storage until August 24, when Koyasan holds a major ceremony in front of the temple, where several Jizō statues, including a *mizuko* Jizō, sit (fig. 1.8). This ceremony is known as the Memorial Prayer for Unborn Babies and Okuribi Rite.[39] It includes the priests chanting many of the same sutras and mantras as in the *mizuko kuyō*; additionally, there is a *goma*, a tantric fire ceremony, wherein the *mizuko* and other wooden tablets accumulated during the year are ritually burned. Whereas the normal *mizuko kuyō* is a private service, this annual event is public and attracts hundreds of onlookers who also engage in throwing water on the Jizō statues, making monetary donations, and similar basic Japanese merit-producing devotional acts.[40]

FIGURE 1.8. *Mizuko* Jizō at Koyasan Buddhist Temple.

Mizuko Kuyō in a Japanese Buddhist New Religious Movement in America

The last tradition I will survey here is Risshō Kōsei-kai, a Nichiren-influenced sect founded in 1938. It is relevant to this project because it shows the involvement of new religious movements, not just traditional denominations, in Japanese-American *mizuko kuyō*.

With the exception of Sōka Gakkai, which developed in the twentieth century in conjunction with the Nichiren Shōshū sect, all of the schools of Buddhism discussed thus far trace their roots to the Heian and Kamakura periods of Japan. These are widely considered the classical periods of Japanese Buddhism, and many commentators have contrasted them with an allegedly more moribund contemporary Buddhism in Japan. Yet Japanese religion has been anything but static in the past hundred years—this "rush hour of the gods" has produced thousands of new religious movements, many of which explicitly locate themselves within the Buddhist fold. One of the most popular of these is Risshō Kōsei-kai.

Risshō Kōsei-kai came to America in the postwar period, with the first center outside Japan founded in Hawaii in 1958. There are now eight formal temples or groups in the United States, including Rissho Kosei-kai Buddhist Church of Los Angeles, located a few blocks from the L.A. Nichiren Shū temple, in a building formerly used by Higashi Honganji Buddhist Temple.

The temples discussed so far have largely second-, third-, and fourth-generation Japanese-American membership, based on waves of Japanese immigration that took place before 1924.[41] Rissho Kosei-kai Buddhist Church of Los Angeles's members, on the other hand, are mostly first-generation immigrants who arrived in the postwar period, in many cases as the wives of native-born Americans.

The story of how *mizuko kuyō* came to this temple differs somewhat from that of other local temples. The Reverend Mizutani Shōkō found that, after his arrival as head minister in 2001, female members sometimes requested special services for pregnancy losses. He felt that there was no need to differentiate between ancestors—the traditional object of veneration for memorial services—and those who died before birth, and therefore encouraged the members to include *mizuko* in the regular observances of the temple. After a few years, however, the Young Mothers Group at the temple decided they wanted a separate *mizuko kuyō* performed. These laywomen felt a need to give special recognition to their lost pregnancies and persisted in their demands, even when Rev. Mizutani explained his opinion that all life should be seen as equal.[42] Relenting, Rev. Mizutani allowed the group to organize the *mizuko kuyō,* which he presided over in 2005. This did not end the story, though. Older women in the temple insisted that they wanted to be included as well. Therefore the service was held again in 2006, with quadruple the attendance (approximately sixty participants). Because of this demand, *mizuko kuyō* has now been made a regular annual event of the temple, held in June, and appears on the calendar and in literature for newcomers.[43]

Participants sign up for the *mizuko kuyō* ahead of time by filling out a form, stating the posthumous ordination names of *mizuko* that they wish to be remembered. In most cases, these *mizuko* will have already received such names upon request to a qualified Risshō Kōsei-kai leader—they are similar to those for ancestors but differ in a few characters because the gender of the fetus is in most cases unknown. The participants arrive ahead of the time set for the ceremony and are greeted by women at welcome tables. Here they receive origami paper and are instructed to go and fold paper cranes, which are then presented as offerings before the *mizuko kuyō* begins. The service itself takes place in the main worship hall, a large room with pews and a raised stage area (called the *seidan*) with seats for leaders, musical instruments, and a tall standing statue of the Eternal Shakyamuni Buddha, the object of devotion in Risshō Kōsei-kai (fig. 1.9). This same room was used as the main worship hall of the Higashi Shin temple when they owned the building, but it was set up 180 degrees opposite of the current layout: in Jōdo Shinshū temples the Amida statue is situated

FIGURE 1.9. Main worship hall at Rissho Kosei-kai Buddhist Church of Los Angeles.

along the western wall, looking east, while in Risshō Kōsei-kai temples the Shakyamuni statue is placed along the eastern wall, gazing west. The main hall set up is also much sparer than that of more traditional temples such as Zenshuji and Koyasan, lacking the golden adornments that hang above and around their main altars. All participants wear white sashes with black Japanese calligraphy that says "Namu Myōhō Renge Kyō Risshō Kōsei-kai Honbu." ("Devotion to the Lotus Sutra, Risshō Kōsei-kai Headquarters").

The service begins with a short welcome message from a woman acting as emcee of the ceremony, followed by three communal chants of "Namu Myōhō Renge Kyō." Next everyone recites the Member's Vow in English:

> We, members of Rissho Kosei-kai
> Take refuge in the Eternal Buddha Shakyamuni,
> And recognize in Buddhism the true way of salvation,
> Under the guidance of our revered founder, Nikkyo Niwano.
> In the spirit of lay Buddhists,
> We vow to perfect ourselves
> Through personal discipline and leading others
> And by improving our knowledge and practice of the faith,
> And we pledge ourselves to follow the Bodhisattva way
> To bring peace to our families, communities,
> And countries and to the world.

This is followed by the Church Anthem, performed in Japanese. Next the main sutra chanting begins. The priest and several lay dharma teachers sit on stage facing the Buddha, while the rest of the congregation sits in the pews. Together they chant a series of extracts from the three main sutras of Risshō Kōsei-kai.[44] During the sutra chanting, the dharma teachers recite the posthumous ordination names of the *mizuko* being remembered in the service. Each participant rises and individually offers incense before the altar, and the liturgical portion of the service closes with a dedication of merit.

When the chanting is finished, several testimonials are given by laywomen. Each goes to a podium to deliver a reflection on her own loss and appreciation toward the *mizuko;* these talks typically last five or six minutes. These are followed by a sermon from the minister, ten to fifteen minutes in length. The congregation chants "Namu Myōhō Renge Kyō" three more times, then takes a five-minute break while soft music plays on the CD player, giving participants a chance to reflect on the ritual. Finally the mourners prepare for the last phase of the event, a group support session called *hōza.*

Hōza is a basic practice of Risshō Kōsei-kai, more or less unique to this movement.[45] Participants sit in a circle and share their personal experiences with one another. During the *mizuko kuyō hōza*, they either move to the front of the hall between the pews and altar area, or they retire to another room where a circle can be more easily created. In the general *hōza*, a dharma teacher guides the discussion, offering suggestions of how the others may relate their experiences to Buddhist teachings and how they might practice those teachings in their everyday lives. The *mizuko kuyō hōza*, however, is slightly different, as the dharma teachers mostly listen without giving much response, allowing each person to simply voice her feelings. As Rev. Mizutani put it:

> Instead of giving some teaching, [the *hōza* leaders during *mizuko kuyō*] more try to listen, because speaking is a very important process towards awareness. So if [a *hōza* participant] feels appreciation, "Oh yes, because of this baby I decided to come, because I feel guilty I remember I decided to come to Risshō Kōsei-kai, then through Risshō Kōsei-kai not only could I offer my prayer to my baby, but at the same time I could learn Buddhist teaching. So the baby actually guided me to the Buddhist teaching." So she may be very appreciative. It is a good opportunity for her to remember [the baby], to appreciate him. But at the same time to make a renewed vow to follow the Buddhist teaching. So by speaking it also is a good way to deepen the feeling, deepen the vow. I think letting them speak is a very important process.[46]

Everyone is given a chance to speak before the *hōza* session is closed. The service portion takes about an hour and the *hōza* lasts approximately thirty minutes, making the total for the *mizuko kuyō* around ninety minutes (but also with origami folding before and brief socializing afterward).

Though the June *mizuko kuyō* is the main service for pregnancy losses, if a member insists that she cannot wait until the public service, the minister will accommodate her. In this case, the *mizuko kuyō* is held in essentially the same manner, though it is conducted in a smaller chapel at the temple or sometimes in members' homes before the home altar.[47] These more informal services lack the testimonials but do include *hōza*—the minister typically asks several other people who have experienced abortion or miscarriage to attend so that a proper *hōza* can be held and the woman receives support.

Analysis of *Mizuko Kuyō* in Japanese-American Buddhism

Now that *mizuko kuyō* at Japanese-American temples in various lineages has been examined, continuities and discontinuities can be explored. All of these

Los Angeles temples perform *mizuko kuyō* in the main worship hall, which is the central sacred space in Japanese and Japanese-American Buddhist temples. A priest presides over the ceremony, and laypeople, whether participants or observers, follow his lead. The primary ritual actions are chanting: *mizuko kuyō* always involves sutra recitation, mantras, and merit dedication verses. Incense is always offered, and in some cases food, flowers, toys, or other trinkets are offered. Participants—priestly and lay—are oriented toward the Buddha statue or mandala, which is the focus of the ceremony. Priests sit with their backs toward the laypeople, facing the main object of worship, unless constraints on space and labor force them to sit sideways. A short talk is always delivered by the priest. In virtually all cases the priest is a male Japanese immigrant, trained in Japan and sent to America to lead services at the temple.[48] If for the moment we exclude the *hōza* conducted at the Risshō Kōsei-kai temple following the formal *mizuko kuyō* service, then none of the ceremonies lasts as long as an hour: thirty to forty minutes seems to be the average length.

Also worthy of note is what *mizuko kuyō* at each of these temples lacks. For one, there is no meditation in any of these ceremonies. Some practices, such as repetitious mantra chanting or quiet reflection accompanied by music, do seem somewhat similar, but none of the temples includes formal Buddhist meditation on the part of either priests or laypeople as part of *mizuko kuyō*. This would not be significant in the context of Japanese Buddhism, in which formal meditation practice—especially by laypeople—is a rather infrequent activity (in all its branches, Zen included), but it needs mentioning because of the unusual focus on meditation by many practitioners and commentators on Buddhism in America. Also, none of these temples has an area with many *mizuko* Jizōs, as are seen at some Japanese temples, especially the ones most often discussed in the context of *mizuko kuyō*. And rather than large outside cemeteries with family grave plots as are found at many Japanese temples—often containing large *mizuko* Jizōs that can be worshipped by laypeople—they all have indoor columbaria (*nōkotsudō*) housing the ashes of temple members.[49]

Overall, the similarities among these *mizuko kuyō* seem greater than their differences, but those differences reveal interesting variations that demonstrate the range of practices and attitudes in Japanese-American Buddhism. Despite their similar general formats, the most obvious differences lie in the actual material culture and ritual practice. All are oriented toward an object of worship, but that object differs from temple to temple, largely for reasons of sectarian affiliation. At Zenshuji Soto Mission it is the historical Shakyamuni Buddha, while at the Risshō Kōsei-kai temple it is the Eternal Shakyamuni Buddha described in the sixteenth chapter of the *Lotus Sutra*. Los Angeles Nichiren Shu Temple also enshrines the Eternal Shakyamuni, but does so along with the monk Nichiren and a large calligraphic mandala he inscribed. Nichiren Shoshu Myohoji Temple of Los Angeles, on the other hand, only uses the mandala, whereas the Jodo Shu North America Buddhist Mission enshrines Amida Buddha and Koyasan has Dainichi Nyorai as its object of veneration. The subaltars at all of these temples also differ widely, enshrining a variety of sect-specific founders and celestial patrons. Thus the image being addressed in each *mizuko kuyō* is different at each temple. Each temple has its own policies about the use of wooden tablets and memorial plaques and the conferral of posthumous ordination names, the basic components of memorial rites in Japanese Buddhism.

The texts used to perform the central portion of the ritual also vary, as each sect has its favorites. The *Heart Sutra* appears at both Zenshuji and Koyasan; all the Nichirenist groups use the *Lotus Sutra;* and the Jōdo Shū temple uses the *Larger Pure Land Sutra.* Each has its own variations on the refuge, dedication, and other standard verses. Perhaps surprising is the relative lack of attention afforded to Jizō bodhisattva, given his prominent place in the historiography of *mizuko kuyō* in Japan. The Sōtō and Shingon rituals include at least the Jizō mantra, whereas the bodhisattva is absent from the other four temples. The desire to include Jizō, whose image does not appear in the main hall, seems to motivate the Zenshuji ritual's post-service tour of the temple's statues, something none of the other temples include.

Only the Risshō Kōsei-kai temple includes significant opportunities for laypeople to share their feelings; it is also the only place where offerings are manufactured by mourners rather than simply bought at a store and brought to the temple. Laypeople have the most participation in the ritual at this temple—they not only perform almost all the chants along with the priest and share their experiences in *hōza,* but they also create their own offerings and some laywomen serve in assistant roles during the ceremony itself, reading *mizuko* posthumous ordination names aloud, emceeing the service, or offering formal testimonials. Lay participation is less extensive at other temples. The two Nichiren temples, Myohoji and Los Angeles Nichiren Buddhist Temple, both expect laypeople to chant all of the sutras, the title of the *Lotus Sutra,* and some of the opening and closing verses. At the Jōdo Shū temple, laypeople generally chant only "Namu Amida Butsu," whereas at Zenshuji and Koyasan the laity are essentially passive observers who do little more than offer incense and say a mantra or two. This reflects common trends in Japan, where the average *mizuko kuyō* participant is an observer of the rite carried out by the priest, whereas Nichiren temples often expect a higher degree of lay participation in the chanting.

Arguably more significant are the differences in how each temple approaches *mizuko kuyō.* For instance, there are a range of attitudes toward the privacy of the ritual. In most cases, *mizuko kuyō* is carried out for a single person or couple, occasionally with a few family members as well. Some of the temples consider these ceremonies strictly private. Others allow or even encourage participants to invite family and friends, and are open to outsiders simply observing the ritual. The Risshō Kōsei-kai temple holds a big annual *mizuko kuyō* where multiple *mizuko* are honored by people unrelated to one another. The Koyasan August fire ceremony, while not strictly speaking a *mizuko kuyō*, also includes some honoring of unrelated *mizuko* in a highly public performance.

Differences also relate to the types of clientele that each temple serves in its *mizuko kuyō*. The typical *mizuko kuyō* seeker at Koyasan and Zenshuji, for instance, is a new Japanese immigrant (Shin Issei) or Japanese student who is unaffiliated with the temple. They appear to seek the temple out only in the wake of an abortion or miscarriage, typically looking the temple up in the phonebook. Koyasan also gets referrals from the several Jōdo Shinshū temples in the area, none of which perform *mizuko kuyō*, and benefits from having a large *mizuko* Jizō statue in front of the temple (located next to the main shopping and dining area in Little Tokyo), which acts to advertise the availability of *mizuko* services within.⁵⁰ Sectarian identity of *kuyō* participants is unimportant to either Koyasan or Zenshuji, and often *mizuko kuyō* seekers have no particular denominational affiliation at all. On the other hand, Myohoji performs services only for members, and the Jōdo Shū temple prefers to serve Jōdo Shū Buddhists or those specifically without affiliation, steering away people who admit to being connected to traditions represented by other local temples. Risshō Kōsei-kai *mizuko kuyō* participants are almost always members, though this is not because of an official policy. Apparently, unaffiliated Japanese in America prefer to seek services from traditional Buddhist denominations rather than from new religious movements, which are often associated with aggressive proselytization. And the L.A. Nichiren Shū temple shows an interesting split in its clientele: members seek *mizuko kuyō* for miscarriages, but *kuyō* performed for abortions are usually done at the request of outsiders. It might be that temple members are embarrassed or ashamed to make their own priest aware of their abortions—he has publicly denounced abortion—and seek to have *mizuko kuyō* performed elsewhere, such as at Koyasan.

Money too divides some of these temples from the others. Although a set fee is never charged, there are different attitudes toward donations, which are in fact expected. At Zenshuji, Koyasan, and the Nichiren Shū temple, it is expected that laypeople who ask for a *mizuko kuyō* will make a donation to both the priest who performs the ritual and the temple itself, with each separate donation equaling about $50. In actual practice, this ranges considerably—a significant number of participants are students, often with limited budgets. Donations of $20 to $25 are not uncommon; on the other hand, some donors provide as much as $100 to both the priest and the temple. The Jōdo Shū mission and Risshō Kōsei-kai, meanwhile, accept money only for the temple, not the priest. Myohoji, the Nichiren Shōshū temple, connects its donations to the *tōba* that is inscribed for the parent, asking for a $10 donation to offset costs. Additional expenses can be accrued at the various temples if the layperson wishes for a formal memorial plaque to be created for the *mizuko,* but in these cases the temple merely acts as the middleman, with the actual money going to the supply shop that creates the plaque upon request.

Money then plays a different role for a temple like Koyasan compared to the Los Angeles Nichiren Buddhist Temple, for instance. Both expect donations to be made to priest and temple. But even though Rev. Kanai at the Nichiren temple is one of the most vocal local advocates of *mizuko kuyō,* he performs the ceremony rarely and receives scant income from these services. Koyasan, meanwhile, conducts *mizuko kuyō* regularly, and conducts other services (such as *senzō kuyō*—memorials for ancestors—and rituals for health or fortune) with about the same frequency.[51] This translates into significant income for priest and temple alike, not a small matter when one considers the precarious financial situation of many American Buddhist temples. They lack the benefits of the parish system of Japan, which ties families more or less permanently to specific temples. They also have to fight the demographics of Japanese-America: Japanese immigration to the United States has been far slower since the major waves of the late nineteenth and early twentieth centuries, and Japanese-Americans have one of the highest intermarriage rates of all ethnic minorities, significantly reducing the number of children raised Buddhist. These factors have led to diminishing membership at many older Japanese-American Buddhist temples and have put some in financial jeopardy. In such a situation, one might expect some temples to market their services, such as *mizuko kuyō,* more actively. But Koyasan does little to announce its willingness to perform such rituals, and the other temples that perform far fewer *mizuko kuyō* show no interest in promoting *kuyō* performance. For most of the twentieth century, these Japanese-American temples faced suspicion and at times harsh persecution from the dominant white Christian community, and they have adopted a low profile in adapting to American realities. With prejudice lighter in the twenty-first century and continuing financial pressures, this stance may eventually be forced to change.

A final area of difference deserves note: attitudes toward *mizuko* spirits and the women who create them. All of the priests consulted for this book stated clearly that abortion is against fundamental Buddhist principles. However, many were more equivocal about its legal status. The majority felt that abortion is wrong morally but is a matter for a woman to decide for herself, and several suggested that it is more wrong for a child to be born into a very unfavorable situation. Rev. Kanai and Rev. Mizutani both felt that abortion should be illegal, though Rev. Mizutani believed exceptions relating to the health of the mother or genetic defects in the fetus should be permitted.

Ideas about *mizuko* spirits also differed. Most felt that *mizuko kuyō* assisted the spirit in achieving Buddhahood or being reborn in a pure Buddha-land (not necessarily that of Amida Buddha). Rev. Tanaka was uncertain about the status of *mizuko:* according to Jōdo Shū doctrine, a being must chant "Namu Amida Butsu" to achieve the Pure Land, yet he felt instinctually that Amida would embrace *mizuko* nonetheless. Rev. Kojima, the Sōtō Zen priest, simply said that he didn't know precisely what happened to *mizuko* and wasn't particularly concerned about the matter. Regardless of the specifics of their ideas about *mizuko,* however, in all cases *mizuko kuyō* remained overtly contextualized by Japanese Buddhist views about the persistence of ghosts after death and the tangible relationship between this world and the spirit realm.

Feelings about spirit interference in the world of the living were not unanimous. All disclaimed the notion of *tatari* (spirit attacks) as having no basis in authentic Buddhist teaching.[52] Here the effects of public criticism of *mizuko kuyō* can be seen—*tatari* has become a dirty word for many Japanese Buddhists, so that even individuals who believe in the phenomenon may avoid directly professing such a belief, especially to an outsider. But when that particular word was set aside during interviews, a range of attitudes readily revealed themselves. On one end, Rev. Tanaka felt that belief in spirits who bother the living was absurd, and he likened it to superstitions picked up from Japanese horror films.[53] On the other end of the spectrum, Rev. Kanai expressed clear belief that *mizuko* spirits may pester a woman's living children to prompt her to conduct *mizuko kuyō*. And though he stopped short of explicitly attributing them to spirit attacks, Rev. Kanai suggested that women who have abortions will suffer symptoms associated in Japan with *tatari:* "Abortion has many harmful influences. It is not always true but it is said that a woman who has an abortion tends to be more stressful and frigid, or her husband cheats or becomes violent, or her child misbehaves or is easy to get sick."[54] However, the priests said that fear of *tatari* was clearly a reason that some women expressed in explaining why they sought out *mizuko kuyō* at Japanese-American temples.[55] They dealt with this in different ways: some priests attempted to convince their clients that spirit attack was a wrong idea, whereas others explained that once *mizuko kuyō* had been performed, *tatari* would not occur.[56]

Acculturation of *Mizuko Kuyō* at Japanese-American Buddhist Temples

Religious acculturation, the process by which a religion shifts from being the product and expression of a foreign culture to being somehow "American," is a major theme in the historiography of religion in the United States. It is arguably *the* theme of studies of American Buddhism, a fact that has both benefits and drawbacks. In examining the practices of nonwhite Buddhists in particular, it can have the effect of rendering Asian traditions practiced in the West somehow "un-American," reifying both Asia and America in problematic ways. Asian-American Buddhism in this critique is only authentically American to the extent that it changes from its culture of origin. I would counter that "American Buddhism" is whatever Buddhist practices are performed in the United States and its territories or by its citizens in whatever locale. A sutra chanted in Japanese or Pali is no less "American" than one performed in English (or, increasingly, Spanish).

An ironic second drawback is that tales of adaptation can make changes by Asian-American communities in their Buddhist practices seem "inauthentic." This is a common implication of comments on the usage of terms such as "church" and "minister" by Asian-American Buddhists or the inclusion of Sunday morning meetings. By taking on elements that are identified by some as inherently Christian, for instance, these Buddhists are charged with having deviated from some purer, essential Japanese Buddhism. This critique is as condescending in its way as the first, not only to Asian-American Buddhism but to that of Japan as well, which is hardly static. It also tends to ignore the ways that such changes have arisen as innovative survival strategies in the face of situations of unequal power exerted by white American Christians. In examining the changes that have been made to *mizuko kuyō* by Japanese-American temples, therefore, let us bear in mind that I am not making value judgments or suggesting that one form is more authentically American or Japanese than another. Rather, the purpose of this exercise is simply to note if and how *mizuko kuyō* practices are impacted specifically by being conducted at temples in the United States.

In fact, Japanese-American temples that perform *mizuko kuyō* have made few deliberate changes to allow these rituals to fit into a new cultural milieu. This contrasts with the significant alterations of the convert Zen communities examined in chapters 2–4 and necessitates some discussion to account for this conservative trend. One important reason that *mizuko kuyō* remains generally intact when it crosses from Japanese to Japanese-American temples lies with the particular clientele for this service. Though the average member of most of these temples is a native-born Japanese-American (usually second or third generation), those who seek *mizuko kuyō* in the United States are often Japanese-born people who have immigrated (Shin Isseis) or those who are here for extended periods of work, study, or relaxation.

The demographics of Japanese-American Buddhism and the history of twentieth-century Japanese religion largely account for this phenomenon. *Mizuko kuyō* rose to prominence in Japanese culture after World War II ended and abortion became a common form of birth control. But Japanese immigration was virtually choked off by racist immigration laws in place between 1924 and 1965. When Japanese citizens could once again emigrate to America, they did so in far smaller numbers than they had before World War II. This means that most Japanese-Americans are descendants of that first wave of pre–*mizuko kuyō* immigrants, among whom the practice was unknown. Even when knowledge of the practice began to arrive on American shores in the latter half of the twentieth century, the majority of Japanese-American temples resisted adding this newly popular ritual to their repertoire because they belong to the Jōdo Shinshū school and therefore oppose the practice of *mizuko kuyō*. Furthermore, as discussed in the introduction, abortion was generally illegal in the United States until 1973. That means that although women in Japan from 1948 onward had recourse to abortion and thus became involved in situations that potentially invited *mizuko kuyō*, an entire additional generation passed in the United States before Japanese-American women had the same options.[57]

The aging of Japanese-American Buddhism, which has shifted in the direction of older membership as the Japanese assimilated into American society, is relevant here. Those first-, second-, and third-generation Buddhists who learned of *mizuko kuyō* and did seek it out had, by the time of the writing of this book (2002–2008), already participated in the ceremony years or decades ago and were past the fertile stages of life when new *mizuko* might be produced. Members of the fourth generation (Yonseis), meanwhile, who are in their productive childbearing years, are a rather small proportion of Japanese-American temple membership, a matter of serious concern in American Jōdo Shinshū and similar circles. On the whole, the traditional Japanese-American community is not a very fertile ground for *mizuko kuyō*. Therefore, it is among the more recent arrivals from Japan—whether here temporarily or as permanent immigrants—that *mizuko kuyō* finds its niche. Unlike the original first generation (the Isseis), these Shin Isseis and visitors arrive from a Japan where *mizuko kuyō* is omnipresent and familiar, and they are less likely to be Jōdo

Shinshū followers.[58] Current or recent Japanese citizens, the Shin Isseis do not need or seek significant alterations in *mizuko kuyō* from how it is performed in Japan. And the priests who provide it to them are in nearly all cases Japanese immigrants themselves; only Jōdo Shinshū, the major traditional sect that has a policy of not performing *mizuko kuyō*, has a significant number of American-born ministers.

The Americanizing changes that occur in *mizuko kuyō*, therefore, are mainly related to indirect factors. These include lack of access to traditional Japanese material objects, restricted space in dense urban environments, and clerical shortages. They affect not only *mizuko kuyō* but virtually all services provided by these temples. Thus even though most of the Los Angeles temples examined in this chapter are major representatives of their sects (Zenshuji, Koyasan, Myohoji, and Jodo Shu North America Buddhist Mission are all the North American headquarters of their sects), they nonetheless occupy smaller spaces, with fewer priests and tighter budgets, than temples of equivalent status would enjoy in Japan. This means that they typically have smaller main worship halls with less room to replicate the main altar and surrounding spaces in a manner similar to Japanese temples. The amount of ritual activity that can take place is therefore restricted (some temples, for instance, cannot accommodate priests performing full prostrations before the altar) and forces some activities to be performed in an altered manner, such as facing in a different direction (perpendicular to the main object of worship instead of facing it, for example).

Some temples omit wooden tablets (*tōba*) and memorial plaques that would probably use them in *mizuko kuyō* if performed in Japan. Myohoji, one of the temples that does employ *tōba*, manufactures their own out of construction paper that can be obtained easily in America, a material that is not used for this purpose in Japan. This adaptation allows the Nichiren Shōshū community to continue its familiar memorial practices without paying to continually import materials from Japan; it also is partially prompted by the environmentalist concerns of American members, who criticized the logging required to produce traditional wooden *tōba*. Lack of resources and space also helps to explain why there are almost no American *mizuko jizōdō* (separate *mizuko* shrines, commonly used sites for *mizuko kuyō* in Japan), forcing *mizuko* rites to be performed in the main worship hall. This also contributes to the rarity of *mizuko* Jizō images and total absence of *mizuko* Kannon images, figures who are common in Japan.

The most significant change to the setting in which American *mizuko kuyō* takes place is the introduction of pews or chairs into the main worship hall (*hondō*). Every Japanese-American temple studied for this project has such a main worship hall arrangement.[59] Compared to the flat, uncluttered gathering spaces of Japanese temples, which lack chairs or pews, this reduces the number of people who can attend services and usually necessitates the elevation of the altar onto a high stage-like area so that the main object of worship will not be at eye level.[60] The effect tends to subtly cut the laity off to a greater degree from the holy image and the ritual actions of the priests. Even when laypeople stand and approach to offer incense, the object of worship is often at a significantly higher relative level that in a Japanese temple, reducing the element of direct personal encounter with the object of worship.[61]

This change needs to be examined more closely, however, because contrary to some reports that lump in the use of pews and chairs with such changes as "church" for "temple," the utilization of these items is not necessarily an attempt by Japanese-American temples to appear more Christian and thus blend in better in America. Many priests said that these innovations had been made simply to accommodate the needs of Japanese-Americans, who were unaccustomed to sitting on the floor in their personal and work lives. The need to make senior citizens comfortable was also cited as a major factor in the current arrangement of temple worship halls. In fact, some modern temples in Japan use chairs (though usually not pews) as the Japanese themselves have moved to a more chair-based culture. Looking at other Asian-American temples shows similar concerns. For example, Won Buddhism of Los Angeles, a temple with a largely Korean immigrant membership, uses pews in its main worship hall to meet the needs of older members, not to mimic American religious norms.

Actual changes to the ritual actions of *mizuko kuyō* at Japanese-American temples are relatively few. Not many of the priests with whom I spoke said they had deliberately altered their style of *mizuko kuyō*. Rev. Kojima of Zenshuji is one of them: he performs the *Daihishin Darani* as the central chant of *mizuko kuyō* at his temple. This is a modification of how he was taught to carry out the ritual by his preceptor in Japan. There, the main text would be the *Jizō Bosatsu Hongan Kyō*, the primary sutra devoted to the bodhisattva Jizō. This text is more than ten times longer than the *Daihishin Darani*. Kojima speaks of such changes as doing things "Los Angeles–style."

AUTHOR What is Los Angeles-style?

KOJIMA SHŪMYŌ Shorter than Japanese style.

AUTHOR So not just *mizuko kuyō*, but many services tend to be shorter?

KOJIMA Right.

AUTHOR Why are they shorter?

KOJIMA I think in Japan, long chanting is traditional. People understand it, and they understand that it is as it is, even longer services they consider they have to be patient, to keep listening to the chanting. But here, the need to be patient without understanding the meaning makes a very difficult time for people.[62]

Rev. Kanai's *mizuko kuyō* at the Nichiren Shū temple contains two obvious American liturgical additions, the compositions *Lord Buddha's Children* and *Golden Chain*. These are English verses with no precise Japanese antecedent; they therefore would never appear in Japanese *mizuko kuyō*. Though they sometimes appear in other services at the Los Angeles Nichiren Buddhist Temple, he makes a particular point of performing them during *mizuko kuyō*, especially the verse about Buddha's children, because of their connection to parenting. *Golden Chain* is one of the most popular original American Buddhist pieces of liturgy: created for use in Hawaiian Jōdo Shinshū temples early in the twentieth century, it is now found in the service books of nearly every Japanese-American Buddhist tradition, regardless of denomination, and is most popular as a children's tune. It is interesting that the two American compositions, intended originally as Buddhist Sunday school hymns, have migrated into services for adults.

The only other changes made in American *mizuko kuyō* were slight alterations to the service at the Rissho Kosei-Kai temple. Rev. Mizutani indicated that he encouraged slightly longer testimonials during the *mizuko* service and more listening rather than discussion in the *hōza* session following the service. He also plays music between the end of the service and the beginning of the *hōza*, a difference from how the ceremony might be carried out in Japan. But these changes seem to be more personal in nature, related to how Mizutani would like such services performed in general. Though first unveiled in America, the changes are related to what he thinks is best for the members and are not a response to the fact that his is an American temple. The L.A. temple is his first appointment, making it difficult to determine precisely what is American innovation and what is simply the experimentation of a new minister with his first congregation.

Conclusion

Mizuko kuyō came to the United States in the 1960s, quietly, before abortion became a major national issue. Even with the subsequent rise in prominence of the abortion debate and the explosion of interest in Buddhism among Americans of the last decades of the twentieth century, the presence of this ritual in select Japanese-American communities remained overlooked. In part this is because of the relative lack of attention given to Asian-American Buddhism by scholars, especially Japanese forms of Buddhism other than Jōdo Shinshū and Sōka Gakkai, both of which are opposed to *mizuko kuyō*.

But it also suggests the general isolation of these temples from non-Japanese outsiders. From a historical perspective, pre-modern Japan was significantly less involved in propagating Buddhism to other countries than many other major centers, such as India, China, and Sri Lanka, and therefore Japanese Buddhism did not come readily to an attitude of transmitting Buddhism to non-Japanese. Furthermore, Japanese people in general and non-Christian organizations in particular were subjected to constant and often intense discrimination as they settled into the United States, reducing their ability and willingness to work with outsiders on making Buddhism available to non-Japanese Americans. Nichiren Shū, Jōdo Shū, and Shingon Shū engaged in little outreach and attracted slight interest from the non-Asian population of the United States. Risshō Kōsei-kai has been slow to target non-Japanese-Americans. Nichiren Shōshū fared a little better, mainly through its pre-1991 partnership with Sōka Gakkai, but happens to conduct only a very minimal *mizuko kuyō*. Furthermore, the average lay practitioner of Nichiren Shōshū–based Buddhism, whether the temple tradition or Sōka Gakkai, has always been a layperson with little to no access to the formal services, such as *mizuko kuyō*, of the small number of Nichiren Shōshū priests operating in America. Meanwhile, Sōtō Zen did manage to attract significant attention from European-Americans beginning in the early 1960s. But as will be discussed in the next chapter, this interest was almost entirely focused on meditation practice and the hagiographies of seemingly liberated ancient masters, not in nonmeditative ritual practice, savior figures such as Jizō, or everyday Japanese temple Buddhism. *Mizuko kuyō* at Japanese-American temples had no influence on the growing European-American practices; their development of *mizuko*-related rites is a separate tale to be narrated in chapter 2.

Viewing these temples through the lens of *mizuko kuyō* reveals facets of Japanese-American Buddhism rarely captured by previous research. In particular, the categorization of Japanese-American Buddhism as "ethnic" or "export" Buddhism tends to flatten out important differences among various groups. Looking once again, we can see that where there is usually expected to be consensus we find considerable disagreement—the two large Jōdo Shinshū temples in Little Tokyo do not perform *mizuko kuyō*, whereas their seemingly similar Pure Land neighbor the Jōdo Shū temple has been conducting services for pregnancy losses since the 1960s. The Nichiren Shū and Nichiren Shōshū communities diverge sharply in the amount of ritualization they believe a pregnancy loss deserves. Koyasan Buddhist Temple has conducted thousands of *mizuko kuyō* ceremonies as part of its wide range of services—including rituals for good luck and selling fortunes (*omikuji*), charms for traffic safety and easy childbirth (*omamori*), and votive tablets (*ema*)—whereas the Risshō Kōsei-kai temple began to hold large public ceremonies only within the last three years.

We also see intriguing details about the participants at these temples. Contrary to the assumption that historic Japanese temples in the United States cater to the descendants of pre-1924 immigration, we find that new immigrants are reshaping the ritual life of these temples by requesting services that are rarely sought by "old-line" members. These Shin Isseis are the x-factors of Japanese Buddhism in America—their practices and religious orientations are largely unknown, and assumptions that they simply fit preexisting patterns of Japanese-American religiosity are clearly flawed. Significantly, they are able to move Japanese-American temples in a more Japanese direction, prompting them to perform new Japanese rituals previously absent from the practice of these American temples—and in this case they did so precisely during the post–World War II period when increasing Americanization of such temples has been assumed to be the trend. Ongoing transnational ties have led to the introduction of new rituals that were not part of the original "baggage" that initial waves of Japanese Buddhist immigration brought with them in the prewar period.

Another point to emphasize is that Asian-American laypeople have considerable influence on the types of practices performed in many temples. Rather than being beholden to priests or goaded into allegedly antifeminist rituals, laypeople (especially women) initiate the performance of *mizuko kuyō* at local temples, sometimes in the face of priestly opposition. Even Jōdo Shinshū priests will back down and try to find a comfortable compromise if a layperson is sufficiently insistent that she wants an unorthodox ceremony performed.

Thus this look at Japanese-American Buddhist temples has shown the diversity of approaches to *mizuko kuyō* and the way in which Americanization proceeds in something less than a straight line. Japanese-American temples show various degrees of Americanization in the ritual, but the introduction of the ritual in the first place represents a kind of partial "re-Japanization" against the backdrop of slow twentieth- and twenty-first-century progress toward the U.S. religious mainstream.

A final benefit of looking at these temples is that it prepares us for a comparative glance into the convert Zen communities. These groups also take their inspiration from Japanese religious customs, but they understand and practice Buddhism in significantly different ways. It is to these new Buddhists and their *mizuko kuyō* practices that I now turn.

2

"A Shadow in the Heart"

Mizuko Kuyō *in Convert American Zen*

This is a world of flows.

—Thomas A. Tweed, *Crossing and Dwelling*

When Zen abbess Jan Chozen Bays wished to introduce Jizō bodhisattva to an American audience in 2001, she did not resort to a history lesson about his place in Asian tradition or a commentary on the texts connected with him. Rather, she sought to put her American readers into direct encounter with him, using the second-person narrative perspective and focusing on emotional cues and visual images:

> A little man of gray stone stands in the garden. His eyes are closed and his lips curve in a faint smile. A fern leaf arches over his head like an umbrella, holding a few bright drops of rain. Someone has made a small bonnet and cape of red cloth for him. A bit of paper peeks out of a pocket sewn on the cape. If you slip it out, you will find it is a message to a child, a dead child. *You had a sweet soul. In your short life you knew pain and love. I miss you.*
>
> A small kite flutters on a low branch. It has a long tail made of twists of bright paper, each bearing a message. *"Uncle Jim remembers your wonderful laugh." "Auntie Jean sends you butterfly kisses." "Bye, bye, baby boy. Mommy loves you."*[1]

Step by step, Bays drew her audience in closer. This garden isn't just for dead children, but for those who were never born. It is a place where God and Jizō alike can be called on in a time of need:

> As you walk around the garden you find other stone figures standing among the slender trees and seated on cushions of green moss. Some have begun to crumble, their features softening, and gray lichen has begun to creep over their patient bodies. You see several thin wooden plaques hanging from a tree and see that they bear names and dates of birth and death separated by only a few months or years. On some plaques are faded drawings, flowers, a teddy bear, a sprinkling of stars and on some, more prayers. *"You are loved and remembered my sweet baby girl. Conceived in love and desired. Died through medical mishap. Never far from our hearts and minds—one of God's smallest angels..."*
>
> At the base of a standing Jizo, there is a little blue doll. It was painstakingly cut and sewn from a favorite T-shirt by a man whose unborn son died when the mother was struck by a car. He had stuffed the doll with paper tissues wet with the tears of friends who came to mourn. There are notes and remembrances from women recalling abortions many years past and from doctors and nurses who assisted in abortions.[2]

Finally, Bays introduced her take on the *mizuko kuyō* ceremony, and revealed that this was not a Japanese scene after all. It was a new development in American religion, a quiet revolution with implications for the abortion issue, Zen in the West, and all who mourn children known and unknown:

> If you came on another day, you might witness a procession of men and women wending their way to the garden carrying tiny garments sewn from red cloth, wooden plaques, and pinwheels or other handmade toys. Led by a woman in a Zen priest's black robes, they chant together, offer incense, then place the remembrances they have made on the statues in the garden. The priest intones a dedication, a list of names of children, including babies whose sex was unknown or who were never named. A few couples hold hands, tears run silently down cheeks, and one woman slips quietly into the trees for a few minutes to sob alone before joining the group for the final chant.
>
> This is a Jizō garden, one of the first in America.[3]

In Japan, Zen is a common purveyor of *mizuko kuyō*. But Zen in America is different from Zen in Japan. Here, some argue, Zen is associated with individualistic meditation practice, disdain for mythology and superstition, antiritualism, liberal social and religious values, and psychological approaches to religion.[4] Some Buddhist apologists who have influenced American percep-tions of Zen have even gone so far as to suggest that Zen is something other than Buddhism—some core, universal insight that transcends the debased ideas of popular religion and the rigid structures of denominational institu-tions.[5] What chance, then, does a ritual associated with appeasing angry ghosts have in the rational world of American Zen?

As it turns out, it is precisely Zen groups in America that have become most active in promoting *mizuko kuyō*. At least a dozen convert-oriented Bud-dhist temples in the United States provide variations on *mizuko kuyō*. A full list of Zen leaders providing such ceremonies is provided in the appendix and includes Yvonne Rand at Green Gulch Farm Zen Center in California; Wendy Egyoku Nakao at Zen Center of Los Angeles; Sevan Ross at Chicago Zen Center; Amala Wrightson at Rochester Zen Center, New York; and Jan Chozen Bays at Great Vow Monastery in Oregon. Together the temples include Sōtō, Rinzai, Sanbōkyōdan, and independent Zen lineages.

Some of these temples have multiple priests who have performed the ceremony, and some of these priests have on occasion offered the ritual at other temples, at national Buddhist conferences, or at private homes as well. Other centers have held the ceremony a single time. These include Zen Com-munity of Oak Park, Illinois, Berkeley (California) Buddhist Monastery, and Zen Mountain Monastery in Mt. Tremper, New York.[6] Furthermore, priests at a number of additional convert Zen temples have expressed their intention to hold "water baby" ceremonies in the future (for example, Sunya Kjolhede at Windhorse Zen Center, in North Carolina), and lay people have discussed having a ceremony performed at centers lacking a resident priest (such as Madison Zen Center in Wisconsin).[7] Some temples, such as Zen Mountain Center outside Palm Springs, California, include prayers for aborted fetuses in annual Jizō ceremonies.[8] Yet other Zen temples (for example, Dharma Rain Zen Center in Portland, Oregon) will hold abbreviated funeral rites for fetuses on request. Though these latter rituals are not truly *mizuko* ceremo-nies, they nonetheless contribute to the growing ritual acknowledgment of pregnancy loss and may come under the influence of *mizuko kuyō*-related ideas and practices as water baby ceremonies gain further prominence in American Zen.[9]

In total, the appendix includes some of the most important teachers and lineages in American Zen—their influence extends far beyond these individual temples to entire networks of branch temples, publishing houses, and sophisti-cated Web sites. It would not be overstating the matter to say that these temples and the networks associated with them represent the majority of Japanese-derived Zen centers in America today.

This chapter traces the process of how these convert American Zen centers came to offer and promote *mizuko kuyō*–derived post–pregnancy loss rituals. As I demonstrate, it is women who have taken the lead in researching, publicizing, and performing these ceremonies. These include not only female priests who lead the ceremonies but also laywomen who prompt male temple leaders to help them ritualize their pregnancy losses. Although the growth of these convert rituals followed in the wake of a *"mizuko* boom" in Japan, the American phenomenon is largely the result of changes in American society generally and developments within American Zen specifically—these rituals demonstrate that domestication of Buddhism involves not only the process of altering imported elements of the tradition, but also takes place in the gradual emergence of new ideas and practices that reflect native concerns. Once these new practices emerge, however, they function as a conduit for information on Buddhism from Asia, thus reversing the usually expected process of importation from abroad followed by adaptation in America. To distinguish American from Japanese ceremonies, I henceforth refer to *mizuko kuyō* in convert temples as "water baby ceremonies" (or, in a few special cases that will be discussed below, as "proto-water baby ceremonies"), a common term used by several of these American groups.[10]

Transmission and Importation: Bringing *Mizuko Kuyō* to America

The first record of Jizō-related memorial rites involving American Buddhist converts dates from 1969.[11] Suzuki Shunryū and his student Yvonne Rand conducted a memorial service at Tassajara Zen Center in California for an adult man, which included placing a Jizō statue atop the man's grave. This does not seem to have been a deliberate attempt by Suzuki to introduce Jizō rituals to America, but nonetheless it was to have far-reaching implications. As Rand explains:

> This, my first meeting with Jizo, affected me deeply. For some years afterwards, I could not explain my pull to the figure of this sweet-faced monk with hands in the mudra of prayer and greeting.
>
> Several years after this funeral ceremony, I terminated an unexpected pregnancy by having an abortion. I suffered after the abortion, but it was not until some years had passed that I came to fully understand my grieving and/or the resolution to which I eventually came.

Subsequently, I began spending time in Japan and became reacquainted with Jizo. Figures of Jizo are everywhere there. I saw firsthand that Jizo ritual and ceremony involved not just graveyards and death in general, but particularly the deaths of infants and fetuses through abortion, miscarriage or stillbirth. Back home, during the 1970's and 1980's, women had begun coming to me and asking if I could help them with their difficulties in the aftermath of an abortion or a miscarriage. In consequence I began doing a simple memorial service for groups of people who had experienced the deaths of fetuses and babies.[12]

Rand's first ceremony was held in 1973.[13] She was not the only American Zen leader struggling with abortion and Buddhist practice during this period. Robert Aitken, one of the first founders of American Zen practice communities in the 1950s, was approached in the late 1970s by a couple who belonged to his center. They asked him to do some sort of ritual for an abortion the woman had undergone.[14] Aitken developed a basic ceremony and then consulted his teacher, Yamada Kōun. Yamada described the process of *mizuko kuyō* at Nichiren, Shingon, and Tendai temples in Japan, and Aitken incorporated some of this information.[15] The result was a ceremony that has only occasionally been performed at the Diamond Sangha, but, because it was published as an appendix to Aitken's *The Mind of Clover* in 1984, has received wider attention.[16]

Establishing the date of the first water baby ceremony is difficult for two reasons. First, records and memories from the 1970s and '80s are imperfect, and my project was made more complicated by serious illnesses experienced by both Rand and Aitken, which hampered my ability to conduct in-person interviews with them.[17] Second, what information I do have of rituals during this initial phase suggests that the ceremonies were different from the format that has become standard for water baby ceremonies in the 1990s and early years of the new millennium.[18] Therefore, I suggest a demarcation between Rand and Aitken's early efforts and these more robust rituals, which evolved after Rand saw participants' reactions to the ceremony at women's conferences in 1988 and 1990 and decided to offer it "as often as possible." In 1991, she took a three-month research trip to Japan to learn more about *mizuko kuyō*, and her return corresponds roughly with the time that the ritual began to attract widespread publicity and was actively adopted by other American Zen communities. It is also at this time that the term "water baby ceremony" emerged and that the general outline of the ritual stabilized into the familiar ritual performed at the temples listed in the appendix.[19]

With these facts in mind, it seems reasonable to differentiate (a) the proto–water baby ceremony period ranging approximately from the early 1970s to the late 1980s, when Rand and Aitken worked on abortion-related rituals that would later influence (b) the rise, at the end of the 1980s, of the model of a full-fledged water baby ceremony that has remained relatively unchanged to the present. Aitken's proto–water baby ceremony differed considerably from the now-standard water baby ceremony; it was far shorter, designed for a single couple, included no sewing or talking circles or offerings, and accorded only a minor role to Jizō. I tentatively date the first true American water baby ceremony to Rand's ritual at the 1988 "Celebration of Women in Buddhist Practice" conference, with the caveat that it is possible to argue for an earlier date because of Rand's history of performing post-abortion ceremonies. An important difference from the earlier events is that they were private affairs, generally for a single person. By contrast, there were thirty-seven participants in the conference ritual.[20] This large, corporate ceremony was a watershed event in American Buddhism and became the model referenced by most of the leaders described later in this chapter in creating their own rituals.

Following Rand's decision to begin offering the ceremony more frequently and expose more people to it, she began to draw attention to it in several ways. Besides conducting it at conferences for Buddhist women, she discussed it at Zen teachers' meetings and wrote articles about the ceremony for such venues as *Inquiring Mind* (the journal of the Vipassana movement in America) and the anthology *Buddhism through American Women's Eyes.*[21] Articles by other Buddhists exposed to the water baby ceremony by Rand appeared in such forums as *Turning Wheel*, the journal of the Buddhist Peace Fellowship, often with step-by-step accounts of the ritual and highly positive reflections on the emotion-healing potential of the ceremony.[22] The publication of scholar William LaFleur's *Liquid Life* in 1992 also helped stimulate interest in *mizuko kuyō*, as did an article he wrote for *Tricycle: The Buddhist Review* in 1995.

Rand was by then conducting the ceremony regularly at Green Gulch Farm Zen Center in Marin County, a branch of the Sōtō-affiliated San Francisco Zen Center; eventually she opened her own center, named Goat-in-the-Road Zendo, which conducts the ritual three to five times each year.[23] The first leader to perform Rand's ceremony elsewhere was Susan Jion Postal of the Empty Hand Zendo, which combines a mix of Zen influences. Postal, a student in the Sōtō lineage of Maezumi Taizan who also studied with the Rinzai teacher Maureen Stuart,[24] was prompted to hold the ceremony by laywomen who asked her for help with their pregnancy losses. She responded by participating in a water baby ceremony held by Yvonne Rand—in part to memorialize Postal's own pregnancy losses—and then holding a ceremony for her own community in

1991. Her temple holds the ceremony only when requested, an average of once every four years. Typical participation is seven to ten people, mainly women.

Sunyana Graef, founder of Vermont Zen Center, was the next teacher to take up the ceremony. She learned of the ceremony from Rand in 1990 and held the first water baby ceremony at the center in August 1992; she has performed a modified form of Rand's ceremony annually ever since, with an average attendance of twenty.[25] Graef was trained at Rochester Zen Center, which draws on Sōtō and Rinzai forms but is independent of any specific Zen sect; its roots lie with the Sōtō- and Rinzai-influenced Sanbōkyōdan, a Buddhist new religious movement, but it broke away in the 1970s. Like many temples, Graef's community created a Jizō garden at the Vermont center to accommodate the ritual.

The next American Zen teacher to incorporate the ceremony into her temple's offerings was Jan Chozen Bays. Bays is the cofounder of the Zen Community of Oregon and a disciple of the late Maezumi Taizan of Zen Center of Los Angeles, who was affiliated with the Sanbōkyōdan as well as mainstream Japanese Sōtō Zen. She had first encountered *mizuko* when Maezumi returned from a trip to Japan with a small *mizuko* Jizō statue, which he placed in the temple's health clinic, where Bays worked.[26] However, Maezumi made no attempt to explain *mizuko kuyō* to Bays or others in his community. Rather, Bays heard about *mizuko kuyō* from Rand, with whom she had become friends by the early 1990s. A longtime child-abuse investigator in Oregon, often confronted with the most tragic and senseless aspects of human cruelty, Bays was moved by the idea of a ceremony for dead infants. In 1993, she took part in a water baby ceremony led by Rand at Green Gulch. She described the effect of the ceremony:

> Later as I looked out the window of the plane heading back to Portland, I realized that my heart was palpably lighter. I hadn't realized how heavy the burden of sorrow was, accumulated over ten years of child-abuse work. Also relieved was the hidden sorrow of my own miscarriage twelve years before. I did not talk or think much about the miscarriage because people could not understand the long-lasting grief over an eight-week-old fetus.[27]

This realization crystallized into resolve: "I thought, 'This ceremony has tremendous power. We have to do this ceremony in Oregon.'"[28] The first water baby ceremony was held at Bays' Larch Mountain Zen Center, east of Portland, on August 8, 1993. There were eleven participants, and a second ceremony was scheduled for October 2, 1993. Since then, Bays has conducted water baby ceremonies three to four times each year at Larch Mountain or at Great Vow Monastery, the community's newer center, founded in 2002. When she is away, another female priest leads the ceremony.[29]

Judith Ragir, of Clouds in Water Zen Center in St. Paul, Minnesota, began to hold water baby ceremonies in about 1997. She learned of them from Rand, who was trained in Minnesota and returned frequently to give lectures and workshops. As she explained:

> I'm a feminist, but I always felt bad about abortion. And I didn't know what to do about it. There's a lot of suffering around abortion. And also I had friends who had miscarriages, and I saw how much suffering there was there too for women. And men. And I thought, wow, to bring up and acknowledge that kind of suffering is really helpful. So I was right on it, because there is a need for this in America. There are many, many abortions, and the suffering around this is never acknowledged. It is amazing what happens when you acknowledge it publicly.

Her first ceremony has been followed by approximately ten more, some scheduled (about every other year) and some in response to requests. They are conducted either at the Zen center or in her home, which has a small zendo and Jizō garden. Attendance is usually eight to ten participants.[30]

In the mid-1990s, word of the ritual at Vermont Zen Center spread back to the head temple of the lineage, Rochester Zen Center, and some laywomen pushed for the ritual to be performed there.[31] However, it took time to convince the priests in Rochester that such a ceremony was worth performing. Eventually, a group of female priests and laywomen began to prepare to hold a ceremony. One laywoman flew to California and participated in Rand's ceremony, and two female priests at Rochester Zen Center received information about the ritual from Graef, including materials about how Bays conducted her ceremonies. Together this ad-hoc committee developed a plan for the ceremony, which was first performed on May 23, 1999.[32] The ritual, led by Sunya Kjolhede, attracted fifteen participants, a mix of both regular center members and non-Buddhists who attended yoga classes at the center.[33] Subsequently, Amala Wrightson took over responsibilities for the ceremony, which was held every May for several years. When Wrightson left in 2004 to found her own temple, it became more difficult to hold regularly scheduled ceremonies (Kjolhede had already left to found her own temple).[34] However, the center continued to offer them upon request, with the male head of the temple or other priests leading it.

Around the same time as the first Rochester Zen Center ceremony, the Floating Zendo of San Jose, California, performed its first water baby rituals. Its leader, Angie Boissevain, had attended a ceremony by Rand at one of the women's conferences mentioned earlier. When students began to ask her for some help with their grief over child and pregnancy losses, she drew on her memories of that past ceremony to create her own ritual. The group has held four more water baby ceremonies since, approximately one every other year, drawing seven or eight people on average.[35]

The Zen Center of Los Angeles held its first water baby ceremony in 2000, led by current abbess Wendy Egyoku Nakao, with twelve participants. As with many of the ceremonies at other temples, this one was prompted by the grief expressed by lay members of the temple. As Nakao described it:

> I facilitated a healing circle on abortion, an intimate gathering of five women and four men. The circle was open to women who have had an abortion, whether therapeutic or by choice, and to men who were partners to an abortion.
>
> No one who has ever had an abortion, or been partner to one, escapes its pain. This is not a loss we grieve openly, if we allow ourselves to grieve at all. Our grief and guilt live, as one person said, "as a shadow in the heart." The cultural, legal, and religious postures around abortion offer little support for women and men who have lived through it. The word "abortion" itself is rather clinical, far removed from the visceral experience that it is . . .
>
> "The thing that most impressed me about the Abortion Healing Circle," one man wrote, "was what a big chunk of repressed anger and remorse it chipped away. I felt the aftershock up to a week later. Who would have thought that the simple acts of telling one's story and making Jizos could bring up so much 'negative' emotion? It came as quite a revelation to discover that, in facing these emotions honestly, I also had to face a few lies I had told myself to keep them stored so neatly away. I've rarely experienced such profound grief, and better understand now how this emotion is necessary to letting go."[36]

Nakao drew on ritual formats already common in her lineage, LaFleur's book, and some knowledge of Bays and Rand's ceremonies in creating her ceremony. The success of the first ceremony led her to hold a second; the temple now holds such ceremonies whenever a need arises.[37]

Laypeople had also begun to approach Sevan Ross, head priest of Chicago Zen Center, and ask for help dealing with their abortions. Ross was trained at Rochester Zen Center and heard about the plans to conduct a water baby ceremony there prior to his move to Chicago in 1996. In June 2001 the first water baby ceremony was held at Chicago Zen Center, with about a dozen participants. The ceremony was based on the ritual forms worked out at Rochester Zen Center, though Ross modified it by staying out of the room during the sewing portion because he had not personally experienced a pregnancy loss.

A second ceremony was held in late summer of 2002, and a third in mid-2006, which was led by one of Ross's male priests. Despite the gap between 2002 and 2006, it is Ross's intention to hold the ceremony every other year.[38]

Finally, the Santa Cruz Zen Center held its first water baby ceremony in 2001. The center's leader, Katherine Thanas, had participated in one of Yvonne Rand's ceremonies at Goat-in-the-Road Zendo a couple of years previously. She also consulted with Jan Bays and had someone from Bays's community assist with the first ceremony. A second ceremony was held a few years later—like many temples, the Santa Cruz center holds water baby rituals as the need arises, rather than regularly scheduling them. Typical attendance is about a dozen people.[39]

As discussed earlier, there are other groups that have a held a first water baby ceremony since 2001, but for the descriptive purposes here I have focused only on those that have made it a part of their ongoing temple practices, whether it be by performing them at specific intervals or by request. With this historical sketch complete, an analysis of what these new ceremonies at American Zen centers can teach us is now possible.

Following the Flows

The transmission of these ceremonies in and through American Zen temples falls into several discernable patterns. First, none of them were transmitted from a first-generation Zen missionary to an American disciple.[40] Suzuki Shunryū, Maezumi Taizan, and the other major Japanese Zen teachers present in America in the latter half of the twentieth century must surely have been aware of *mizuko kuyō*, one of the most dramatic phenomena in postwar Japanese religion. Yet none felt a need to pass along knowledge of how Japanese Zen routinely memorializes aborted fetuses and other pregnancy losses. This is true even though these and other major figures had numerous female students, many of whom had experienced pregnancy losses.

How can this be accounted for? With all of these figures now deceased, it is only possible to speculate. I must therefore be cautious, but a number of possibilities do present themselves. First, most of the missionaries were radicals by Japanese standards and preached a sort of neo-Zen based on formal seated meditation for laypeople, rather than the normal temple Zen of Japan. They may have felt that *mizuko kuyō* was superstitious and/or exploitative, and intentionally chose not to pass the practice on to Americans. Second, many of these Zen missionaries were quite savvy about the cultural attitudes of their Western students, and they may have perceived that praying to a supernatural savior to alleviate the attacks of angry fetal ghosts would not offer a particularly attractive image of Zen. Third, it may be that these teachers, all male, were at times inattentive to their female students' feelings or uncomfortable discussing such intimate and gendered issues with them.[41] Finally, it may be that in the context of early convert Zen, when Americans were only beginning to understand some of the forms and purposes of Buddhism in Japan and typically approached Zen as a form of personal meditation practice, female students did not consider their Zen teachers an appropriate resource for dealing with the issues around pregnancy loss. For now, all that can be said for sure is that the first generation of Japanese Zen teachers did not transmit *mizuko kuyō* and that nevertheless the ritual has found a place in major Zen centers run by their direct disciples.

Rather than from their teachers, the Zen priests who offer water baby ceremonies developed their rituals from a number of other sources. One of these is printed accounts: all of the American priests I interviewed had read something about *mizuko kuyō*, whether it was accounts by American Zen priests; scholarly works such as *Liquid Life* or Helen Hardacre's *Marketing the Menacing Fetus in Japan*; or articles in such popular periodicals as the *New York Times*, *Harper's*, or *Yoga Journal*. A second source was contacts with other American Buddhists. Some of these came via intralineal linkages, such as the flows between Rochester Zen Center, Vermont Zen Center, and Chicago Zen Center—all part of the network of temples founded by Philip Kapleau and his students—or through interpersonal relationships. In fact, there is a rather tangled web woven among these individuals. For example, Jan Bays, who had a very close relationship with Maezumi Taizan, is now married to Hogen Bays, the ex-husband of Sunya Kjolhede, who is the sister of Bodhin Kjolhede, the main successor of Philip Kapleau and an occasional presider at water baby ceremonies in Rochester.[42] The goal here is not gossip but to make a crucial point about Buddhism in America: despite the presence of several million Buddhists in the United States, in the upper echelons it is quite a small pond, and many of the big fish know one another and have personal entanglements that go beyond shared lineage. In tracking the transmission of knowledge about Buddhism through these communities, be it about a practice, a doctrine, or an icon, it pays to give attention not only to the obvious connections of lineage but also the more subtle but often more important shared histories of the actual individuals involved.

There is one more important source for these rituals: the individual creative imagination. To a certain extent, these teachers just made them up. While all of them drew on some knowledge of Japanese Buddhist ritualism and modified their ceremonies as more information about *mizuko kuyō* became available over time, they readily filled in the gaps in their knowledge with their own invention. Angie Boissevain, the leader of the Floating Zendo, explained this attitude toward ritual in general to me:

> [Kobun Chino Roshi] taught us very little. He taught us *oryoki*, and the *Heart Sutra*, how to do the ceremony at the altar, and that's about it. As some of us got older and were asked to teach at various places, we were eventually asked to do weddings and things like that. We would go to Kobun and ask how to do them, and he would say "Make it up." ... So my own way of learning has been a lot of making it up. I just met again a woman in Switzerland, a woman who I had met before, and we got to talking about rituals and she said that she didn't know how to do anything and Kobun told her just to make it up. And she's now transmitted and has her own place, so I bundled up and sent her all the things we've accumulated. So I think that's what we mostly do, is pass around what we've done. I found that I had two new baby ceremonies that people had sent me, and an eye-opening ceremony that someone had sent me. A couple of weddings. In the AZTA [American Zen Teachers Association] listserve, people just write back and forth: "Hey, does anybody know how to do a house blessing?" And then several people write back with their versions of how to bless a house. So it's very curious how we're doing this. There is a book, Shasta Abbey has a book with all the ceremonies in it in the Sojiji style. But most of us I think are just kind of winging it.[43]

There is something remarkable about this attitude. Few American water baby purveyors have seen a *mizuko kuyō* performed, whether in America or Japan. They discuss it informally among themselves, sometimes as a committee, and some merely read about it in a book and proceed. Indeed, Jan Bays's *Jizo Bodhisattva* gives step-by-step instructions with the assumption that readers can then go off on their own and do it. And some believe you can just make up ritual. This contrasts sharply with their idea of meditation. These same teachers push the idea that meditation must be done in the context of a teacher-student relationship, that it must be formally practiced with precise postures and procedures, preferably at a temple among a community of co-practitioners. Many assert that one can read about it in a book but will never truly succeed without personal guidance. In Japan, on the other hand, a priest would most likely receive instruction and sanction for both meditation and *mizuko kuyō* from a teacher, such as his preceptor. This dynamic can be seen, for example, in the experiences of Kojima Shūmyō of Zenshuji Soto Mission, discussed in chapter 1, who received his *mizuko kuyō* from the teacher who raised him.[44]

There are two important points for future researchers that should be gleaned from this. First, American Buddhist communities are not necessarily good representations of Asian Buddhist practices. This means that investigation of convert activities has the potential to create misunderstanding of Asian Buddhist practices, especially when comparable research on practices is not performed in Japan or other Asian Buddhist countries. There is an obvious application of this point for classroom pedagogy as well. Many professors enjoy bringing in local convert Buddhist leaders to speak on Buddhism to their undergraduate students. However, we must be aware of the potential for misrepresentation of Asian forms by American converts. An American convert in a Japanese-derived Zen lineage may understand *zazen* meditation, for instance, in ways significantly different from how actual Japanese practitioners would, and thus may offer a sincere but highly inaccurate portrait to a class on Japanese religion.

Second, the presence of a ritual within American convert temples does not necessarily mean that it was derived from an Asian practice, even when an analogous practice exists within Japanese or other Asian traditions. Researchers must bear in mind the need to directly investigate the source of all practices within convert Buddhist temples—what seems at first glance to be a transplanted activity may well turn out to be a wholly original ritual that just coincidentally bears a resemblance to an Asian practice. The Americanization of Buddhism includes adapting Asian rituals; it also includes the creation of wholly original ones, at times reinventing the wheel, so to speak.

In examining the lineage links, we see other surprising disjunctions. Not only did none of the purveyors of water baby ceremonies receive the ritual from a Japanese missionary priest, none received it from his or her own American teachers either. None of the Americans described earlier in this chapter is a disciple of any of the others. They are all what we might loosely call "dharma brothers and sisters," priests of the same generation and mainly the same rank, who studied parallel to one another, in some cases together in the same communities.[45] This generation gap between the founding Japanese Zen missionaries (and those pioneer Zen teachers such as Philip Kapleau, who trained in Japan) and their American disciples is an important element of the story. Water baby ceremonies are a product of the first full generation of native-born Western Zen teachers and thus represent a direct example of how the tradition began to change as authority shifted from foreign to American leaders, and from the WWII to the baby boom generation.

Though there are cases of the ritual subsequently being passed from American master to American disciple once it is established in a community—from Jan Bays to her priests (who represent the second generation of leaders trained in the United States), for example—we also see surprising examples of back-flow *up* the ladder of Zen hierarchy. Thus, Bodhin Kjolhede, abbot of the American Zen flagship temple, Rochester Zen Center, conducted a water baby ceremony after being taught about it by subordinate female priests and laypeople at his temple.[46] Likewise, practices initially introduced at branch temples may flow back to the lineage's main center—as with Rochester Zen Center picking up the water baby ceremony from its affiliate Vermont Zen Center—rather than the main temple necessarily serving as the "mother ship" from which orthodox ideas and practices are spread out to the smaller, newer temples of the lineage.

Zen practitioners did receive some information about how *mizuko kuyō* is conducted in Japan, and all justify their water baby ceremonies by reference to the Japanese ritual. So even after the death of the founding Japanese teacher, convert Zen communities remain pervious to new ideas and rituals from Japan. In fact, American-created rituals provide new avenues for knowledge about Japanese traditions—it was only after a desire for abortion-related rituals arose in convert communities that they began to learn about *mizuko kuyō* in Japan. Yet none of these convert Zen practitioners learned about the ceremony from Japanese-American Buddhist communities. As explained in chapter 1, there are a number of mainly Japanese-American temples in the United States that have been performing *mizuko kuyō* at least since the 1960s. Zenshuji, in fact, is the oldest Zen temple in mainland America and is presided over by the bishop of all American Sōtō Zen establishments. Less than four miles away, Wendy Nakao of the Sōtō-affiliated Zen Center of Los Angeles was unaware of the practice at Zenshuji.[47] In some situations, at least, it seems fair to observe that convert Zen practitioners are more likely to interact with Japanese temples fifty-five hundred miles across the Pacific than with Asian-American Zen Buddhist communities in their own cities.

Forces Driving the Spread of Water Baby Ceremonies

Both external and internal forces have played a part in the rise of American Zen rituals for pregnancy loss. It was soon after the U.S. legalization of abortion in 1973 that Yvonne Rand and Robert Aitken began to offer the first convert Zen rituals for dealing with abortion. The number of American abortions rose from 1973 to 1990, peaking at 1.61 million in 1990 before declining to the level of approximately 1.21 million today.[48] This period after 1990 also roughly corresponds to the greatest expansion of convert Buddhism in America. The women's movement, both influential in legalizing abortion and stimulated in turn by the new possibilities unleashed by broader reproductive options (and the new need to vigorously defend them from conservative opposition) also expanded and diversified during this period, and during the 1980s feminism brought about significant changes in attitudes within American Zen, especially toward models of leadership.[49] With so many more abortions occurring and with growing cultural attention paid to women's needs and opinions—as well as gradually increasing opportunities for female leadership in American Zen—the situation developed in directions favorable to the emergence of ceremonies recognizing traumatic pregnancy losses.

The growth in the number of water baby ceremonies performed reflects forces of both supply and demand. In many cases, it was laypeople who prompted their community leaders to offer some sort of ritual recognition and healing of pregnancy loss. Zen priests followed up on this demand by studying preexisting models for water baby ceremonies or developing their own. At the same time, supply is clearly a driving force behind this growing phenomenon. Some leaders heard about or participated in water baby ceremonies in other locations around the country and then decided to offer them to their own students on a trial basis to see if there was sufficient interest. Books like *Liquid Life* and *Jizo Bodhisattva* set off waves of new ritualization as communities learned about previously unknown facets of Buddhist practice. The fortunes of the water baby ceremony have also risen and waned with changing local supply and demand. Some communities do the ceremony infrequently because their membership is small: after a certain time, everyone who might want to memorialize a previous abortion or miscarriage will have already done so, and the slow rate of growth means newcomers with potentially unresolved pregnancy losses are rare. Others have members who would like to do a water baby ceremony but no longer have resident priests dedicated to providing the service. The continued spread of the ceremony, at least in its current form, thus relies both on more priests becoming involved in offering the ritual and in ever more temple members, especially laypeople, desiring the ceremony.

One interesting detail about the water baby purveyors is that prior religious affiliation is not a good predictor of which convert Zen practitioners will favor such rituals, or perhaps other rituals as well. For instance, Jan Bays grew up in an active Disciples of Christ family that disliked religious icons or elaborate rituals. Her initial reactions to Jizō at the Zen Center of Los Angles were ambivalent. She liked a simple statue out in the garden but balked at a more ornate *mizuko* Jizō:

> [Maezumi] went to Japan, and he brought back a golden Jizō statue with some children, like a *mizuko* Jizo, for the clinic. We put it up in the clinic. But I was raised Protestant, and I looked at these images,

and I was like, "Um, hmmm, that's a little dicey there, these images!" [chuckles] So I didn't really personally relate to it, but we had a lot of poor Mexican-American immigrants at the clinic, and I think they liked it. It was like a saint.[50]

Yet today Bays is arguably the most prominent missionary of Jizō bodhisattva. Leaders of water baby ceremonies come from a wide variety of backgrounds, including Protestants, Catholics, and smaller religions such as Tenrikyō.

Bodhisattva Movements in Convert Buddhism

The rise and spread of water baby ceremonies also owes much to the development of bodhisattva-oriented movements within American convert Buddhism. Not unified factions but rather a confluence of loosely connected currents running through (and out of) American Buddhism, the growth of interest in such bodhisattvas as Jizō and Kuan-yin has contributed to increased performance of water baby ceremonies and, in turn, has been reinforced by the spread of these rituals. The presence of bodhisattva devotion in convert American Buddhism has not received scholarly attention, but it is among the more intriguing developments in Western Buddhism since the 1980s.

Knowledge of bodhisattvas, especially Avalokiteshvara and Manjushri, has been present to some degree in convert Buddhism from the beginning. Nonetheless, what I wish to call attention to is the rise in devotion by convert Buddhists to particular Buddhist mythological figures. Whereas in earlier periods of American Buddhism bodhisattvas were relatively marginalized, appearing as a statue here or there or as a few words about what this or that bodhisattva represents, they are now a visibly growing presence in American Zen and other traditions, with a substantial industry of bodhisattva-related products, books advocating devotion to such figures, and large numbers of converts claiming Jizō or Kuan-yin as integral parts of their Buddhist practice. Many bodhisattva devotees are quite self-conscious in their attempts to attract newcomers to these movements and increase the profile of their favorite figure in Buddhist circles. Moreover, this shift corresponds roughly to the periodization of proto– and full water baby movements, and attention to one development helps shed light on the evolution of the other.[51]

The rise in attention to bodhisattvas in American Buddhism can be seen in the popularity of Taigen Dan Leighton's book *Bodhisattva Archetypes: Classic Buddhist Guides to Awakening and Their Modern Expression*. Leighton is a priest in the American Sōtō Zen lineage of Suzuki Shunryū. Explicitly conceived as a way to encourage appreciation of bodhisattvas by Westerners, Leighton's book focuses on seven figures from the Buddhist tradition, such as Siddhartha Gautama (the Buddha prior to his awakening), Avalokiteshvara (Kuan-yin), and Kshitigarbha (Jizō). Although he presents them as psychological forces and role models, the book nonetheless contains many miracle stories and significant information about devotional practices associated with these bodhisattvas, from pilgrimage to Kuan-yin's Pure Land of Putoushan to Jizō and the rituals of *mizuko kuyō*.[52] The book thus reinforces the tendency of American Zen to psychologize Buddhism and simultaneously undercuts it with elements often perceived as "superstitious" in convert Zen. Furthermore, while preserving a prominent place for modern reconstructed ideas of the historical Buddha—a perennial icon in Western Buddhism—it also decenters him by offering multiple alternative (and ahistorical) objects of veneration in the form of cosmic bodhisattvas. This work of the late 1990s represents a bridge between an earlier "Protestant Zen" that resisted elements other than meditation and avoided savior figures and ritual, and more recent reappraisals of ceremony, saviors, and devotion. *Bodhisattva Archetypes* reflects growing interest in these figures among American Buddhists and also contributed significantly to greater interest among priests and laypeople.[53]

The first bodhisattva movement to consider is that of Kuan-yin, which, as the most widely spread and popular one, as well as the one that appears first in the historical record, provides a useful model that can then be applied to the Jizō movement and perhaps others that may arise in the future.[54] Avalokiteshvara, the Indian bodhisattva of great compassion, is widely revered in Buddhist Asia. One specific form of Avalokiteshvara has enjoyed a particularly high profile in American Buddhism. This is Kuan-yin, the bodhisattva as understood in East Asia and, specifically, Kuan-yin depicted as a woman.[55] This bodhisattva is increasingly favored by convert Buddhists for some very obvious reasons. The first is gender: among a constellation of male Buddhas, bodhisattvas, and arhats, Kuan-yin stands out as a *female* bodhisattva. She thus attracts the attention of many convert Buddhist women, particularly those who are actively looking for feminist or at least overtly woman-friendly approaches to Buddhism. For both women and men, Kuan-yin's female gender makes her more approachable than the Buddha or Manjushri. Beyond gender, two closely connected aspects of the bodhisattva make her particularly appealing to convert Buddhists. First is her status as the embodiment of compassion. Second is her ability to take on any form in order to help those in need. This is a characteristic of her compassionate activity, which is implicitly tied to her gender by Americans (women are often assumed to be the more caring and helpful sex by Americans, Buddhist or otherwise), and together these qualities of adaptable female compassion stand out as uniquely Buddhist contributions to religion.[56]

Finally, Kuan-yin is valued because she not only embodies these valued traits, but, unlike ancient goddesses such as Athena or Isis, she has an enormous body of worshippers in the modern world. The sheer number of Kuan-yin devotees in East Asia enables new devotees in the United States to feel that they are in solidarity with a large group rather than with scattered individuals subsumed in an American culture that overwhelmingly affirms the male image of deity.

Kuan-yin has been present in American Buddhism since the arrival of the Chinese in the late 1840s, but her ascension in convert circles dates to a much more recent time. Though traces of her can be seen in earlier decades, the Kuan-yin movement really began to snowball in the late 1980s and 1990s. In 1997, Sandy Boucher published *Opening the Lotus: A Woman's Guide to Buddhism*. Boucher's book specifically singles out Kuan-yin as an ideal object of devotion for American Buddhists. Boucher followed up in 1999 with *Discovering Kwan Yin, Buddhist Goddess of Compassion: A Woman's Book of Ruminations, Meditations, Prayers, and Chants*. The book is a manifesto of sorts that asserts through numerous examples the importance of the bodhisattva in the lives of many American women, Buddhist and otherwise. She proudly proclaims that

> as the feminine reasserts itself in Western spirituality, a towering female figure has arrived on our shores from Asia. Her name is Kwan Yin. She is the most revered goddess in all of Asia, and Chinese, Japanese, Korean, and Vietnamese immigrants naturally brought her with them when they came here. But her presence has also reached beyond the immigrant communities to enter the lives of countless European-Americans.[57]

Boucher now leads workshops on Kuan-yin around the country. Other recent Buddhist works on Kuan-yin include *Kuan Yin: Myths and Revelations of the Chinese Goddess of Compassion*, by Martin Palmer and his colleagues and *Compassion: Listening to the Cries of the World*, by Christina Feldman. There have also been a host of New Age titles that purport to channel or otherwise reveal secret teachings of the bodhisattva goddess.[58]

One of the interesting aspects of the Kuan-yin movement is the prevalence of Kuan-yin devotion among Vipassana (Insight Meditation) practitioners. Textbook descriptions of Buddhist traditions would suggest that Kuan-yin should not be present in the Vipassana movement, which is derived from reformist trends in modern Theravada Buddhism. Not only is Theravada Buddhism supposedly uninvolved in the worship of transcendent bodhisattvas, but the Vipassana movement in particular is alleged to be aniconic and disdainful of more "religious" elements in Buddhism. Yet Kuan-yin is venerated by converts committed to Vipassana practice, such as Sandy Boucher and Christina Feldman, and appears regularly on the altars of Vipassana centers and individual practitioners in America. Wendy Cadge notes, for instance, that Kuan-yin was specifically introduced to the Cambridge Insight Meditation Center to balance the male images of the Buddha; it is her female gender that the center members value.[59]

The Jizō Movement

The Kuan-yin movement is important to understanding the Jizō movement and water baby ceremonies for several reasons. First, it demonstrates a growing interest in transcendent bodhisattvas on the part of both convert Buddhists and non-Buddhists. This interest, sparked initially by Kuan-yin, provides an opening for additional figures such as Jizō. Avenues of transmission established by the Kuan-yin movement—books on single bodhisattvas, images sold through Buddhist supply catalogs, workshops or projects devoted to a specific figure—are followed by subsequent movements. Avenues not yet taken by Jizō, such as Kuan-yin's widespread adoption by elements of the New Age movement, point to potential future developments in the Jizō movement. Most intriguing, the adoption of Kuan-yin by participants in the non-Mahayana Vipassana movement suggests the possibility that the Jizō movement will influence convert strains of Theravada Buddhism as well. This potentially could lead to the creation of Theravada water baby ceremonies. Whether they would remain largely as is or would be substantially changed in the process of leaving the realm of Mahayana Buddhism is an open question. It is worth noting that the first venue in which Yvonne Rand publicized her water baby ceremonies was *Inquiring Mind*, a Vipassana periodical. Also noteworthy is the participation of convert practitioners of Tibetan Buddhism. One example is Kimberley Snow's account of her participation in one of Yvonne Rand's ceremonies described in *In Buddha's Kitchen*.[60] Perhaps convert Tibetan water baby ceremonies will become yet another development of *mizuko kuyō*.

Second, these figures are often closely associated by Western Buddhists. Both are described as healers, comforters, and figures of compassion. The Kuan-yin movement has a direct effect on the Jizō movement by encouraging more feminine depictions of Jizō—many of my consultants intentionally or inadvertently used the pronoun "she" in describing Jizō, and Jan Bays switches between "he" and "she" frequently in *Jizo Bodhisattva*. There is a tendency among Americans to think of Jizō as androgynous-leaning-female rather than male-leaning-androgynous as typically understood in Japan, a phenomenon that appears not only in use of the feminine pronoun and conceptual pairings of Kuan-yin and Jizō, but also in material culture, such as the decidedly feminine garden Jizōs sold by Great Vow Monastery and used by many Zen centers for their water baby ceremonies.

A third reason for paying attention to the Kuan-yin movement is that although this book focuses on Jizō as the preeminent water baby bodhisattva, Kuan-yin too plays a role in the ceremony. Most centers include the *Enmei Juku Kannon Gyō*, a chant dedicated to Kuan-yin, in their water baby ceremonies, and images of Kuan-yin are often present in "Jizō gardens" at American Zen centers. Although with less frequency than Jizō images, these Kuan-yin images do receive offerings and veneration as alternative figures to Jizō. Those who prefer Kuan-yin are encouraged to direct their attentions during the water baby ceremony to this figure instead.[61] Devotion to Kuan-yin thus plays a role in the spread and development of water baby ceremonies, albeit a minor one compared to that of Jizō.[62]

Kuan-yin enjoys greater overall popularity in both Buddhist and non-Buddhist circles in America, and she has a far longer and stronger history in American Buddhism and is a more frequent object of devotion in Asia than Jizō. She is a female figure depicted as a goddess or queen and thus fills a void in Buddhism, attracting a natural constituency of women. Jizō, on the other hand, is a male monk with few flashy incarnations who received very little attention for most of Zen's history in the United States. Jizō does not appear frequently in convert Buddhism prior to the rise of the water baby ceremony. When he did appear, it was primarily as a sort of patron saint of and *for* children. For instance, Rochester Zen Center developed a celebration for the children of the community and shaped the festivities around the figure of Jizō, with candy, stories, and so on. Jizō was not often presented as a bodhisattva for adults, however, who make up the overwhelming majority of participants in the convert Buddhist community.

This orientation began to change, however, in connection to the water baby ceremony during the 1990s. As documented above, Jizō had a connection to death and ritual from the beginning for Yvonne Rand, the foremost American proponent of the water baby ceremony, and her rituals for pregnancy loss have always centered on this bodhisattva. It is largely from this initial source that the interest in Jizō has grown. Knowledge of Jizō and the water baby ceremony have gone hand in hand, with interest in one leading naturally to awareness of the other. Just as Kuan-yin has a particularly prominent promoter in Sandy Boucher, Jizō plays a major role for Jan Bays, whose particular interest in Jizō originally stems from participation in Rand's ceremony. Jizō has a strongly noticeable presence in Bays's community, not least because her monastery houses a collection of more than a thousand Jizō figures of various shapes and sizes and performs the water baby ceremony at least four times a year. Zenworks, the Buddhist supplies service run by Bays's community, annually sells approximately three hundred home-crafted Jizō images in more than a dozen different styles, including *mizuko* Jizōs and related designs (fig. 2.1).[63] Her book *Jizo Bodhisattva*, which includes full instructions on holding water baby ceremonies, helped introduce the bodhisattva to many Americans just as Boucher's *Discovering Kwan Yin* has done with that figure.

However, while providing the historical impetus for the Jizō movement, the water baby ceremony is now only one manifestation of this rising American interest in the bodhisattva. For example, in 2005 Bays's community carried out a project that dramatically contributed to the meteoric rise of this bodhisattva in the consciousness of American convert Buddhists. After a visit to Hiroshima in 2002, Bays decided to return three years later on the sixtieth anniversary of the atomic bombings and present 270,000 Jizōs to the Japanese, one for every person who died in the first year from the Hiroshima and Nagasaki bombs.[64] She called on Buddhists and sympathizers everywhere to create Jizō images, pray for peace, and send their Jizōs to her for presentation in Japan. Publicized both by word of mouth and convert Buddhist associations such as the Buddhist

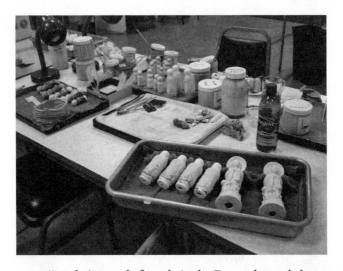

FIGURE 2.1. Jizōs being made for sale in the Zenworks workshop at great vow Monastery. The two on the right are *Mizuko* Jizōs, the only images Zenworks manufactures that are based on a statue imported directly from Japan.

Peace Fellowship, the project was successful beyond anyone's expectations. At least a hundred Buddhist temples and meditation groups from twenty countries, including every state in the United States, contributed more than four hundred thousand Jizōs.[65] Bays led a forty-person pilgrimage group to Japan and gave Jizōs away as a gesture of peace and reconciliation on the anniversary of the American attacks, and the remaining Jizōs have toured as exhibits in the United States, Japan, and Europe.

The wider interest in Jizō can be seen by the bodhisattva's presence in Buddhist supplies catalogs. Not only Zenworks but also DharmaCrafts, Dharma Communications, and many others now offer Jizō statues for sale. Some come from workshops in the United States, whereas others are imports from China, Taiwan, or Japan. The material culture of Jizō is often on display in Jizōs for Peace pictures, cloth panels, or banners that hang in many convert Zen temples.[66] Jizō also appears in the ceremonies of non-Buddhists, as will be further discussed in chapter 6.

In conclusion, the Jizō movement originated in the water baby ceremony, and though now encompassing more than just this ritual, continues to spread interest in both the bodhisattva and the water baby ceremony specifically (fig. 2.2). The Kuan-yin movement also contributes indirectly to the spread of information about Jizō and Buddhist pregnancy loss rituals. Together they show a growing demand for bodhisattva-related merchandise and practices among Americans, especially convert Zen Buddhists.

FIGURE 2.2. Jizō altar at the house of a laywoman who helped introduce the water baby ceremony to Rochester Zen Center.

Exportation: Water Baby Ceremonies beyond America

There is one final channel to explore in tracing how Jizō and his post–pregnancy loss rituals have come to the United States. As I will discuss in the next chapter, the water baby ceremony has been modified from *mizuko kuyō* in many ways to adapt it to American convert Zen temples. While having partial roots in Japan, it is now a distinctly American Buddhist practice. But even though the ceremony has only recently been created and settled into place at a number of American centers, it is already being transmitted abroad to new communities of Buddhists in other countries.

Sunyana Graef, who leads water baby ceremonies at Vermont Zen Center, is the spiritual head (but not the resident leader) of the Toronto Zen Center. Having learned the ritual from her, the Toronto temple now holds water baby ceremonies that follow the same general format as those in America. Graef also maintains a Zen temple in Costa Rica, known as Casa Zen. She holds water baby ceremonies in this majority Roman Catholic country where abortion is illegal. Future international sites likely to perform water baby ceremonies include New Zealand, where Amala Wrightson has established a Zen temple, and Poland, where Stamen Trejner, who held water baby ceremonies at Chicago Zen Center under the direction of Sevan Ross, has recently returned and intends to promote the ceremony.[67]

Both the Canadian and Costa Rican temples received their water baby ceremonies directly from the United States, not Japan, and the format (and accompanying logic) of the ceremonies is the same as that of the American rituals. Here is an example of a significant phenomenon emerging in American Buddhism: though still very much a missionary field for Asian Buddhists, the United States has also become the launching pad for missionization of new countries with uniquely American forms of Buddhist practice. In the twenty-first century, the United States both imports and exports Buddhism. It will be interesting to see if the Canadian, Costa Rican, and other ceremonies eventually depart in noticeable ways from those of the United States. Such differences could point to aspects of the ceremony that are more specific to the United States, as well as shed light on unique elements of Canadian and Costa Rican Buddhism. It is to the consideration of these ceremonies as *American* forms of Buddhist practice that I turn in the next chapter.

3

"We Need to Free Ourselves"

Adaptations of Convert Mizuko Kuyō

Translation, of course, is not something abstract—it always involves a practice.

—Robert J. C. Young, *Postcolonialism:*
A Very Short Introduction

So far I have discussed how *mizuko kuyō* came to convert Zen communities; it is now time to explore the actual procedure of the ritual. It is in the comparison of these American rituals with their Japanese counterparts that the never fully completed process of Americanization can be discerned.

The Process of the Ceremony

To understand the water baby ceremony, it is necessary first to get a sense of it "from the inside." This section presents a narrative of the water baby ceremony held at Great Vow Monastery in Clatskanie, Oregon, on Saturday, November 4, 2006. Here I attempt to give as full a description of the ritual as possible, based on my participant observation of the ceremony, and extensive field notes written immediately after it concluded. This chronicle is intended to provide a sense of how a "typical" water baby ceremony might proceed at an American Zen center.

But the offering of a template narrative for this or any ritual must be interrogated before I go further. First, it must be noted that the format of the ceremony at Great Vow differs in some particulars from that at other convert Zen centers. In fact, no two Zen temples in America perform the ceremony in precisely the same manner, though there is significant overlap between all of the ceremonies. Therefore, the narrative will be interspersed with observations about how other groups perform the ritual, creating a more comprehensive understanding of the various approaches taken to this ceremony. Furthermore, the production of any ritual is always specific and unique. No matter how tightly controlled and carefully planned, rituals in actual practice always go "off script" to some degree: outsiders barge in by accident, priests fumble and drop ritual implements, cell phones ring, sick participants disrupt proceedings with loud coughing, and so on. Perfectly executed rituals exist only on paper. Thus this description of the water baby ceremony, even a specific ceremony conducted on a particular date, can offer only a broad suggestion of what the experience of any given ritual will be like.

Second, my own position as the author must be explored. All sightings of human activities, religious or otherwise, are made only from one person's particular vantage point. This has implications for what is observed and what is overlooked, even before the active process of selection and refinement of data begins. Researchers are not privy to others' inner thoughts and emotions during rituals and must rely on observation and, later, consultation to develop an opinion about what seems to have taken place. In an attempt to work through this problem, I consulted several participants afterward, both priests and laypeople, to get their impressions of the ceremony. But comprehensive reports of human activities are impossible no matter how many accounts are collected. Ultimately, the choice of how this and other ceremonies are represented rests with the author—in this case, a man at a ceremony primarily conducted for women, a researcher with more than a dozen years of interaction with Zen in America who does not self-identify as a Zen Buddhist. In the following narrative, I do not emphasize my own experience, as my goal is primarily to present an account of the ritual, not an autobiographical vignette. But these are nonetheless the observations and reflections of one person, with one angle of view, subject to influences both known and unknown in the process of spinning a tale.

The ceremony took place at a former public school that has been partially converted into a Zen monastery. This was the fourth water baby ceremony held at Great Vow that year; the previous one was conducted twelve weeks earlier, in mid-August, while the next one took place eleven weeks later, in mid-January.[1] An hour before the arrival of outside participants on that rainy afternoon, a room was already prepared for the first part of the ceremony (fig. 3.1). Near the entrance to the monastery, this high-ceilinged room with light-colored cement walls was once the school's music room. It is now called "the musical zendo"

FIGURE 3.1. Great Vow Monastery room prepared for the water baby ceremony on November 4, 2006.

by the current inhabitants, who use it to store marimbas and other instruments that they play in local parades. Besides musical instruments, the walls are lined with cabinets, maps, and chalkboards. On a counter by the entrance lay books about grieving and pamphlets from organizations dedicated to counseling parents who have lost children. The room is carpeted and has three sofas, and multiple chairs were brought in for the ceremony. In the middle of the room sat a round table covered with cloth, yarn, thread, and additional materials for making bibs and other offerings; in the center of the table a copy of the abbess's book *Jizo Bodhisattva: Modern Healing and Traditional Buddhist Practice* was prominently placed. Toward the back wall a low table in a corner held tongue depressors, construction paper, and other materials. Also at the back of the room was a small table with a wooden altar on top, enshrining an image of Manjushri, the bodhisattva of wisdom, a common patron of Zen. A second small table, slightly more prominently placed but still on the margins of the room, was covered with red cloth and supported a large white figure of Jizō made by the monastery. Also on this table was a book of photographs showing Jizō statues and the offerings made for them, and nearby on a stand a memorial book for the ceremony lay open.

The first three people—two men and a boy of about twelve—arrived early at 1:35 P.M. for the 2 o'clock ceremony. A robed resident priest met them at the door. They introduced themselves to her, explaining that they were familiar with Zen Buddhism but had never visited the monastery. One man declared that he wanted to buy a couple of Jizō statues and was told to wait until after the ceremony. They were given tea and allowed to wait in the dining hall.

By 1:45 several more people had arrived, and the abbess took the opportunity to provide a tour of the monastery, ending up at the room for the water baby ceremony. At 2 o'clock sharp the ceremony got under way. In the beginning, there were fourteen participants, including me, plus the abbess and a female priest who acted as an assistant facilitator; a fifteenth participant arrived about a half hour later. Altogether, eight of the people at the ceremony were men, nine were women, and their ages ranged from twelve to the mid-sixties. Everyone there was white except for one Native American female participant and the co-facilitator, who is of Filipino heritage. The two priests wore formal robes, but everyone else was dressed casually. Other than the two ritual leaders, none had been present at the previous ceremony in August. This was an average attendance level for the ceremony, both at Great Vow and other centers in general, though the percentage of males was higher than at many such ceremonies. Occasionally water baby ceremonies at Great Vow attracted as many as thirty-five participants, whereas some had only a handful—and rarely, at other centers, ceremonies held by special private request have had only a single participant plus the ritual leaders—but twelve to fifteen is normal.

We sat in a circle on the sofas and chairs. Jan Chozen Bays, the abbess, stood and introduced herself, beginning a twenty-five-minute explanation of the ceremony. "This ceremony is based on the *mizuko kuyo* in Japan. At the same time, we have adapted it for our own needs in America." She narrated how she first heard about the water baby ceremony from Yvonne Rand, and participated in the ritual at Green Gulch Farm Zen Center as a way to deal with the pain of being a full-time child abuse investigator.

Bays explained that ceremonies for children who have died go back many centuries in Japan, and that the water baby ceremony, which is the core of this ritual, dates from the end of WWII, when abortion became common. She described a water baby as someone who died before being born, whether from abortion, miscarriage, or some sort of accident. She emphasized the water imagery, pointing out how in Japan people are cremated after they die and their five elements return to the earth and from there to the sea. "They may merge with the water and be part of the rain falling on us today." Japan is surrounded by water and gets most of its sustenance from water, and babies come from water, she said:

> In Asia there is a different understanding of life and death than in the West. Here we think of life as beginning at a specific moment: at conception, or after conception. And we think death happens at

a certain moment. But in Asia they understand that birth and death are processes, with no exact beginning or end. We can think of it like waves on the ocean. A person appears as a single wave which arises, changes, and returns to the ocean in the course of things. But a wave is never apart from the ocean, and whether it is in the form of a wave or has merged and disappeared into the ocean, it is always water. With this kind of thinking we can understand how the Japanese were able to think of incidents such as abortion as returning water to water because the causes and conditions were not right for it to be a wave at that time, and how they might then go on to pray for that wave—that baby—to come again when the time was right.[2]

Next, Bays picked up the photo book and began to point out various pictures as she explained that Jizō is the bodhisattva of travelers, women, children, and those who die before being born. All eyes were on her, with many people nodding their heads as she described how Japan offered a more humane and intelligent approach to pregnancy loss than America does. Bays began passing around many photos of Jizō. "Jizo can appear in any realm to offer aid," she said. She explained the process of making offerings for Jizō, calling them "tokens of remembrance," and told the participants to write the name of the person they were honoring in the memorial book, along with the person's age and cause of death. We were also invited to write a message on the bibs or plaques we were about to make. The boy asked if he had to memorialize a specific person. Bays replied no, that it could be general. "In the past, people have done it for abortion, miscarriage, stillbirth, SIDS [sudden infant death syndrome], and children who died young. Some have also done it for adult children, or for kidnapped children lost through divorce. One man did the ceremony for his pet turtle that he left in the sun as a child, and still hadn't forgiven himself for. There have also been cats and dogs, and people have done it for the victims of the tsunami, or for their own lost childhood due to abuse."

After thirty minutes, just at the end of the abbess's explanation, the last participant straggled in. Bays took her outside for a few minutes to recap the explanation of the ceremony, while the rest of us prepared to make offerings. A couple of people did not start to make things right away: rather, they sat on the floor for a few minutes in silence, apparently meditating. Some centers schedule a period of meditation in their water baby rituals.

Most people began by making bibs or hats. The favored color was red. Participants used patterns to cut cloth, paper to make pinwheels, and tongue depressors to make memorial tokens with messages and names on them. A few made dolls out of clothespins. Many people sewed buttons onto their bibs or wrote messages. The more technically adept participants—in general, the women—were able to make several items, while others struggled to produce a single bib.

Throughout the period of sewing, all participants remained silent. Communication occurred nonetheless. A man stroked his wife's hair and rubbed her back; two young women who arrived together surreptitiously gestured to each other in sign language. Another woman sighed deeply from time to time and sniffled as if she was trying to hold back tears. Occasionally someone got up and went out to the bathroom. Some people drank tea. Every twenty minutes or so, Bays reminded us to hold the person we were memorializing in our thoughts. Although nothing was read aloud during this time, some Zen centers will read a poem to set the mood.

The silence of the sewing marks the Great Vow ceremony as exceptional, because at most other American Zen centers participants are encouraged to talk. However, even in such cases there are strict rules: people may voice their feelings and say a little something about the child they are remembering, but they are not to engage in conversation. There is no replying to another person's words. In essence, the leaders at these other ceremonies seek a series of short, expressive monologues, rather than dialogue between participants. Usually, the leader must prompt the other participants by offering his or her own feelings—others then feel more comfortable and empowered to share. In a few cases, participants actually go around the circle stating their names and giving a somewhat more extensive explanation of why they came to the ceremony. Ceremonies using this model are more likely to restrict participation to actual members of the Zen community and family members.

After ninety minutes elapsed, Bays began to explain the process of the second part of the ceremony, to be conducted in the Jizō garden. We spent several minutes finishing up our tokens and writing in the memorial book as Bays and her assistant gathered some additional personnel to hold rain coverings. Then the abbess solemnly led us single-file through the monastery and out through a back door. The assistant priest took up the rear, and both rang small hand-held bells every few seconds. I was asked to carry a small table. Outside, most participants opened umbrellas and maintained the single line as we walked through the rain, up a path, and a short distance into the woods. All around us, little figures lurked in the leaf litter and tree branches: Jizōs, several dozen of them, adorned with old clothing and deteriorating ornaments from previous ceremonies (fig. 3.2). In all, the slow walk took about five minutes.

In a slight clearing below the trees, we assembled in another circle, standing this time, while the small table I had carried was set up and altar implements placed on top. Three men from the monastery—including Hogen Bays,

FIGURE 3.2. A portion of the Jizō Garden at Great Vow Monastery, with offerings made during water baby ceremonies.

the abbot and husband of Chozen Bays—joined us to hold a tarp over Bays and the altar. She passed out sheets of paper covered in plastic, containing the chants for the final part of the ceremony. When everyone was ready, Jan Bays began the opening invocation, calling out in a singsong chant voice:

> Because of cause and effect, reality is shown in all its many forms.
> To know this fully liberates all suffering beings.
> All beings appear just as we all do, from the One, and pass away as
> we all do,
> after a few flickering moments of life, back to our Original
> Pure Nature.
> Truly our lives are waves on the great ocean of True Nature
> which is not born
> and does not pass away.

> In gathering today we remember children who have died
> and express our love and support for their parents and friends.
> Here these children are in complete repose, at one with the mystery
> that is our own birth and death, our own no-birth and no-death.

And together, we launched into the *Heart of Perfect Wisdom Sutra,* performed in English:

> The Bodhisattva of Compassion, from the depths of Prajna Wisdom,
> Clearly saw the emptiness of all the five conditions,
> Thus completely relieving misfortune and pain,
> Know then:
> Form is no other than emptiness,
> Emptiness is no other than form.
> Form is exactly emptiness, emptiness exactly form.
> Sensation, conception, discrimination, awareness are
> likewise like this.
> All creations are forms of emptiness, not born, not destroyed,
> Not stained, not pure, without loss, without gain.[3]

Next, we chanted the *Enmei Juko Kannon Gyō* three times. Finally, we chanted the Jizō mantra nine times: "Om Ka Ka Ka Bi San Ma E Soha Ka." As our voices died away, Bays began a chant to dedicate the merit of the chanting:

> Vast ocean of dazzling light,
> marked by the waves of life and death
> the tranquil passage of great calm embodies the form of new
> and old, coming and going
> in chanting the *Prajna Paramita Heart Sutra*
> the *Enmei Juku Kannon Gyo*
> and the Jizo *Dharani*
> we dedicate our love and prayerful thoughts to . . .

Bays began to intone the names of those being remembered. Almost all of those being honored were fetuses or babies, but the list also included a preteen, a young adult, and some more abstract mass categories, such as "all children who have died because of war." Some of the unborn were given full names, whereas other parents had chosen to simply designate their lost pregnancies as "water baby." At many ceremonies the fetus or child being remembered is given a Buddhist name as well, but this is left out at Great Vow, apparently because it can make non-Buddhists uncomfortable.[4] Bays next asked the participants to silently or aloud say the names of people, either on or not on the list, if they wished. One woman called out a name, but it was drowned in the sound of the falling rain. After a few moments of silence, Bays continued:

... and all beings in the Dharma worlds.
The bright sun of wisdom shines forever, banishing the dark night of ignorance.
Let all karma be wiped out and the mind flower bloom to bring the spring of enlightenment.
May we all practice, realize, and manifest wisdom and compassion together.

The final merit dedication began. Although the words were not printed on the handout, several other people joined Bays, such as participants with previous Zen experience who already knew the commonly chanted text.[5] Next, Bays lit a number of incense sticks. One by one, the participants approached the altar, bowed, and took a stick from Bays. Each then raised the stick to his or her forehead, stuck it upright in the burner, waved the bibs and tokens through the smoke, and bowed again. The abbess had explained that this action purifies the tokens, and that in Asia spirits are believed to receive nourishment from scents.

After leaving the altar, each person went off into the woods in search of a figure to dress and give offerings to. Most were Jizō figures, but the forest garden also included two statues of the Virgin Mary and two of Bodhidharma, the semilegendary founder of Zen in China. Each participant spent a few minutes alone with their chosen figure, in some cases praying or talking softly to it. Though here the dressing took place after the chanting, at some other Zen centers it is performed before the service portion of the ceremony. Some centers do not keep Jizō figures outside year-round, meaning they must be carried out to the site by participants before the service can be conducted. Also, some cluster the statues together around the altar and have participants one by one come up and dress them in front of the group, rather than wandering off to choose a statue and spend a few moments alone with it. Although not part of this rainy Great Vow ceremony, some temples include a washing of the Jizō statue as part of the ritual.

Slowly, people trickled back to the clearing to re-form our circle. Bays read aloud the story of Kisa Gotami, a woman of the Buddha's time who went mad after her baby died. This story is very popular in American Buddhist circles and is recited during water baby ceremonies at several temples. The tale describes how, carrying her dead child on her back, Gotami went to the Buddha to ask him to heal the boy. The Buddha told her he could do it only if she brought him a mustard seed from a household where no one had ever died. Gotami went from house to house in the village, but at every turn she found only families who had experienced the death of a child or adult. Eventually she understood that grief was an experience shared in common by everyone and she was able to bury her baby, enter a nun's order, and eventually become enlightened.

Returning to the water theme, Bays closed the formal part of the ceremony with a few remarks about how the rain was our loved ones returning to greet us, and read a poem by an American titled "Jizo the Sky Is Crying." We bowed to one another and one by one began to head back to the monastery; at some centers, participants bow more formally to the altar and then to one another. Approximately twenty minutes had passed since the procession outside. Not everyone returned immediately—one woman lingered for several minutes in front of her Jizō, and a couple stood huddled by theirs for about five minutes. Back inside, people drank tea, munched brownies, and admired the monastery's extensive Jizō collection. Several people bought Jizō statues. The woman who had stayed outside for a while approached and talked to Bays, then broke down sobbing. The couple talked to Bays as well, and the woman cried while her husband listened. Many people said how grateful they were for the ceremony. Eventually the participants began to leave, but some lingered until it was nearly time for the evening meditation period, three and a half hours after the water baby ceremony had begun.

From *Mizuko Kuyō* to Water Baby Ceremony: Changes in Ritual Practice

The first changes to pay attention to are organizational logistics related to the water baby ceremony. First, it is noteworthy that in nearly all cases, American Zen communities do not charge fees for water baby ceremonies.[6] Nor are participants expected to pay money for supplies, such as bibs, votive plaques, statues, and so on. The Zen centers provide materials for making offerings free of charge or ask participants to bring cloth and thread. The centers also allow the use of temple Jizō statues during the ceremony; alternatively, participants may elect to bring in and use their own Jizōs, but this is not required or expected. Thus *mizuko kuyō*, which is often associated with profiteering and exploitation in Japan, is in America a non-exploitative service offered to the community. American Zen practitioners want the ritual to be available to anyone who needs it, and they are generally opposed to the idea of charging for religious services.[7] This contrasts with the Japanese situation, where virtually all religious services—from a short visit to pray at a shrine to a full *mizuko kuyō*—require a monetary donation. In Japan, paying money, even if only tossing a few yen in the collection box, is a common way in which religious practitioners demonstrate the authenticity of their sincerity and respect.[8] But for American Zen adherents, accepting money from participants cheapens religious activities and implies greed and insincerity.

This does not mean that money is completely divorced from American water baby ceremonies. Leaders sometimes suggest that participants consider providing a voluntary donation after the ceremony. In many cases, the temples that perform the ceremonies also sell related books or statues after the ritual. Putting on water baby ceremonies increases the exposure of the Jizō movement in the United States and therefore helps those who benefit from it financially, such as Great Vow Monastery with its extensive product line of homemade Jizō figures. And because some people's first exposure to Zen comes through participation in the ceremony, and they may subsequently go on to become full-fledged Zen practitioners, holding these open ceremonies does over time contribute to greater membership and therefore increased revenue from member dues. On the whole, however, water baby ceremonies are probably a roughly even trade-off in terms of money, since the donations received, modest amount of books and statues sold, and small number of new members gained are balanced by the many hours spent planning and performing the ritual, as well as the considerable initial outlay for Jizō statues and the unrecouped costs of materials for making offerings.

A second important organizational difference relates to restrictions on who can observe and participate in water baby ceremonies. In Japan, restrictions on the attendance of outsiders at a *mizuko kuyō* vary. In many locations, I was readily allowed in as an observer of the ceremony, in some cases before I had a chance to identify myself as a researcher. Many such ceremonies are held in public places where no real policing of attendance is possible. I was usually allowed to take photographs, digital movies, and audio recordings. I was never asked if I had a *mizuko* to memorialize, nor was I required to participate. Even the people sponsoring the *mizuko kuyō* did not have to participate: most just paid a priest and then silently watched as he performed the ritual.

By contrast, participation in American water baby ceremonies is severely restricted. To attend, a person *must* agree to be a full participant—sewing, chanting, and so on. Observers are strictly prohibited, and no one is allowed to photograph or record the ceremony—I was not even allowed to surreptitiously take notes while participating. Some leaders, such as Yvonne Rand, go further, insisting that all participants first discuss their participation with her prior to receiving permission, and only those who wish to memorialize a young or unborn child are admitted.[9] Sometimes ceremonies have been held for women only, with no male participation allowed.[10] These restrictions are intended to heighten the effectiveness of the ceremony by preventing the distraction of outside observers and to insulate participants who may feel uncomfortable about strangers' knowing that they have had an abortion. The restrictions ensure that, even if one has not met the other participants before, there can be a reasonable assurance that everyone has had a similar experience and that therefore there will be no judgments against those who participate. Also, the fact that all participants have had similar experiences is seen as making the ritual more meaningful and efficacious.

This restriction has some practical consequences. For one, in Japan *mizuko kuyō* is available every day and often with no prior notice. Anyone who feels a need for such a ritual can walk into a temple and request services. If a certain temple does not perform *mizuko kuyō,* there is almost always another temple within easy traveling distance that will provide it. In America, water baby ceremonies are held infrequently and typically are announced well in advance, sometimes with a requirement for preregistration. Even if the ceremony is initiated at the request of a grieving layperson or couple, it is often scheduled for some time in the future and preceded by announcements to the community in the hopes of attracting more participants. This is in part because the temples are unprepared to do these rituals readily and in part because they feel that, from the mourners' standpoint, participating alone is far inferior to participating with others who have had similar losses.[11] Thus the American restrictions that are intended to ensure the integrity of the ceremony and privacy of participants also make it somewhat less accessible to the public and decrease its frequency.

The first difference in the ritual itself that can be observed is the addition of formal seated meditation (*zazen*).[12] *Zazen* is not a common component of *mizuko kuyō,* but it is present in several of the American Zen water baby ceremonies, either as part of the ceremony itself or as a spontaneous activity on the part of individual participants. The addition of *zazen* to such ceremonies is hardly surprising, since, for the majority of adherents, Zen in America is formulated around the idea of individual meditation practice or spiritual/mystic experience as the core of Buddhism.[13] To hold a Zen ritual in America without any meditation, especially one that explicitly includes reference to traditional savior figures, is potentially to suggest that something other than one's own effort is involved in proper Buddhist practice. Though some are comfortable with this, for others this flies in the face of American Zen's fundamental self-understanding, and the incorporation of meditation into the ceremony makes it fit more easily into the Zen temple's procedures. On an even more basic level, for many Americans Zen practice *is* seated meditation. It is the default to which

Zen practitioners revert automatically, prompting it to be included in ceremonies as often by habit as by conscious attempts to enforce a "self-reliance" orientation in the ritual.

Parallel to the addition of seated meditation is the relative downgrading of prayer. Prayer is an integral part of *mizuko kuyō* in Japan, including formal rituals presided over by a priest and especially in more informal rites conducted by solitary women in cemeteries or before Jizō statues. But prayer—understood as petitionary communication directed at an exterior entity—is a fraught issue for American Zen practitioners, many of whom assert that prayer is not a Buddhist activity. Again, it borders uncomfortably on a model of religious practice that places the practitioner in an inferior position, asking for assistance from an outside force. Even in a ritual such as the water baby ceremony that is structured around the idea of petitioners seeking help from Jizō, attempts are made to reduce this aspect of the ceremony. While participants do write messages of love or sorrow in some ceremonies, there is little beseeching made toward Jizō or water babies; it seems worth noting that there is less reason to actively pray to a bodhisattva primarily conceived as a symbolic archetype that represents aspects of your own nature, as described later in this chapter.

The dual location of the ceremony is another important change from the usual Japanese model. In Japan and the Japanese-American temples described in chapter 1, *mizuko kuyō* generally takes place in a single location, be it the temple worship hall, a *mizuko* Jizō shrine, or a cemetery plot; at all of these locations, the action takes place in front of and oriented toward Buddhist statuary. By contrast, virtually all of the American ceremonies are two-stage events, with the majority of the time spent away from altars and images. The actual chanting before the Jizō statue, reading of names, and presentation of offerings is the smallest portion of the ceremony. Most of the time accorded to the water baby ceremony is spent during the sewing and talking first stage. For those centers with tea after the chanting, even less time is proportionally spent in front of Jizō. Jizō is thus almost peripheral for much of the ceremony, an abstract presence that provides the catalyst for the ritual but not necessarily its heart.[14] Rather, one could argue that the longer first portion, with its shared space of group solidarity, productivity, and emotional catharsis, displaces the bodhisattva icon as the focus of the ritual.

This sewing and sharing portion is intriguing, especially since it is absent from Japanese rituals. Japanese people rarely sit in circles during religious rituals, and they never do so during *mizuko kuyō*.[15] The form is entirely American, a direct cultural adaptation to fit the preferences of Americans who find circles egalitarian, aesthetically appealing, and conducive to sharing sentiments with others.[16] In Japan, lay participants collectively face the altar or image, while the priest sits or stands with his back to the "congregation."

Likewise, in America water baby participants sew their own bibs and manufacture offerings to present in the second portion of the ritual. This is not part of the ritual in Japan. Rather, Japanese women typically buy their bibs from the temple itself, or purchase them elsewhere and bring them to the ritual site (fig. 3.3).[17] Nevertheless, proponents of the water baby ritual routinely—erroneously—describe Japanese women as sewing bibs as part of *mizuko kuyō;* virtually no ceremony fails to include mention of this "fact."[18] Conversations with American Zen practitioners suggest that they are unaware that Japanese women do not ritually sew their own offerings, including even those minority of Americans who have observed aspects of *mizuko kuyō* in Japan. This major element of the water baby ceremony seems to have arisen in large part from misunderstanding of the Japanese precedent: Americans saw that there were bibs, assumed that they were manufactured during the ceremony, and proceeded to do so themselves. Having done so, they then spiritualized the practice, creating a religious rationale that asserts the healing properties of manufacturing one's own offerings.

A second likely source for this addition of sewing into the ceremony is the precedent set by the creation of *rakusus.* Sewing is already present as a valorized practice in American Zen centers: when a practitioner prepares to receive lay ordination (*jukkai*), he or she is instructed to sew a *rakusu,* a small apronlike

FIGURE 3.3 Bibs, *mizuko* Jizō-sized hats, votive tablets, and other items for sale at Zōjōji in Tokyo.

cloth adornment that represents the robes worn by Buddhist monks.[19] This process typically takes days, weeks, or months of labor. Because several people often take *jukkai* at the same ceremony, and because laypeople typically need assistance in sewing an unfamiliar religious garment, it is common for groups of American Zen practitioners to gather and sew their *rakusus* at the same time. This group arrangement comes about in part through brute necessity: American Zen centers lack the resources (staffing, time, material resources) to conduct frequent *jukkai* ceremonies, thus they hold them infrequently and bunch several people together in one ceremony, and Americans do not know how to sew *rakusus*, so they often do it together where they can get advice and feedback on their work. A second source for these sewing groups are twentieth-century reformist strains of Zen that sought to popularize the practice of sewing robes. The Japanese nun Kasai Jōshin was a follower of one of these movements and passed the practice on to the San Francisco Zen Center in the 1970s.[20] From there it has spread widely through American convert Zen, giving rise to the idea that sewing your *rakusu* expresses Zen ideals of self-sufficiency, attention, and commitment. Participants in these sewing groups bond with one another through the shared practice and discussions that take place during sewing, leading to greater group cohesion at the *jukkai* ceremony and afterward.[21]

All of this takes place in a partial vacuum of knowledge about Japanese Zen practice. First of all, *jukkai* as part of practice is, proportionately, a far less common event in Japanese Zen than in American Zen. The average Japanese Zen devotee receives *jukkai* posthumously during the Buddhist funeral rites.[22] Non-priestly American Zen practitioners (the large majority of Zen adherents) are generally ignorant of this fact, though some longtime priests are aware of the Japanese situation. In the American situation, *jukkai* becomes an important practice during one's lifetime as a way of demonstrating one's commitment to the religion. This is a more pressing concern for Americans, who unlike the Japanese are mainly converts to Zen and subsist in a cultural environment that does not reinforce their religious identities. Among other functions, *jukkai* undertaken during life helps Americans relieve anxieties about personal and group identification, and offers them a way of attaining greater status within Zen communities, where *jukkai* is often an unspoken demarcator between "serious" practitioners and dilettantes. This differs from the Japanese Zen practice, in which *jukkai* is mainly used to transform a deceased layperson into a sort of monk and thus into a Buddha; if undertaken during life, *jukkai* is often contextualized as a merit-generating practice that confers benefits on the practitioner and his or her family.

Second, once again contrary to American assumptions, those Japanese who do take *jukkai* during their lifetimes, as well as clergy who take full ordination, do not usually participate in groups to sew their own *rakusus*. *Rakusus* and clerical robes are usually purchased from Buddhist goods merchants or, much less often, received as donations from groups of laywomen who sew the robes on behalf of the ordinand and then offer them as a way to make merit. The American sewing groups that produce rakusus for their own use, introduced by Kasai, are following a small minority practice with little precedent in premodern Japan, a fact that is generally unknown by American Zen converts.

To return to the issue of sewing bibs and other clothing for Jizō at water baby ceremonies, it is possible to conjecture a likely connection between sewing *rakusus* and this component of the ceremony. American Zen centers are already used to the idea of sewing items for practice, and the meanings they give to this process for *rakusus* show up in their explanations of why bibs are sewn for Jizō. Furthermore, the bibs sewn for Jizō statues are strikingly similar in basic appearance to *rakusus,* and when placed on the monastic Jizō figures, the appearance of a monk wearing a *rakusu* is arguably more immediate than that of a baby or young child wearing a bib. Proponents of the ceremony are aware of this visual effect and have commented on it in interviews, increasing the likelihood of a direct connection between *rakusu*-sewing and the later development of Jizō bib-sewing.[23] This also probably influences the form the bibs themselves take, since patterns are recommended by priestly leaders of the ceremony, who have already sewn a *rakusu* at some point. Thus partial knowledge of Japanese practices related to robes feeds into ignorance about the production of *kuyō* offerings and supports the (unwitting) creation of entirely new models of ritual practice.

This change in ritual practice—adding in a long period of communal sewing while seated in a circle, away from the main site—leads to additional, significant changes in the meaning and function of the overall ceremony. At most centers, participants are encouraged during this sewing period to verbally express their feelings and reasons for performing the ritual. The protracted nature of the time needed to sew is conducive to self-searching and leaders claim that it naturally leads to emotions "welling up" that can then be released into the shared space. Weeping often occurs during this process, and the sharing of these emotions aloud with others is presented as a major motivation for the ritual in the first place, a phenomenon I will return to in greater detail below. For now, it is worth noting that in Japan *mizuko kuyō* does not include a segment in which participants are encouraged to express to strangers their feelings or reasons for their presence at the ceremony. Though some people cry, this is not common at Japanese *mizuko* rituals.[24] Americans who discussed the ritual assumed, wrongly, that it was as highly emotional an occasion in Japan as it is in America.

Bibs are not the only material items associated with the water baby ceremony that display a degree of difference in comparison to *mizuko kuyō*. American Zen ceremonies do not use *tōba*, the stupa-shaped slivers of wood on which Japanese priests write calligraphy; these are one of the most common elements of *mizuko kuyō* and indeed *kuyō* of all types in Japan. Americans also do not use *ihai*, the inscribed memorial plaques that in some sense provide a substrate for the deceased person's spirit to live in, nor do they use *ema*, the painted votive tablets used to send messages to the realm of gods and spirits. In fact, *ihai* and *ema*, primary forms of material culture for Japanese Buddhism, are generally absent from American convert Zen. However, the messages written on bibs and tongue depressors and in memorial books do serve a roughly analogous function.

The roles and relationships of priest and laity are altered in the American ceremonies. In Japan, it is the ordained Buddhist priest who transfers merit to the *mizuko*. He is the one who has the authority, the ritual initiation, the preceptural purity, and the training to perform the rite correctly and produce the desired result. In general practice, he is also the one who does most or all of the merit-generating chanting, while laypeople look on or sporadically try to keep up with his rapid chant pace. Laypeople do sometimes, though infrequently, participate in the merit-dedication chants; priests always do so. In American ceremonies, every member of the group performs the same chants and mantras, and often the merit dedication is done together as well. Even when, as at Great Vow Monastery, the ritual leader performs part of the merit dedication solo, such rituals conclude with communal merit dedication. Unordained laypeople who have lost a child to abortion are put more or less on the same level as priests, and there is no implication that these two types of participants generate different amounts of merit. The participatory nature of practice is stressed here: the water baby is only effective if someone actively performs it—no one can do it for you. The Japanese logic is nearly opposite: the priest is necessary but the layperson is not, and in fact when Japanese become too elderly to travel to temples where their *mizuko* are enshrined they may continue to send money so that *kuyō* will be performed by the priests in their absence.

Even when the same elements are used in Japanese and American rituals, we need to be attentive to subtle differences in use and different ways of understanding them. For example, the *Heart Sutra* is a commonly chanted text in both countries. However, in Japan the sutra as performed is difficult for many Japanese to understand. As T. Griffith Foulk explains in the official Sōtō liturgy book for Americans:

> [Sutras] are written and recited in classical Chinese, albeit using
> Japanese phonetics (*on yomi*), which means that the chanting
> is incomprehensible to the average listener. Most well-educated
> Japanese can read classical Chinese to some extent, so the chanting

may be understood if they also have a written text to follow or if, having memorized the text by chanting it many times, they can visually
recall the Chinese characters as they are intoned. When sutras are
studied, they are usually read in Japanese translation. While many of
the teachings and beliefs expressed in them are very important for
the Zen tradition, the main reason for chanting sutras in liturgical
settings is not to broadcast their meaning but rather to produce spiritual merit (*kudoku*) for subsequent ritual offering and dedication to a
variety of beings and purposes.[25]

Use of the *Heart Sutra* in Japanese Buddhism is often talismanic in nature,
with no expectations that its doctrinal content be understood. Laypeople copy
out single characters to gain merit, and it is not unusual for bibs offered to
mizuko Jizō to have the entire sutra written on their front—these sutra bibs are
not intended for reading but for their magical and meritorious powers.[26]

By contrast, the *Heart Sutra* is usually performed in English in America
specifically so that everyone can understand. This moves the sutra from being a
meritorious or even magical text to one with a teaching role. Americans are not
only supposed to perform the sutra, they are to learn from it. The ceremony is
not allowed to be "merely" one of forms and expressive gestures, but is made to
include didactic elements that help reconcile the ambivalence many American
Zen practitioners feel about "empty ritual." We can see this further in the case
of Great Vow Monastery, where the abbess has gone so far as to alter the word-
ing of the sutra in order to carry a meaning that she hopes participants will take
away with them. For instance, she changed the sutra to read that nothing is
born or *dies,* rather than *created* or *destroyed,* an obvious allusion to the ceremony's genesis as a rite for pregnancy losses. Tinkering with chanted texts can decrease their effectiveness as merit-generating engines according to mainstream
Mahayana thought; the change here suggests that merit is not a primary concern
and takes a subservient position to the communication of specific philosophical
ideas. On the other hand, the *Enmei Juku Kannon Gyō* and Jizō mantra are not
translated and thus remain unintelligible. Explanations for using them include
that they serve to focus attention—compared to formal seated meditation by my
consultants—and that they evoke the energies of Kannon (Kuan-yin) and Jizō.

New Orientations: From Fear of Spirits to Healing the Self

Direct changes to the performance of water baby ceremonies versus their
mizuko kuyō antecedents are not the only notable alterations. Perhaps even
more significant is how Americans dismiss the idea of spirit attacks. In Japan,

fear of spirit attacks is one of the primary reasons for *mizuko kuyō*. As R. J. Zwi Werblowsky noted, "In fact, the key words to be found in all Japanese manuals for *mizuko kuyō*. . . are *osore* (fear), *tatari* (spirit attack), and *sawari* (envious revenge), and *shizume* (pacification)."[27] But in American Zen discourse on the water baby ceremony, these ideas are completely left out. The priests do not publicize their events by suggesting that people need to exorcize or pacify water baby spirits, or that they will take care of physical symptoms or bad luck. In fact, none of them seriously believes that spirit attacks are even possible, and some are unaware that this exists as a motivating factor in Japan. In the same way, the laypeople I spoke with were dismissive of this idea:

AUTHOR   In Japan there is an idea that the spirits of dead babies can actually attack and harm the living. In some ways that makes the water baby ceremony almost like an exorcism. Is there anything like that idea here?

LISA HUNTER   No.

AUTHOR   Do you think that's a possibility, that the spirit of a deceased fetus could harm the living?

HUNTER   Do you mean the whole spirit thing?

AUTHOR   Yes.

HUNTER   [snort of derision] No. Do you mean that it might really happen, or that people might think it is happening?

AUTHOR   Do you think that could in fact ever happen?

HUNTER   No.

AUTHOR   Did anything that anyone said or did during the ceremony suggest that any Americans might think it could happen?

HUNTER   I don't think so.[28]

As one female priest at Rochester Zen Center explained, "We live in a rationalistic society which doesn't believe in ghosts. And ghosts don't fit into Buddhism at all. They have no place in it. It's really not part of the worldview of Buddhism. And I don't think it's part of the way most Westerners think about things, all those ideas about malevolent spirits."[29] The aborted or lost fetus has been transformed from menacing to harmless in the reproduction of *mizuko kuyō* in America.

It is certainly possible to take issue with the assertion that ghosts are absent from Buddhism. All Asian Buddhist traditions contain significant amounts of ritualization and concern around ghosts and what Robert DeCaroli calls "spirit-deities."[30] From the oldest accounts of the Buddha's activities in India to the spirit boom in contemporary Japan, the deceased and elemental spirits have been one main focus of Buddhism. Indeed, in Japanese Zen the funeral and ongoing memorials for a deceased person (both formal periodic ones at temples and daily rites performed before the home *butsudan*) are the primary form of religious practice, far outstripping meditation or other activities. And Sōtō Zen clerics' competency at performing exorcisms (along with such things as faith-healing, rain-making, and rituals to save women from hell) is precisely one of the main factors in the schools' successful growth and popularity.[31] Ordaining and pacifying local ghosts was an important domestication strategy for Sōtō Zen in Japan.[32] It is instructive, therefore, to observe the unanimity with which American Zen practitioners approach this issue. From my interviews I learned that some American Zen adherents do believe in spirits; many do not, whereas others leave the possibility open but in actual practice never think about them. But all converts interviewed for this project and every publication on the water baby ceremony agree that the dead pose no threat to the living and that there is no need for religious intervention to ward off disaster or misfortune.

Related to this development is a significant shift in the rhetoric on the woman's sinfulness. In Japan, this is a common aspect of the *mizuko kuyō* phenomenon, where abortion is described as a violation of Buddhist morality and even miscarriage and stillbirth may be seen as reflecting faults in the mother. Furthermore, the associations of death, illness, and blood with pregnancy loss render it a polluting event in the context of Japanese religion, necessitating purification. But in America the Zen teachers involved with the water baby ceremony are careful not to suggest that the participants might be immoral or impure in any way. Even if they do not agree with abortion, they seem not to see any usefulness in linking it to rhetoric about the woman's culpability.[33] Thus, what in Japan is a strongly shame-based practice becomes a relatively nonjudgmental one in America—the only judgments are the ones the woman brings to the ceremony herself, which are neither encouraged nor discouraged by the clergy. *Mizuko kuyō* loses its aspect as a critique of contemporary female sexual or reproductive practices, therefore, and is abandoned as a method to control or direct female agency regarding these issues. Rather, water baby ceremonies encourage and affirm women's agency and right to make difficult decisions.

One of the most commonly alleged differences between American convert Buddhism and its Asian antecedents is the role of women in reshaping Buddhism along feminist lines. Despite the frequent allegation of difference, there are remarkably few sustained scholarly studies of how exactly the women's movement has changed American Buddhism, other than impressionistic assertions that women occupy a greater proportion of leadership roles and have developed a "more feminine" style of teaching and nurturing their communities. It is as if the impression is so strong that no one feels a need to actually demonstrate in concrete terms how women are specifically altering Buddhism.

The water baby ceremony, of course, is a case study tailor-made to explore this impact. In Japan, the *mizuko kuyō* is often associated with right-wing politics and frequently has a misogynistic tone. As explained in the introduction, male Buddhist priests have been active in promoting *mizuko kuyō* as a practice that reminds women of their shame and places them in a proper position of submission and humility.[34] By contrast, in America the Zen purveyors of water baby ceremonies are mainly champions of women's equality and advocates of liberal political views.[35] Although some American men—all of whom are pro-choice on the abortion issue and liberal in political orientation—have led water baby ceremonies, it is women (both ordained and lay) who have taken the lead in introducing the ceremony into their own communities, publicizing it to others, and acting as ritual facilitators. The average leader of a *mizuko kuyō* in both Japan and Japanese-American temples is a man; the average leader of a water baby ceremony is a woman. All in all, in America the ritual appears to appeal to an entirely different segment of society, one arguably diametrically opposite from that in Japan. The American women driving the spread of the water baby ceremony all hold feminist views to some degree, and in their reproduction of this Japanese ritual they reconstitute it as empowering, nonjudgmental, nonpunitive, and supportive of women's power over their bodies and lives. Fetuses are no longer potential antagonists and mothers are conceptualized as mourners, not criminals or murderers.

If American water babies are nonthreatening, then what exactly are their qualities? And who is Jizō, if he is not a supernatural savior needed to pacify and rescue fetal spirits? Perhaps surprisingly, American Zen adherents who had gone through the water baby ceremony—including leaders of the ceremony—often had difficulty articulating the concept of a water baby when asked directly. Sometimes, the water baby was described as a spirit or being who had died and/or was trapped in another existence. More commonly, however, the existence of such an entity was questioned or contextualized in particular ways. Water babies were frequently described as "energies" or treated in nonanthropomorphic ways, such as stressing the "water" imagery over that of a baby or individual entity. Many consultants had never given serious thought to what the concept "water baby" referred to, indicating that their reasons for participating in the ritual were not strongly connected to a desire to do something for such beings.

By contrast, most people were more confident in their understanding of Jizō. For some, Jizō played, at least in part, the role of protector or savior, helping beings in need:

> AUTHOR   Is Jizo an actual entity on some level?
>
> RYUSHIN CREEDON   There have been times [I've felt that way]. We used to rent a house down the road from the Zen center in Larch Mountain. It was a short little half-hour walk if you weren't taking a car. So occasionally I would walk back at night, and being from the city, when I'm all of a sudden in the country there's all sorts of things in my head that are going to jump out and get me: cougars and bears and everything. So how I would soothe myself would be to imagine two large seven-foot Jizos walking behind me, like my bodyguards: big, blue, carrying their staves, *cintamani* jewels, and walking behind me. I would do the Jizo mantra as I was walking, and I would feel more at peace. So that's one way that I see Jizo. There have been times when I have done bowing practice, doing a hundred thousand bows, and when I've been doing it very vigorously and starting to get back pain, starting to get knee pain, then I'll imagine that as I am starting to come up, Jizo is reaching over and helping me up. And then I'll feel lighter as I do that. That's very vague to know whether this thing that I can't see, whether it's physically lifting me up or whether it is mental, but I do know that it does help.[36]

Nonetheless, this role tended to be confined to specific segments of the water baby ceremony and was not the dominant way that Jizō was usually talked about. Much more often, Jizō was described as a role model to be emulated by the practitioner.[37] Jizō was often described as an aspect of oneself, such as the practitioner's Buddha-nature or compassion. As Wendy Egyoku Nakao put this point:

> The way that we always talk about the bodhisattvas is that the bodhisattva is me. It can only be me. Of course, we have all the qualities of all the bodhisattvas, but we tend to have more of one than the others, perhaps. We just tend to manifest in the world in particular ways, you know. And so for me, those who really naturally seem to be Jizos, I ask them to really study Jizo, and really look at what that manifestation is in your life. So it's not that you become Jizo, you *are* Jizo. You yourself are Jizo. Jizo only is alive through you, really.[38]

This sometimes meant that Jizō was an archetype, essentially a fictional character designed to represent subtle parts of the human personality or Buddhist practice. Just as often, this was conceptualized as "energy," though this energy was described in highly nebulous terms, leaving open the question of whether to take such ideas literally or metaphorically.[39] Perhaps it is best to say that both modes were present: Zen adherents generally felt that unseen but affecting (and typically nonanthropomorphic) forces do pervade the universe and lurk within the body and mind, but they also used this terminology to speak more abstractly about the power of vows, intentions, and feelings.

Bodhisattvas are interpreted in a wide variety of ways in Japanese Zen, and all of the above ideas can be found in some form. The degree of emphasis on some interpretations is quite different from what it is in America, however. Jizō is for most Japanese people an actual savior—in the case of children and the unborn, the supernatural protector par excellence. He is beseeched for help by millions daily, and in the *mizuko kuyō* is often expected to actively rescue lost spirits and remove them to the Pure Land. He is believed in as an actual living—if nonetheless transcendent—entity first and foremost in Japan. Presumably few Japanese Zen participants would state that they are only praying to or getting in touch with their "inner Jizō" or "Jizō energies" via *mizuko kuyō*.

Most of the differences between Japanese *mizuko kuyō* and American water baby ceremonies documented so far lead toward what is the most important change of all, the key to understanding not only why the ceremonies take on an altered form but why American Zen practitioners have adopted this ritual in the first place. In Japan, the basic point of the *mizuko kuyō* is to placate the *mizuko*, to apologize to it and try to make amends by dedicating merit on its behalf. Ultimately, the spirit who has been wronged—whether it is imagined as actively disgruntled or merely the victim of unfortunate circumstance—is the focus of the ritual. Though some participants hope to derive benefit from the performance of *mizuko kuyō*, the ceremony is primarily designed to benefit the *mizuko* ghost. Again, the example of elderly patrons who pay for *mizuko kuyō* to be performed in distant temples is relevant, as it clearly shows that the focus is the spirit being memorialized, and there may be no lay participants in the ceremony at all.

In America, on the other hand, the focus of the water baby ceremony is completely reoriented. Here, the point of the ceremony is the mental and spiritual health of the grieving mother (and/or father). This came out clearly in conversation with the abbess of Zen Center of Los Angeles:

AUTHOR In the Japanese context, there's a feeling that maybe these *mizuko* beings can haunt people, that they're trapped in-between somehow.

WENDY NAKAO I don't know if these beings are trapped. I think the thing is that for us, *we're* trapped. We're trapped in our abortion or the death of our child. That's really for me what is being liberated.

AUTHOR   So it's really more of a ceremony for the people who are participating in the ritual, not for the ghosts.

NAKAO   Yeah. I think so. Of course, you can't separate yourself from the child that's been aborted. So they're really together. But I would say the emphasis is more on "we need to free ourselves."[40]

This is the crucial fact to grasp in understanding these rituals, and it differs on the most basic level from how *mizuko kuyō* is approached in Japan. As another female promoter of the ceremony described, "It's about creating a space in which one can experience what one is feeling. Because one can experience it and live it, it's no longer ruling them. It's no longer a burden. It's something that has its own life beyond you. . . . That's why we have ceremonies, in order to create a space for these very, very powerful, very deep, primal things we feel, and often don't know we feel and can't give shape to."[41] For this woman, the water baby ceremony does not accomplish the exorcism of the wrathful fetal spirit or the alleviation of the mother's bad luck. Rather, the result is an opening to powerful and hidden emotions akin to that sought through seated meditation. Or, as I will discuss shortly, through psychotherapy.

That the grieving participant, not the water baby, is the new central focus of the ritual can be most easily seen in the range of persons being memorialized in the ritual. Most participate in the water baby ceremony to remember an abortion, miscarriage, stillbirth, or the death of a young infant. But having adopted the ritual, many priests are willing to allow other uses if there is felt to be a need. Thus, some people participate in the water baby ceremony to memorialize deceased adult children, who also receive normal funeral rites. More unexpectedly, some participate in the ceremony to honor runaway children, children given up for adoption, children lost through post-divorce custody disputes, or adult children alienated from their parents. And yet others participate on behalf of their own "lost childhood" or "all children in the world."[42] In many of these cases there are certainly no fetal spirits to direct merit toward because the subjects are still alive, while in others there are no beings—living or dead—to speak of at all. In all of these cases, the ceremony is solely for the benefit of the participant; most of these would not be considered to require the performance of *mizuko kuyō* in Japan. Even when there are indeed fetuses and young children as the imagined water babies, proponents are clear that it is the parent who is the main object of concern in the ritual. The point is to produce healing for these mourners.

One reason for this is that meditation, ritual, and psychotherapy are closely aligned in American Zen thought. Although some of the people with whom I spoke took pains to explicitly state that the water baby ceremony is not therapy, the connections are clear. All consultants used psychotherapeutic language to describe the ceremony, employing such terms as "repression," "unconscious" and "subconscious," "neurosis," "healing," "defenses," "processing," "taboo," "active listening," "working through," "catharsis," and "aversion," as well as terms originating in psychotherapy that are already common currency in American Buddhism, such as "ego." Actual forms of therapy and famous therapists were often referenced in conversation, particularly Carl Jung—hardly surprising since Jizō is persistently explained as an "archetype" by American Zen adherents.

Historian Eva Moskowitz has traced the rise of psychotherapy as a model for American self-understanding in her book *In Therapy We Trust: America's Obsession with Self-Fulfillment*. Moskowitz describes a "therapeutic gospel" with three key tenets that rule contemporary American culture: (1) happiness is the supreme goal in life; (2) problems once thought to be political, economic, or educational are now believed to be psychological; and (3) psychological problems lie at the base of our unhappiness and failures, problems that must be addressed on the individual and corporate levels.[43] As she says, "Today a psychological point of view dominates our political, economic, and cultural life. . . . The therapeutic gospel celebrates all that promotes self-realization and condemns all that promotes psychological harm. . . . [Thus] the therapeutic gospel assumes that mental health and happiness require that we become aware of the underlying and often hidden emotions that determine our outlook."[44]

This therapeutic gospel is clearly present in the water baby ceremonies. In explaining the effectiveness of the water baby ritual, consultants always said that it allowed hidden emotions to come into the conscious mind, where they could be acknowledged, expressed, and released. They also frequently said that this was one common purpose for meditation practice, which involves deep introspection to discover and "work through" places where people are "stuck," "attached," or "conditioned." In many cases, consultants said that during meditation practice, emotions connected to past pregnancy losses had bubbled up unexpectedly, and they then sought relief through the water baby ceremony, where they could "process" these developments in a more active manner than simply sitting with them.[45] From a certain vantage point, much of the water baby ceremony could be interpreted as a series of psychotherapeutic exercises performed in a religious venue. For instance, the sewing of bibs, making of memorials, and drawing of pictures appears as a type of art therapy, while sitting in a supportive circle of fellow sufferers seems rather similar to group therapy. As previously discussed, this sort of circle sitting and group expression is absent from Japanese Zen and *mizuko kuyō* in general. Rather, there are indications that this element was adopted by Americans from self-help and twelve-step programs, such as Alcoholics Anonymous, that have roots in modern notions of therapy, with further influences from so-called "Native American talking stick circles" popular in many New Age groups.[46]

Conclusion: Swapping Cultural Luggage

The striking degree to which water baby ceremonies display the marks of influence from elements of mainstream early-twenty-first-century American culture—such as psychotherapy, liberalism, modern skepticism, and non-Buddhist religious and self-help groups—suggests a need to rethink the frequent assumption that converts seek to divorce Zen from "cultural baggage" and articulate a Buddhism closer to the Buddha's original intention than the Asian traditions that evolved over the millennia after his death.[47] Rather, it seems that in rhetorically attacking the baggage of Japanese-American immigrant Buddhism, commentators sometimes overemphasize the handbag of Japan while missing the suitcase of American culture. In quite explicit terms, what many Zen leaders are seeking is not to de-culturalize Buddhism but simply to re-culturalize it for a new society, as Robert Althouse, the founder of the Zen Community of Oak Park, stated affirmatively to me during an interview:

> We've received wonderful things from the Japanese, and we've also received things that aren't particularly helpful. And I think that some maturing is happening as Western Buddhists are having some discernment around what is cultural and what isn't, and being able to separate the two. And in that process I think what's also happening is that Zen is kind of marrying with science and psychology and social justice.[48]

In reflecting on the adaptations that have been made in the water baby ceremony, I suggest that it is not simply that these changes were made, consciously or unconsciously, by the mainly female priests who have developed the water baby ceremony in America. I believe that these changes were necessary for the ritual to be accepted and utilized within a convert Zen milieu. Currently, if the *mizuko kuyō* were offered as is (i.e., contextualized by Japanese spirit beliefs and so on) by a convert Zen temple without these sorts of Americanized adaptations, it likely would not appeal to the members and would fail to attract support for its continuance. Furthermore, it might have even greater difficulty attracting non-Buddhists, a significant clientele for the ceremony at many Zen temples.

And yet, the growing popularity of the water baby ceremony is itself an indication that changes are occurring in these convert Buddhist communities as the bumpy road of Americanization continues on its way. It is hard to imagine that a long and ritualistic ceremony drawing on ideas of savior bodhisattvas and fetal ghosts, even if significantly modified along the lines described above, could have enjoyed such a widespread popularity in the convert Zen groups of the 1960s and '70s. It is the implications of this newly popular ceremony's emergence that concern the next chapter.

4

"Branching Streams Flow On in the Dark"

Rethinking American Buddhism in Light of Mizuko Kuyō

Americanization occurs under the guise of a sincere belief that one is following Japanese Zen tradition.

—G. Victor Sōgen Hori, *The Faces of Buddhism in America*

"Branching streams flow on in the dark," wrote Chinese Zen patriarch Sekito Kisan in his classic text *Sandōkai*.[1] In ways recognized and unrecognized, American practitioners have often branched away from the stream of Zen that has flowed to them from Japan. At the same time, the rivers of Zen flowing through America have themselves branched off in many unnoticed directions from the master narratives of scholars writing about Western Buddhism. Now that we have explored how the water baby ceremony arrived in American Zen centers, how it is conducted, and what modifications have been made to fit it into an American context, we can consider the implications of the ceremony for both the future of American Zen and the future of academic historiography of Buddhism in the West. Do convert Zen groups most resemble traditional temples in their lineage or new religious movements? Why has ritual, including the water baby ceremony, been largely overlooked, and why is it on the rise? In this chapter, I also highlight four key elements of the water baby ritual—places, objects, bodies, and emotions—and examine how they point to new narratives in the study of Zen in America.

Comparing American Buddhist Post-Pregnancy Loss Rituals

When considering water baby ceremonies in light of Japanese-American practices, some interesting phenomena are revealed. The most natural comparison
is with Zenshuji, the downtown Los Angeles Zen temple that serves as the
North American headquarters of the Sōtō denomination. While most interpreters prefer to stress the differences between Japanese-American and convert Zen communities (and especially the innovative nature of the latter), some
similarities are in evidence as well. Both communities are willing to memorialize pregnancy losses and have worked out rituals to do so. Both afford a prominent place in such rites to Jizō, including incense offerings to images of the
bodhisattva and repeated performance of his mantra. The *Heart Sutra* is used
as liturgy in the post–pregnancy loss rituals of both groups, and merit dedica-
tions are chanted. Ordained Zen priests lead the rituals in both communities.
Specialized material objects are created for post–pregnancy loss rituals in both
cases: origami "babies" and memorial plaques (*ihai*) by the priest at Zenshuji,
and bibs, hats, capes, pictures, and/or messages by all the participants in water
baby ceremonies.

Yet there are noticeable differences as well. In particular, *mizuko kuyō* at
Zenshuji is merely one of several types of *kuyō* that can be sought at Zenshuji,
and its performance—while including unique elements such as gathering before each of the temple Jizō figures in turn—is similar to other such rites. It is
striking mainly for the object of the ritual—aborted and miscarried fetuses—
rather than the process of the ritual itself, and exists comfortably within the
matrix of memorial ceremonies that are among the most common practices at
the temple. Water baby ceremonies, on the other hand, are noticeably divergent
from other convert Zen activities. On no other occasions do large groups of Zen
practitioners gather to manufacture offerings. This includes funerals for adult
community members, which differ considerably from water baby ceremonies.
The water baby ceremonies are much longer than most convert Zen activities,
including normal periods of communal meditation practice.

In fact, the Zenshuji *mizuko kuyō* and the convert Zen water baby ceremonies make a rather poor match in many ways. But there is another Japanese-
American Buddhist community described in chapter 1 whose *mizuko kuyō* is a
much closer counterpart to the water baby ceremonies: Rissho Kosei-kai Buddhist Church of Los Angeles. Among all the *mizuko kuyō* rituals at the wide
range of denominations described in the first chapter, it is only at the Risshō
Kōsei-kai temple that women manufacture their own offerings for the service.
It is the only place where large groups of individuals (mostly women) gather

to meet and memorialize *mizuko* with one another. It is the only temple that includes portions specifically designed for participants to voice their hidden feelings over pregnancy loss aloud. Nowhere other than the Risshō Kōsei-kai temple are the *mizuko kuyō* rituals broken into two clearly discernable halves, and it is only here that people sit together in supportive circles. Rissho Kosei-kai Buddhist Church of Los Angeles is the only temple that consistently includes women as prominent coleaders of the ceremony and has laypeople fully participating in all elements of the ritual. It is the only temple where the ceremony takes well over an hour. And finally, it is the only temple that includes *mizuko kuyō* as a regularly scheduled event advertised on the public calendar, rather than a private ceremony held only when an individual or couple petitions the priest.

It seems significant that convert Zen ceremonies share so much in common with a Buddhist new religious movement, while demonstrating noteworthy differences from rituals in their own tradition. In many aspects, convert Zen functions more like a new religious movement in American society than like Zen in Asia: as a large movement, it emerged in America only a few decades ago, has shown rapid growth, attracts individual seekers disenchanted with the religious and cultural mainstream, and is significantly tied to the charismatic personalities of first- or second-generation lineage leaders (such as Suzuki Shunryū and Maezumi Taizan). Both Risshō Kōsei-kai and Zen outside of the Japanese-American community are primarily composed of converts, and both are explicitly oriented toward evolving Buddhism to meet the needs of the laity in a late-modern context, rather than focused on maintaining traditions and monastic orientations found in historical Buddhism.[2]

Furthermore, in light of this comparison it can be noted how Risshō Kōsei-kai *mizuko kuyō* is much more similar to convert Zen post–pregnancy loss rituals than it is to other Japanese-American *mizuko kuyō*. At least in the case of *mizuko kuyō* it becomes difficult to talk about a monolithic "ethnic" Japanese-American Buddhism that contrasts with white convert Buddhism. Some Japanese-American Buddhist communities clearly operate, at least at times, in ways that are far more similar to convert temples than are usually acknowledged. Also, Risshō Kōsei-kai considerably complicates Jan Nattier's well-known typology of import (brought in by converts), export (arriving as missionaries), and baggage (carried along with immigrants) forms of Buddhism in America. Risshō Kōsei-kai is in some ways a baggage form of Buddhism, but it is also very much an export type as well, proselytizing actively within the Japanese-American and (less successfully) non-Japanese-American communities. Yet in the case of *mizuko kuyō*, it looks fairly dissimilar to other baggage Japanese-American Buddhisms, and is nothing like the classical export Buddhism of Sōka Gakkai, which does not conduct *mizuko kuyō*.[3] Instead, in form and function it is closer to the import Buddhism of the American Zen converts. Attention to rituals such as *mizuko kuyō* across denominational and racial lines reveals many ways in which previous scholarly classifications, though useful in many situations, break down in others, failing to be either descriptive or predictive. They serve as helpful reminders that new perspectives are continually required when dealing with a subject as rich and various as American Buddhism.[4]

Reassessing the Place of Ritual in American Zen

The water baby ceremony is a rapidly growing phenomenon in a form of religion that has often been depicted as antiritualistic. How are we to understand this? Is Zen more amenable to ritual than many have described? Has there always been more ritual in American Zen centers, but it was overlooked or downplayed? Has there been a change in American Zen communities, so that they have become more open to ritual and incorporated more ceremonies into their temples and meditation centers? Has American culture itself changed to become more "ritual-friendly?" All of the above can be answered affirmatively, I believe.

The assertion that Zen does not involve ritual or is opposed to ritual in its basic orientation cannot be supported by a look at actual Zen activities, either historical or contemporary. Zen, whether in Japan or in another country where it is widely practiced (such as China, Korea, or Vietnam), is dominated by ritual activity. For example, Duncan Williams, in his study *The Other Side of Zen*, has done a terrific job of retrieving the actual practice of early modern Sōtō Zen Buddhism. As he points out, the main activities of Zen priests were "praying for rain, healing the sick, or performing exorcistic and funerary rites,"[5] not formal seated meditation. In fact, "the vast majority of ordinary Sōtō Zen monks and laypeople never practiced Zen meditation, never engaged in iconoclastic acts of the Ch'an/Zen masters (as described in hagiographical literature), never solved *kōans*, never raked Zen gardens, never sought mystical meditative states, and never read Dōgen's writings."[6] This statement is as true of modern-day Zen as it was of Edo period Zen.[7] Thankfully, the work of recent scholars on Asian Buddhism seems to be influencing historiographers of American Zen. Though one can still find numerous popular accounts of Zen as "unritualistic," academic studies of Zen in the United States are now more likely to acknowledge ritual as a normal part of Zen practice.

If Zen has always had ritual as a basic component, how is it that earlier historiographers failed to account for it? In part, the blame must be laid upon the emphasis on formal seated meditation (*zazen*) in American Zen communities. This practice is marginal in everyday Japanese Zen, but it is the raison d'être for nearly all American Zen groups, particularly those dominated by converts. Most American Zen practitioners are attracted to Zen as a way to perform meditation, which is usually described as lowering one's blood pressure, helpful in dealing with everyday stress, productive of greater patience and self-insight—and conducive to Buddhist enlightenment. The convert groups that have spread across the continent since the middle of the twentieth century all take extended silent seated meditation as their primary communal activity. American Zen has widely perpetuated a belief that meditation is not just the core but the only necessary aspect of Buddhism, that *zazen* is not ritualistic, and that liberated spontaneity—often directly contrasted with "empty ritual"—is the essence of Zen.

Reliance on American Zen rhetoric deflected attention away from other elements of Zen practice that were nonetheless present from the beginning. This is true both of outsiders who took Zen rhetoric at face value and insiders already indoctrinated to focus on seated meditation to the detriment of other practices. This dynamic is clear, for instance, in the reflections of one of my consultants, a longtime member of the Rochester Zen Center:

> People were just manic [laughs] about practice—formal meditation practice. But that does not mean that actually in those early years we didn't develop a lot of ceremonies—we did! We developed a lot of ceremonies. It was a very rich ceremonial year, and that was the start of sort of adapting Buddhism into what was already here, in the ceremonial life of American culture. For instance, Thanksgiving is a very big ceremony for us here in America. New Year's Eve is another big one. We adapted and kind of transmogrified [laughs] the existing ceremonies into something that had meaning for us as Buddhists. Halloween was a big one. And then, of course, we had Wesak [the celebration of the Buddha's birth, awakening, and death], which was uniquely Buddhist. And we used to do a kind of Buddha's birthday ceremony.... There are ceremonies for lots of different things. And we've done plays of the Buddha's life. In the early years we had some incredibly creative people. We did this real big piece of theater in the '70s, it was music and singing.... Not everybody goes or can go to *sesshin*! And if they don't, what happens here is that they feel that their practice is less than valid. Because there's this model of staff where you dedicate your life to this constant going to *sesshin* and many hours of sitting a day, somehow that's seen as the only way, the only valid way to practice.[8]

Furthermore, the notion that *zazen* is not ritual must be interrogated. What does *zazen* actually consist of in practice at hundreds of meditation centers across the country? It is an activity typically performed according to a repetitious community schedule and for an exact set amount of time, whose bodily postures and orientations are rigidly prescribed by traditional texts. It is carried out by a group in a religious setting with a religious goal, is accompanied by bells, drums, incense, and bowing, with special equipment, and is connected to a set of religious legends and myths. It is followed by communal chanting of venerated texts, and often with a designated leader wearing clerical garb and carrying out additional devotions in front of an altar holding the images of cosmic entities and semideified lineal ancestors. Surely all this is the very description of a model ritual. That Zen practitioners in America have generally been unwilling to admit as much seems to be linked to at least two phenomena. The first is the classical Protestant critique of Catholic ritual (and often by extension, ritual in general) as the meaningless and corrupt development of scheming priests, antithetical to the intent and practices of the religious founder, that substitutes mere gestures and formality for genuine spiritual feeling and belief—what Zen studies scholar Paula Arai aptly terms "the 'Protestant Undercurrent' that has dominated most Western practice of Zen."[9] This view has had force in American religion since the time of the British colonies, and though its grip on our culture has diminished somewhat with the rise of pluralism and other factors, it was still operative during the first waves of convert Zen in the 1950s and '60s.[10] This was also a time of rising countercultural attitudes that in some ways took the Protestant orientation even further, searching for authentic religious experience outside of the framework of Christian dogma and practice altogether. Savvy Zen missionaries and spokespersons, such as Suzuki Daisetsu and Philip Kapleau, marketed Zen as pure experience and a process of self-understanding, deflecting attention from *zazen's* ritual aspects.

A second reason for this failure to identify *zazen* as a ritual seems to have been a strong but not fully articulated connection of ritual with more ceremonial practices—"ritual" was associated with large, liturgically oriented ceremonies such as the Catholic Mass.[11] Because seated meditation is a relatively quiet practice that can be interpreted as individualistic rather than communal, it lacks some of the more grandly ceremonial aspects that have drawn the ire of persons influenced by the Protestant critique.[12] Moreover, with a shortage of qualified priests, limited schedules, few dedicated sites for practice, a dearth of ritual implements, a young clientele of individual seekers needing few funerals or family rituals, and incomplete knowledge of common practices in Japanese Buddhism, early convert Zen communities naturally did not include many of the ceremonies that drive Zen in Japan. A situation where few ceremonies were performed, quietistic seated meditation was emphasized, and pure experience was championed as the uniquely defining characteristic of Zen, led to a perception that Zen was unritualistic by *nature* rather than by contingent American *circumstance,* and created feedback pressure not to acknowledge the ritualized elements of meditation and other practices.

So early convert Zen practitioners really were temporarily *less* involved in certain types of ritual compared to both their Japanese parent lineages and many other American religious groups, and they simultaneously failed to perceive the ritual nature of those practices they did engage in. But while the perception of Zen as nonritualistic has remained strong for some, over the years the frequency, variety, and impact of ritual in American Zen communities have increased significantly. All of the flagship convert Zen institutions—those large and stable enough to own their buildings and to support one or more permanent teachers—now perform a weekly, monthly, and yearly cycle of ceremonies and rituals. These differ somewhat according to lineage but commonly include *zazen, oryoki*-style meals, celebration of the births and deaths of founders, Wesak, Segaki, New Year's, devotions to bodhisattvas such as Kannon and Jizō, *jukkai,* Coming of Age ceremonies for teens, atonement ceremonies, Sunday services, and many other rituals. And, increasingly, the water baby ceremony.[13]

I have tried to account for why ritual did not seem to be part of Zen in earlier decades, but why is American Zen now filling up with ritual? A number of factors seem to be in play here. One is that many Zen communities now have sufficient size and resources to perform rituals that would have been difficult or impossible in earlier, leaner times. Ritual on anything beyond the most basic scale tends to require a certain minimum of free time, usable space, specialized equipment, and participants. These were often not available to Zen centers during their formative periods. Material culture is particularly relevant here: historically, many Buddhist implements have had to be imported from Asia at considerable cost. But now with a flourishing industry of American Buddhist products—from meditation cushions to Jizō statues—access to such items is far greater, and reasonably priced instruments can be obtained.

A second factor is that with the growth of Zen in America has come greater knowledge of Asian Zen, including the dawning awareness of the common role of ritual in Japanese religious life.[14] Some convert Zen practitioners have become critical of what they see as watering down of the tradition as it crosses into an American milieu, and ritual appears as an important element that helps maintain and express Zen attitudes and forms. This leads to a point that I have tried to gesture toward in previous chapters: the need for a corrective in the narrative of Buddhism's adaptation in America. It is possible to imagine that adaptation involves a progressive unidirectional shift over time away from Asian elements and toward phenomena seen as more "Western" or "American," such as away from ritual and toward meditation, away from belief in spirits or karma and toward skepticism, and so on. But in fact, the scale slides in both directions, and the process is considerably more complex and less teleological. Attention to the growing favor toward ritual in American Zen highlighted by the water baby ceremony suggests that the timeline can in some cases be read as becoming *more* Japanese over time, rather than less, as Americans learn more about Japan. Perhaps a new term could be coined here—*Reconstructionist Zen*—to refer to the tendency in some quarters of Zen to explore and re-appropriate aspects of the tradition that were ignored or excluded in the early period of assimilation to America.[15] This highlights the parallel to Reconstructionist Judaism, which has encouraged the reevaluation of rituals and other elements of Judaism abandoned in the rush to modernize, yet does so in a manner that does not require literal belief in the supernatural aspects of Jewish religion.

One of the ironies of studying Buddhism in America is the eventual realization that *ignorance*, the bugaboo of Buddhism, is at times just as responsible as *understanding* for the creative development of distinctive forms of Buddhism that allow Zen and other groups to become acculturated and grow. For instance, not knowing that Japanese Zen practitioners don't make bibs or engage in cathartic circle sessions, Americans readily conjure up entirely innovative "traditions" and then retro-project them onto an Asian parent lineage that they both deeply value and sometimes only partially comprehend. This further complicates the trope of adaptation in Buddhism's transmission to the West. Adaptation is often not a process of taking a preexisting model and changing it to meet a different cultural understanding. Instead, it involves inventing new forms from whole cloth—pardon the pun—and then perhaps modifying them later to better reflect Asian models when knowledge of Japanese practices increases.[16]

Demographic changes are a third factor that may account for shifts in the amount and types of ritualization taking place in convert Zen. The baby boom generation that provided so many Zen practitioners in the 1960s–'80s is aging, and as the Buddha pointed out, with age comes illness and death. Most of the pioneer convert priests were ordained as a way to deepen their personal spirituality and spread the meditation techniques with which they were enamored. Yet many of those who have gone on to run major Zen temples find that rather than spending their days meditating like a legendary master of old and delivering enigmatic statements encapsulating true reality, they are increasingly called upon to perform funerals as their peers age and die. Thus the simple passing of time leads to greater incidence of illness- and death-related rituals, and with the acceptance of one type of ritual comes greater tolerance of others as well.

A fourth factor in the increase of American Zen ritual is the emergence of positive valuations of ritual itself within these communities. My consultants expressed appreciation for ritual in the abstract as a positive activity, one needed in order to communicate teachings on a somatic level, to honor and remember major figures in the lineage, to effect real healing, to psychologically usher participants into new stages of life and commitment, and to mark for the community important milestones or bring attention to communal values and desires. Many cited the water baby ceremony as a ritual that fulfilled one or more of these needs. Whereas some consultants professed to have appreciated ritual since the beginning, many others indicated that they had gradually come to reject the early anti-ritualism of American Zen. Factors in this turn of opinion included greater distance from the negative religious experiences of childhood, exposure to ritual in other Buddhist lineages (such as Tibetan Buddhism) or in trips to Asia, and the emergence of new concerns not addressed directly by seated meditation, such as unresolved emotional issues, growing awareness of one's mortality, and the death of temple members or family. One frequent story told in many slight variations was of the consultant as a headstrong young meditator who defiantly eschewed "smells and bells," yet over years and decades learned to love Buddhist ritual as it became more familiar and comfortable, augmenting or even supplanting formal seated meditation as their primary orientation in practice. Some indicated that the very anti-ritualism of earlier American Zen had eventually driven them to investigate ritual as a potentially useful side of Buddhism; according to Buddhist psychology, aversion is ultimately as dangerous as attachment, and the rejection of ritual and many aspects of Zen other than meditation began to seem extreme or somehow indicative of deeper unresolved issues to some consultants.

These changes have parallels in other convert communities. For example, Wendy Cadge found a similar dynamic at the Cambridge Insight Meditation Center (CIMC):

> In the early days, the teachers and lay practitioners at CIMC focused only on meditation practice, believing that any other branches of the Theravada Buddhist tree were just the sapwood and would only get in the way. Over the years, however, the teachers and practitioners have come to realize that the tree cannot survive with only the heartwood and have gradually introduced other branches through rituals and ceremonies, regular gatherings to take the precepts, and holiday gatherings. These branches, they increasingly believe, support the meditation practice, and combined with meditation can lead to the complete end of suffering in this lifetime.[17]

One piece of this puzzle of ritual's rise is the proliferation of Zen in America, which drives inevitable change. As Zen adds to its client base, it must serve new niches; meditation simply cannot meet the wishes of all people potentially interested in Zen. Experiments such as the Jizō movement provide other ways for Americans to interact with Zen. Furthermore, with the increase in the number of Zen centers, there is greater opportunity for different expressions and models. When Zen was concentrated in a small number of central sites— San Francisco Zen Center, Rochester Zen Center, Zen Center of Los Angeles— it could be more easily policed. But today most small cities and even many rural areas have Zen groups, and voices that were subaltern now speak. Women and priests amenable to ritual lead temples in many locations. There has been a parallel explosion in the number and visibility of media venues available for championing ritual and other previously marginalized aspects of Zen, including the Internet and such print publications as *Tricycle: The Buddhist Review* and *Buddhadharma*. The very success of convert meditation-oriented Zen guarantees the emergence of postmeditation developments.

The role of women in promoting a more ritualistic Zen is also related to a wave of scandals that shook American Buddhism, especially Zen, in the 1980s and '90s. Virtually every major convert Buddhist lineage—including the San Francisco Zen Center, Zen Center of Los Angeles, Minnesota Zen Center, Kwan Um school, and Shambhala—experienced crises related to male leaders (often married or allegedly celibate) inappropriately having sex with students, extravagantly spending temple funds, or engaging in similar misuses of power.[18] Many students, disillusioned by all-too-human flaws on the part of supposedly enlightened masters, left Buddhism altogether, and others formed breakaway lineages or sought to dramatically restructure the way American temples were governed. One significant outcome of this turmoil was a substantial increase in the attention paid to female Buddhists' issues, including a concerted effort by many groups to put women into leadership positions that were often unavailable to them before. Most of the women priests described in the previous two chapters came to their current leadership positions in the wake of the biggest crises in American convert Zen. They thus brought not only new perspectives but also a particular determination to find ways to offer Zen forms that were gentler, more sensitive to practitioners' needs beyond the meditation cushion, and less given to the strict hierarchical duality of master and pupil. Communal rituals offered one attractive avenue of such exploration.

Finally, American Zen does not operate within a vacuum. Despite the lingering Protestant critique, the profile of ritual in American religion has risen steadily since the 1970s. Attributable in part to the explosion of religious diversity in the second half of the twentieth century and concerns over the corrosive effects of modernity, this reevaluation and approval of ritual is at least partly owed to the emergence of the academic discipline of ritual studies itself.[19] Although internal forces account for much of the rise of ritual in American Zen, other American groups have also adopted an increasingly favorable attitude toward ritual. This is particularly important because American Zen practitioners are frequently involved in other religious communities as well, from which they receive ideas, attitudes, and even practices. For instance, one common area of member overlap is with the New Age movement, which is highly positive toward ritual and ceremony. As scholar of American religion Sarah Pike notes, "Neopagan and New Age rituals heal by externalizing suffering and loss and helping individuals to process painful aspects of their lives within a supportive group setting."[20] A more succinct description of the water baby ceremony could hardly be imagined.

Places, Things, Bodies, Feelings: Other Sightings of American Zen

The water baby ceremony highlights many elements of Zen that have not been sufficiently examined in previous studies and provide particularly fertile sites for the investigation of Americanization in Buddhism. In particular, four tightly interwoven themes stand out as prominent in this ritual and require closer attention: place, material culture, body, and emotion. Against images of Zen as an aniconic, self-controlled, and mind-oriented sect, the ritualization of pregnancy loss reveals the presence of other experiences of Zen. Cast into particularly high relief by the water baby ceremony, once these alternate narratives are recognized we may begin to perceive how they manifest in other aspects of American Zen as well, providing a more well-rounded picture of the true life of convert Zen centers.

Place: The water baby ceremony requires certain types of places for it to be performed. The first thing to note is that water baby ceremonies take place at Zen temples. They are rarely carried out at homes, hospitals, public parks, or cemeteries, all sites that could potentially be used for the ritual. Producing the ceremony at a temple ensures a certain level of privacy and control over the proceedings and makes it easier to assemble resources and draw on the labor of the Zen community for assistance. It also imbues it with greater force by connecting it with the sacred nature of the site.

The next thing to note is that at these temples, the ritual is usually conducted in two different locations: a sewing room and a Jizō garden. The rooms for sewing are not dedicated to this activity: they are libraries, storage rooms, worship halls, or other spaces normally used for other purposes. It is the ceremony itself and the bodies of grieving participants that form the important parts of the "ritual container" during the sewing, not the walls and ceiling. No rites are conducted to mark out the space of sewing or special boundaries established—American priests feel no need to demarcate an inner, pure space for this portion of the ceremony. We should also note that there is one prominent space that is rarely utilized for water baby ceremonies: the main meditation room (*zendō*). This space is typically reserved for meditation, the ritual activity at the heart of American Zen. And unlike the Japanese-American temples described in chapter 1, little ritualization takes place in the main worship hall (*hondō*) for one simple reason: whereas most Zen temples in Japan have *hondōs* but not *zendōs*, all convert Zen groups in America have a *zendō*, but few have a formal *hondō*.

The second portion of the ceremony takes place in a more specific location: a garden with Jizō figures. During this part of the ritual, where Jizō is directly approached, given offerings, and merit is dedicated to lost children, there is a need to be out of doors, close to the soil, as the participants move symbolically from the constrained space of the sewing room into the freedom and open air of the garden. Whereas the sewing portion is done indoors for purely practical reasons (it is easier to sew without the interference of weather), even in pouring rain, bitter cold, or oppressive heat the offering will take place outside if possible. A type of birth occurs as the indoor womb is left for the outside world, and Jizōs standing in for the unborn are encountered in a place of life and growing things. At the same time, this birth is a type of death and funeral, as the offerings are left behind to rot and return to the earth—Rochester Zen Center actually buries the dilapidated remains of former offerings during the ceremony—and the difficult emotions expressed in the ritual are left behind in the pastoral environment of the garden. Though the first part of the ritual could be performed in practically any large space at the temple, the second part usually requires that Zen centers interested in offering the ritual set aside ground that can be maintained as a Jizō garden. This garden then becomes a place of memory, returned to by some participants to reconnect with the beings symbolically laid to rest there or the feelings expressed on that site during the ritual.

Material culture: The water baby ceremony cannot be performed without *stuff*. The core of this ritual is the manufacturing of bibs, hats, capes, toys, and messages to be presented to a childlike statue simultaneously representing a powerful bodhisattva and a lost child. Interacting with objects during the ceremony is believed by proponents to have tremendous healing power. By making an item of clothing they are able to do something on behalf of their lost loved one, and by writing out messages, a form of communication with the dead takes place.

Dressing the statue, the participants appropriate the identity of parents caring for their children (fig. 4.1). The Jizō image provides a stand-in for a child who is gone and perhaps was never present to begin with, a proxy that can be seen and felt. At the Chicago Zen Center, Jizō statues are actually wrapped in swaddling clothes and brought home to be kept in a crib for a month before being returned to the temple. Pregnancy losses thus are moved from the realm of the imagination into the perceptible world, just as the participant's grief and sadness are moved from the shadows of the heart out into the shared circle of the ceremony.

Participants don't just see and touch bibs and statues. Incense is used to purify the offerings; sutra books help guide participants through the chants of the ceremony, which are punctuated by ringing bells; tea and cookies are strategically employed during the final phase of the event to comfort participants and perhaps encourage them to linger and express the feelings evoked by the ceremony. Thus all five senses are attended to by material objects in the course of the ceremony, providing a full experience that lasts in the mind, considered the sixth sense in Buddhism. As Paula Arai puts it in her study of women's Zen rituals in Japan: "Rituals work through the senses to cultivate wisdom in the bones."[21]

The need of material objects for the ceremony creates new developments at American Zen centers. Most of those that perform such ceremonies regularly had to first make or purchase Jizō statues, increasing the presence of icons and raising the profile of figures associated with the water baby ceremony. The increased demand has contributed to a greater supply—as reported in chapter 2,

FIGURE 4.1. Jizōs with water baby ceremony offerings at Rochester Zen Center.

Buddhist supply catalogs now carry Jizō statues, including ones specifically intended for the water baby ceremony.

Material objects are also a site of noticeable hybridity in American Zen, where even within the context of the supposedly thoroughly Buddhist water baby ceremony other influences appear and suggest alternative understandings of the ritual. Many Jizō gardens, for instance, house more than just Buddhist figures. One frequent inhabitant of such gardens is the Virgin Mary, whose statues can be found festooned with the same red bibs and memorial tokens left during water baby ceremonies (fig. 4.2). She appears as an alternative to Jizō in

FIGURE 4.2. *Mizuko* Mary: Virgin Mary image with water baby ceremony offerings in the Great Vow Monastery Jizō garden.

the gardens of temples ranging from the strictest to the most liberal about pre-screening participants and delineating what the ritual is for. Mary is female and a mother; more important, she is Christian, and many participants at American Zen centers are Christians. As demonstrated by the objects associated with the water baby ceremony, Zen centers are entangled with other religious communi-ties and seek to minister to Christians and other non-Buddhists, going so far as to purchase Christian statuary and make a permanent place for non-Buddhist icons on their grounds. Great Vow Monastery's Jizō garden houses two Virgin Mary statues because the first was so popular that it was being smothered by water baby offerings. A second statue was placed in the garden specifically to provide comfort to a greater number of Christian participants, and the abbess points out this statue to participants and encourages them to worship in front of it if they wish.[22]

Messages left on tokens by participants speak of God, angels, heaven, and other non-Buddhist concepts, suggesting that many participants utilize the rit-uals strategically, taking part in Buddhist ceremonies when an equivalent ritual is unavailable in their own religious tradition. It may also be that like some of the women in the Japanese-American temples discussed in chapter 1, who sometimes go to an unfamiliar temple so their own priests won't know that they have had an abortion, some non-Buddhists seek out water baby ceremo-nies not because they cannot get help in their own churches but because they do not want their pregnancy losses known to their own religious communities. Perhaps more than any other aspect, the water baby ritual shows the extent of American Zen's religious pluralism, which compels it to include outsiders and even accommodate their beliefs and objects of devotion. As one priest whose temple does biannual water baby ceremonies said, "For this June, what will be put out will be that anybody can come to this, as long as we have enough Jizōs. Sounds silly, but it's true, it's limited by the number of Jizōs we have. These [non-Buddhists] can come, anybody can come. To me, the fulcrum is the loss. The fulcrum is not Buddhism. I'm always going to tip it to the loss, it's the loss that counts."[23] Non-Buddhists too have losses and thus are welcome, as shared suffering allows theological boundaries to be crossed.

Although material culture becomes a place for building bridges to the non-Buddhist community, it also functions at times as a site of potential conflict and antagonism with outsiders. For example, the Zen Community of Oak Park wanted to build a Jizō garden behind its temple (a converted house in a resi-dential Chicago suburb) and store the ashes of cremated babies in hollow Jizō statues. This is a common practice in Japan, where virtually every temple has a cemetery or columbarium, whether the temple is located in the inner city, sub-urbs, or rural countryside. Japanese-American temples usually house remains as well, such as in the columbarium at Zenshuji mentioned in chapter 1. In fact, the cemetery or other such space is a basic site for Japanese and Japanese-American Buddhist ritual. But the board of directors at the Oak Park temple determined that they would run afoul of very strict codes regulating the handling and use of human remains in their area, and so they ultimately scrapped the plan.[24]

Body: Theorist of religion Thomas Tweed has noted, "Religion begins—and ends—with bodies."[25] Nevertheless, American accounts of Buddhist practice tend to stress the mental effort of meditation. In contrast, the mind is put on the back burner in some ways while the body moves to the forefront in the water baby ceremony. The space of the ritual is populated by sitting bodies; the hats and bibs are painstakingly manufactured by loving hands that then dress and caress little statues. While the leader occasionally exhorts participants to recall their lost children, most instructions are specifically about physical activities. Participants are led through a series of actions: sewing, writing, walking, standing, bowing, chanting, and presenting gifts. Bodies are carefully stage-managed in orientations designed to evoke or reinforce different elements of the ceremony: point them inward in a circle to get them to talk, face them toward the altar to make them pay homage to Jizō. The statues and their clothing are used as stand-ins for a crucial absent body: that of the fetus being honored in the ceremony.

Consultants often proclaimed that "mind and body are not two" and attempted to disclaim dualistic concepts that pit the mind and body against one another as separate or even antagonistic. Nonetheless, it was striking how strongly they felt about the importance of physicality in Zen and specifically that it is in and through the body that the water baby ceremony effects its healing. Repeatedly, grief was reported to be something carried within the body, a hidden festering that must be cleansed by actions that work on the body and thus on the underlying emotions. During the ritual, the body may seem to take over while the mind disappears altogether, as one laywoman described:

AUTHOR   Is there a specific moment in the ceremony that stands out for you as the central part of where that change really happens?

NORMA CREST   For me, I would say it was the making of something. It was almost like I was watching my hands make something. Yes, I was really watching. They were working on their own. It wasn't like my brain was saying, "Do this"—it just sort of developed.[26]

The effects of the ceremony were almost invariably reported in somatic terms, especially as "lightening," the release of tension, a sense of being cleansed, and feelings of energy moving within the body.

At least in part, the emphasis on the body was part of a strategy to correct a perceived imbalance in the Zen communities. Many people I spoke with use the water baby ritual to implicitly criticize aspects of American Zen that they disagree with. For instance, most felt that the body was or had been discounted in Zen practice in favor of ideas of the disembodied, enlightened mind. Some described this as a "patriarchal" mind-set linked to notions of control and aggression and contrasted it with a more "feminine" approach that respected the body—in the process they turned the misogynistic tendencies of Japanese *mizuko kuyō* upside down.[27] Thus the pro-female, bodily practices of the water baby ceremony were subtly contrasted with and even at times set in opposition to the pursuit of enlightenment in the meditation hall. Or, it could be said, in opposition to certain interpretations of the meditation hall, because these consultants also emphasized the physicality of seated meditation and activities such as prostrations, an increasingly popular practice in convert Zen communities.

Emotion: If there is one element even more central to the water baby ceremony than the body, it is emotion. Yet emotion is a difficult subject for many American Zen practitioners, some of whom view meditation as a way to destroy or control negative emotions. Desire and anger are frequently described as poisons, two of the three basic evils of the human condition that lead to suffering and whose elimination is the goal of Buddhism. Displays of strong emotions are subtly but persistently discouraged at most convert Zen centers. Strong emotion can be taken as an indicator of inadequate religious practice and contrasted with the perfectly calm, self-possessed image of the Buddha seated in quiet meditation. Emotion may be seen as disruptive of practice—it is hard to meditate when someone is crying, laughing, or cursing nearby—and expressions of negative and even positive emotions seem to make many convert practitioners uncomfortable. We can see this in the disapproving initial reactions of some participants in the water baby ceremony:

AUTHOR   Do you recall your reaction when you first heard about [Zen water baby ceremonies]?

LISA HUNTER   *"Oh, please! This is so fricking touchy-feely I can't believe it!"*[28]

Into this atmosphere of emotional restraint, the water baby ceremony enters as a countervailing force. According to proponents, this ritual exists to heal the wounded hearts of grieving parents and to purge or diminish feelings that arise in the wake of abortion, miscarriage, and losses of pregnancies or young children. Consultants and published accounts of the ritual emphasize the presence of grief, loss, sadness, regret, and in some cases anger or shame in connection to the water baby ceremony. These emotions are negatively valued and viewed as a threat to mourners' physical and mental health, as well as dangerous to one's marriage and interpersonal relationships; they are not, however, usually directly described as explicitly threatening to one's spiritual state. During the ceremony, these negative emotions are brought into attention and acknowledged, a process believed to be healing, and new expressions of positive feelings—especially love, gratitude, and hope—are encouraged.[29] From the memorial book at Rochester Zen Center, here is one example:

> My child,
> I am so deeply sorry that I had to make the choice not to give you
> life—please forgive me. May Jizo Bodhisattva guide you on your way
> and may we both attain the most profound understanding so we may
> together lead others to understanding. I accept full responsibility for
> the choice I made and now give you the love I couldn't give you then.
> Your name is _____.
> In gratitude,
> Your mother[30]

Emotions are not just referred to in the water baby ceremony: they often manifest in dramatic displays. People cry, shake, sometimes completely break down and have to leave. Consultants described seeing "explosions" of emotion during ceremonies and described the ritual as "heartrending."[31] Some wept themselves in recounting the pain of others they had witnessed during past ceremonies. At one ritual, the participants were all women who had abortions. The level of deep hurt surprised the male leader of the ceremony, who said in an interview:

> It was just unbearable, the pain....I had no idea how much there was
> around this. I was shocked. And also how much of a stigma there is
> around it. And I heard women saying that they had lived with this
> all their lives. It was a secret that they couldn't talk about. And they
> really thought that they were the only bad person in the world with
> that, that they sort of carried it with an enormous amount of burden,
> thinking that they had done something terribly wrong, and they
> couldn't talk about it with anyone.[32]

Still, he affirmed the rightness of their emotions. "Grief is a wonderful, rich part of our human experience. It's OK to cry, it's OK to be sad." Unlike the normal American Zen ethic of subdued emotion, emotional expression is encouraged in these ceremonies.

The water baby ceremony thus aligns in some ways with the predominant attitude of controlling or removing emotion (the point, after all, is to manage grief that has become unhealthy), and at the same time pushes back against it. For most of the people with whom I spoke in my fieldwork, the ritual suggests that emotions cannot be directly controlled by mental effort or meditation but must be released by fully experiencing them. Attachment and anger are contextualized as natural—perhaps not desirable, but nonetheless part of life itself, aspects that are managed only by paradoxically embracing them and allowing them to pass on their own. With the issue of emotion, once again the water baby ceremony becomes a site of subtle resistance to the dominant logic of the meditation hall.

We should not misunderstand this resistance as simply that of laypeople resisting the orthodox interpretations of priests, or of women resisting the institutional power of men. Though many of the women I spoke with criticized interpretations of Zen as mind-oriented, antiemotion, meditation-centered— interpretations that they viewed as widespread and dominant—the men I spoke with also voiced such criticisms. Furthermore, many of the people expressing such critiques of the meditation hall are themselves priests and even founders and leaders of their own temples, who in other contexts emphasized the importance of formal seated meditation.

This phenomenon should be viewed in two ways. First, there is *some* direct resistance to priests and male leadership in these critiques, especially on the part of longtime female lay members at older Zen temples. In other cases, the critiques seem to be the rehearsing of past battles—leaders voicing resistance to earlier authorities are rehashing old roles of rebellion, often with the memory of the above-mentioned scandals in mind, with a certain amount of disconnect with their present situation as the new authorities. But a second interpretation of this resistance is that it is itself a performance that explores the boundaries of acceptable American Zen behavior without fundamentally changing the meditation-favored orientation of convert communities. Water baby ceremonies provide an occasional vessel for the expression of emotions that are deemed inappropriate for the meditation hall, thereby allowing the zendō to remain the central presence in Zen practice. When a female Zen priest laments the lack of attention to body and emotion in Zen and performs a water baby ceremony in the garden outside, she is fleshing out the Zen experience and at the same time not changing or challenging the paradigm of practice in the zendō itself. Rather, alternative approaches to Zen are being advanced as infrequent corrective measures that heal damaged practitioners and put them back into a state fit to carry out calm, concentrated seated meditation.

Summing up, and not forgetting the many adaptations made in the process of adapting *mizuko kuyō* reviewed in the previous chapter, I nonetheless suggest that the emergence of the water baby ceremony can be taken to represent a new stage in the development of American Zen, one which in some ways moves in an opposite direction from the primary features identified in the current literature on Zen in the United States. This new stage builds on ritual practices that go back to the beginnings of convert Zen, but as a confluence of forces have converged in the late 1990s and 2000s, a change in quantity has resulted in a change in kind, and American Zen has been partially reinvented in significantly more ritualistic modes than those displayed in earlier decades. Even as the *mizuko kuyō* is disciplined along psychological and anti-supernatural lines within convert Zen centers, it adds to the increase of ritual in American Zen, reveals a hesitant step toward greater engagement with cosmic savior figures and Buddhist spirit culture, and points to a revaluation of emotional needs within what has heretofore been a rather subdued and controlled middle-class religious culture. It clearly highlights the importance of women—both priests and laypeople—in changing aspects of American Buddhism. Though still a far cry from the way Zen is practiced and understood in Japan, American Zen is nevertheless moving in some ways toward its parent lineage as it incorporates ever more ritual and gently displaces the meditation cushion as the sole location of true Zen practice. Thus, while *mizuko kuyō* has been altered to make it conform to an American understanding of Zen, it is also part of a series of changes that alter what American Zen is, pushing it closer to Asian forms. The end result could be that some future ritual transplantations will not need to go through the same process of adaptation.

Attention to space, objects, bodies, and emotions in the water baby ceremony—and likely other places in American Zen as well—leads to seeing that, rather than a single set of coherent attitudes or logic, Zen practitioners both embrace and reject feelings, love and resent meditation, value and ignore their surroundings. They want freedom from emotions and freedom to feel emotions; they want to become stoic Buddhas and to remain living human beings; they want mental clarity and full embodiment; they want to just sit and also to engage in elaborate religious celebrations and rituals. They want to get over their lost children, and they want to never let them go. They disapprove of abortion and want to keep it legal. They disbelieve in ghosts and send messages to their dead; they disclaim the supernatural and pray to cosmic bodhisattvas. They want spontaneity and formality. They are feminists who import antiwoman rituals. They want a tradition outside words and letters, and they want to study and chant holy scriptures. They want a Zen adapted to American culture and an authentic representation of the ancient tradition. They belong to a venerable lineage and act like members of new religious movements. They want to be modern and progressive, and they want to practice precisely as the Buddha himself did in long-lost India. Ultimately, these are more than seeming contradictions. They are the real stuff of lived religion, of Buddhism as it crosses into a new cultural arena, of a story of Japan and America that will continue to shift and change as long as Americans seek meaning in the religion of the Buddha.

5

"Without Biblical Revelation"

Rhetorical Appropriations of Mizuko Kuyō
*by Christians and Other Non-Buddhist
Americans*

People appropriate religious idioms as they need them, in response
to particular circumstances. All religious ideas and impulses are of
the moment, invented, taken, borrowed, and improvised at the inter-
sections of life.

—Robert Orsi, "Everyday Miracles"

"Well before I came to my faith in Christ, I traveled to Tokyo,"
explains actress and longtime Cover Girl model Jennifer O'Neill. As
she further recounts in her evangelical post-abortion manual *You're
Not Alone: Healing through God's Grace after Abortion,* "I found myself
taking a tour bus out into the countryside to visit one of the largest
Buddhist temples."[1] It's no mistake that this passage starts out with
passive verbs and the assurance that she wasn't yet born again. They
serve to safely bracket her exposure and interest in a non-Christian
practice she discovered on this trip: *mizuko kuyō*. Disclaimers in
place, she can now proceed to passionately describe *mizuko*, which at
this temple are represented by children's pinwheels:

> When I arrived at the temple, *the image before me stopped me
> dead in my tracks....* Speckled across acres of property, as
> far as the eye could see surrounding this incredibly ornate
> temple, were little pinwheels, no bigger than six inches tall,
> all stuck in the ground. There were literally thousands and
> thousands of these tiny, odd structures planted over the

rolling landscape.... What was more curious than the pinwheels themselves was what was propped next to each little pinwheel—groupings of mementos, empty picture frames, knitted baby booties. It was very odd to me, as I didn't understand their significance. With not a clue about what I was observing, I couldn't quench my curiosity until I finally found someone who spoke English who explained to me that I was viewing the burial ground for the Japanese aborted babies. *It took me a moment to catch my breath, I was so stunned.* All my emotions surrounding my own abortion flooded back as I tried to digest the display of love and loss that spilled across the field before me. My mind suddenly filled with the images of babies who might have filled the empty picture frames. *Paralyzed*, I stared at the spinning landscape, trying desperately to marry the tenderness of the moment to the savagery of abortion.[2]

Her mind moved from Japan back to America, which seemed to provide a stark contrast:

Back home in those days, I had never seen abortions recognized with mementos. Worse, I had never heard of any recognition of loss at all concerning the millions of our aborted babies. Remember, we who have had those millions of abortions were told that it was "nothing" that we were carrying... just a problem to discard. So what was this thing I was looking at? I remember thinking that Buddhists believe in reincarnation, so perhaps this display of recognition and love may have emotionally eased the expectant mother's and father's loss... a loss made by their own decision to abort their babies. I'm speculating—but what I do know is that they were allowed to openly grieve and honor their children taken by abortion, for whatever reason.

Grieving is part of surviving loss and is an integrally crucial part of the healing process. Grieving is not a step you can skip if you want to heal.[3]

Frozen by this Buddhist scene, O'Neill reflects on her own anguish over abortion and wishes that America would provide religious recognition of pain such as hers. Even though she stops short of explicitly recommending *mizuko kuyō*, her description, one of the longest and most vivid passages in the book, provides such clear visual imagery that readers seem to be invited to mentally encounter the field of *mizuko* just as she did. Later in *You're Not Alone*, she explicitly tells her readers to ritually memorialize their aborted children.

This scene is a window into a realm totally different from the one that has been discussed so far in this book: the presence of Jizō bodhisattva and *mizuko* in the imagination and rhetoric of non-Buddhist Americans. As knowledge of Jizō is reaching the very different religious world of North America, he is being selectively called upon to speak to traditions outside of Buddhism. In this and the next chapter I discuss how non-Buddhists also participate in the discussion and ritualization of *mizuko kuyō*, and thus add their own unique and often unacknowledged contributions to the process of Buddhism's Americanization. A survey of both general and religious literature over the past three decades reveals a persistent fascination with *mizuko kuyō* among segments of the wider American culture, particularly those invested in the rancorous debate about abortion issues. My investigation turned up more than one hundred published works in popular (nonacademic) venues by non-Buddhist Americans that discuss the Japanese practice of *mizuko kuyō*, most of them written in the 1990s and 2000s.[4] Additionally, many of these articles were also republished repeatedly in other forums (including some of the most important and widely read pro-life and Christian publications) and continue to circulate informally among networks of pro-life activists and women dealing with pregnancy loss.

Jizō and *mizuko kuyō* have appeared in articles, books, and sermons by American Catholics, evangelicals, mainline Protestants, Jews, Unitarian Universalists, Mormons, neopagans, secular feminists, bioethicists, and others. In fact, Jizō and *mizuko kuyō* have been drawn into the American debates surrounding issues as diverse as abortion, miscarriage, stillbirth, birth control, infertility, stem cell research, cloning, genetic engineering, and laboratory use of human tissue.

In investigating these American Christian and other appropriations of Buddhist elements in this chapter, I uncover some of the paths that Buddhist practices and ideas take into non-Buddhist settings. There has been much speculation about Buddhism's increasing impact on American culture over the past several decades, but little sustained attention to the channels of influence and how non-Buddhists actively disseminate selected information about Buddhism. Research on the transmission of Buddhism to the United States in the nineteenth and early twentieth centuries by scholars such as Thomas Tweed and Richard Seager has shown the important role that non-Buddhists once played.[5] But as the story of American Buddhism evolves into the later twentieth and twenty-first centuries to include significantly more actual Buddhists—both American converts and new Buddhist immigrants—the current historiography seems to lose sight of the continuing importance of non-Buddhists in the story. In fact, there has been a significant historiographical shift—especially in works focusing on the present or recent history—from attention to "how Buddhism arrives here" to "who here can claim a Buddhist identity and to what extent."[6] This is good and necessary work, to be sure. But there is still much work to be done on how non-Buddhists *today* are making considerable contributions to knowledge

and attitudes about Buddhism in America. Perhaps we might do well to expand
Jan Nattier's description of "import Buddhism" to observe how non-Buddhists
package and disseminate elements of Asian Buddhism for consumption by
other non-Buddhists, with no intention of conversion to formal Buddhist practice or adherence.[7] The closest that current historiography comes to noting the
role of non-Buddhists in contemporary American Buddhism are a few suggestive lines in one of Thomas Tweed's articles on night-stand Buddhists. Tweed
makes brief allusion to people he calls "Buddhist opponents" and "Buddhist
interpreters," terms that could be applied to many of the figures whom we will
meet in this chapter.[8] Certainly they are closer approximations of many of the
actors in our story, whom, as we will see, do not fit comfortably in the more
widely used category of "Buddhist sympathizers." But until this present work,
Tweed's suggestions have remained largely pointers to investigative paths not
taken.

Channels of Knowledge and Appropriation

Like Jennifer O'Neill, many other Americans have stumbled across this seemingly alien religious approach to abortion and pregnancy loss by accident while
working or vacationing in Japan. Since 1945, American travel to largely Buddhist Japan has increased steadily, with hundreds of thousands of tourists, students, and businesspersons visiting the country each year. Japan's lovely historic
temples are a major draw, and *mizuko* Jizōs are among the most common and
prominent sights throughout the country, whether at major temples or road-
side shrines. Many Americans pass by these colorfully decorated little statues
without a second thought; others, however, pause to examine them. Sometimes
a guide explains their purpose, or a pedestrian stops to offer a friendly explanation. Many popular English guidebooks on Japan—including the Lonely Planet,
Fodor's, Frommer's, Rough Guide, and Insight Guide series—carry information
about *mizuko* Jizō. Says *Frommer's Japan*:

> Hase Kannon Temple (Kamakura): Although this temple is famous
> for its 9m (30-ft.) tall Kannon of Mercy, the largest wooden image
> in Japan, it's most memorable for its thousands of small statues of
> Jizo, the guardian deity of children, donated by parents of miscarried,
> stillborn, or aborted children. It's a rather haunting vision.[9]

Based on the accounts of American travelers, there seem to be a number of
temples where tourists most frequently come face to face with *mizuko* Jizō,
especially Hasedera Kannondō in Kamakura and Zōjōji in Tōkyō (fig. 5.1).[10]

Each of these temples is heavily involved in *mizuko kuyō*, and displays hundreds of *mizuko* Jizōs at any given time. It is this visual tableau, as much as the unfamiliar concept of *mizuko* and Jizō, that seems to arouse American tourists' curiosity—a possibility suggested not only by the numerous and detailed descriptions of *mizuko* Jizōs, but also by the frequent inclusion of large photographs of row upon row of *mizuko* Jizōs in American articles that mention Japanese abortion or miscarriage memorials.

A striking similarity between many American travelers' accounts is the effect of their initial exposure to the idea of *mizuko* and Jizō. Time and again, the American tourist surveys a field of hundreds or thousands of *mizuko* Jizō statues, intrigued but unsure of their meaning (fig. 5.2). Informed by a companion or passerby, she or he is suddenly stuck fast, arrested by the disorienting knowledge that the Japanese memorialize their abortions and miscarriages in such a public and religious way. We see this "*mizuko* arrest" in O'Neill's description at the beginning of this chapter, for instance. Notice her language: "the image before me *stopped me dead in my tracks....* It took me a moment to *catch my breath,* I was so *stunned...I tried to digest* the display of love and loss.... *Paralyzed,* I stared at the spinning landscape."[11] This freezing effect is often followed by

FIGURE 5.1. *Mizuko ema* left at Zōjōji by an American who had an abortion.

FIGURE 5.2. Rows of *mizuko* Jizō at Hasedera Kannondō in Kamakura.

a rush of emotion—wonder, grief, thankfulness, or some combination of the three. Though these visitors are not Buddhist, the image haunts them, and they feel compelled to paint the scene for readers and friends later on. Sometimes this simple encounter with the unexpected is sufficient to transform their feelings toward abortion and other pregnancy losses; sometimes the moment goes further, and the American visitor actually conducts a brief *mizuko kuyō* by leaving a talisman, ritually washing a statue, and/or saying a prayer over one of the *mizuko* Jizōs, a phenomenon I explore further in the next chapter.

A second class of Americans who encounter *mizuko kuyō* in Japan are missionaries and theologians who have deliberately arrived in the country to spread and support Christianity. They too are often brought up short by the unfamiliar practices and ideas around *mizuko*, and they must articulate a response that explains the phenomenon without suggesting too strongly that their own religion is somehow inferior or deficient in the face of this Buddhist phenomenon. This dynamic can be seen in the narrative of Thomas P. O'Connor, an American Maryknoll Catholic priest who served for many years in Japan:

> Some friends took me to a small country temple in Oita Prefecture to
> see the mountain cherry blossoms....We turned a corner and beheld

quite a sight! There were several hundred tiny statues on the hillside,
a veritable army of *Jizo-Bosatsu* climbing up the bank. Rank upon
rank, they stood straight and silent like soldiers in formation. This
was my first encounter with *mizuko-kuyo,* or memorial services for
deceased infants.... Several years later I visited Hasedera in Kamakura
and again was overwhelmed by the cascade of metal and stone *Jizo*
statues flowing down every hillside.... In each local area I received
a different explanation of the reason for the practice, or witnessed a
different reaction by Japanese friends. I found these reactions interesting and as I pursued the negative feelings toward the practice was
informed that many of the services are performed for aborted souls.
Suddenly the tremendous increase in statues made sense.[12]

O'Connor, like O'Neill and many others, is struck by the visual tableau
and unusual practice of *mizuko kuyō.* As a missionary writing for a Christian
audience in Japan and dedicated to moving Japan from a Buddhist to a Catholic
base, he feels a need to contextualize it in a way that clearly proves the superiority of Christianity:

If one considers the plight of the dead from the view of Christian anthropology, there appears to be no necessity for consoling spirits; and moreover, in the hullabaloo raised in the practice of these memorial services
and corresponding advertisements, a much more serious and basic
issue of humans being-in-the-world is in danger of being overlooked....

Although abortion is legal and socially acceptable, the propa-
gandists on behalf of *mizuko-kuyo* play on the emotion of fear,
stressing the anger and potential threat of revengeful "murdered"
souls.... The result is the recent public display of infant memorials
throughout the whole country.... The type of Buddhism in Japan that
recognizes the true problem tends to deal with the visible superfi-
cialities. Through a variety of ceremonial activities it responds to
the immediate needs of these women in need. Christianity, intent
on transmitting the teachings of Jesus and the message of Jesus'
cross and resurrection, is not willing to participate in a questionable
practice even if its immediate results bring happiness and consolation for some and generates great new revenues for religion.... For
the above reasons and others, *mizuko kuyo* is not a practice within
Christianity. Christians should teach that infant's souls are received
into the eternal life of God, and being consoled by this merciful
God find themselves strengthened to actively engage in bettering
the world.... To seek to spiritualize the evil consequences of human

injustice and remedy them with mere ceremonies is to ignore the
challenge of conversion and change.[13]

Information on *mizuko kuyō* also reaches large numbers of Americans
who never visit Japan. One major source is articles about *mizuko kuyō* in mainstream newspapers and magazines, written by reporters who have observed
the ritual in Japan or read about it. For instance, Sheryl WuDunn's article "In
Japan, a Ritual of Mourning for Abortions" appeared in 1996 in the *New York
Times*. WuDunn describes men and women who perform regular *mizuko kuyō*
for abortions carried out years earlier, connecting the ceremony to a range of
emotions: sadness, fear, grief. She seems most intrigued by the phenomenon
of public mourning despite abortion's legality and near-noncontroversial nature in Japan.[14] Martha Shirk displays a similar fascination in her 1997 *St. Louis
Post-Dispatch* article "Temples Show Japan's Ambivalence toward Abortion."
She pays particular attention to the offerings that mourners leave—a plastic
Donald Duck, a teddy bear, a pinwheel, a windsock—and takes note of the
money that temples make from the ritual. Nonetheless she concludes that *mizuko kuyō* satisfies "an emotional or spiritual need for thousands of women
who have undergone abortions."[15]

Many nonscholars first learned about the ritual through reading academic
treatments of the subject. By far the most commonly cited source for information on *mizuko kuyō* is William LaFleur's *Liquid Life: Abortion and Buddhism
in Japan* (1992), followed by Helen Hardacre's *Marketing the Menacing Fetus
in Japan* (1997). A variety of articles are also sometimes referenced, especially
Elizabeth Harrison's articles "Women's Responses to Child Loss in Japan: The
Case of Mizuko Kuyō" and "Strands of Complexity: The Emergence of *Mizuko Kuyō* in Postwar Japan," and Bardwell Smith's "Buddhism and Abortion
in Contemporary Japan: *Mizuko Kuyō* and the Confrontation with Death."[16]
These and other scholars also have brought information about *mizuko kuyō*
to the wider American community via lectures and other public appearances.
An example is LaFleur's interview on National Public Radio in 1994, in which
LaFleur contended that *mizuko kuyō* can knit together family bonds damaged
by the act of abortion.[17] LaFleur's frequent appearance as a chief source of information for nonscholarly works on Japanese Buddhist abortion recognition is
particularly intriguing because of his stated intention that *Liquid Life* contribute
in some way toward reorienting the American abortion debate and provide a
resource for entrenched pro-life and pro-choice partisans to discover common
ground.[18]

Besides general articles that mention or describe *mizuko kuyō*, some particular forums with targeted audiences have been vigorous in disseminating

information about Japanese Buddhist attitudes toward pregnancy and pregnancy loss. Not surprisingly, publications that deal with abortion as an issue have repeatedly brought *mizuko kuyō* to the attention of the American public. But perhaps there will be some surprise that both pro-life and pro-choice venues promote knowledge of *mizuko kuyō*, and pro-life Christians and pro-choice feminists are equally as likely to make reference to the ritual.[19] Thus, we find Richard John Neuhaus, Catholic priest and major architect of American Neo-Conservatism, editorializing about *mizuko kuyō* in a 1994 issue of *First Things*, one of the leading journals for conservative religious discussion of "culture war" topics. For Neuhaus, the grief of Japanese *mizuko kuyō* serves as a damning cross-cultural indictment of America's individualistic approach to abortion laws.[20] Meanwhile, we also find feminist Eve Kushner discussing the ritual in her 1997 book, *Experiencing Abortion: A Weaving of Women's Words*. In her account, *mizuko kuyō* is also used to critique American culture, but this time it is to point out that only "New Age or Eastern" religions, not those of "mainstream America," choose to ritually acknowledge abortion or even death in general.[21] From these partisan platforms, readers may then spread the information further by discussing it in sympathetic local forums. For instance, in their flier "He Who Frames the Question, Wins the Argument!," New Jersey-based evangelical Gateway Pregnancy Centers offered a quote on *mizuko kuyō* as evidence that abortion is a religious concern, not merely a personal choice.[22]

Another source of *mizuko kuyō* information that reaches targeted audiences is publications that cater to grieving parents in the wake of the death of a child, especially those that specifically center on post-abortion or post-miscarriage grief. Anthropologist Linda Layne, in her book *Motherhood Lost: A Feminist Account of Pregnancy Loss in America,* describes the rise and evolution of this phenomenon: "I discovered that the first pregnancy-loss support groups had been established in the United States in the mid-1970s and that during the 1980s such groups spread quickly about the country. By 1993, there were more than nine hundred pregnancy-loss support groups, and similar groups had been established in Canada, Australia, Israel, Italy, England, West Germany, South Africa, and the Virgin Islands."[23] Layne lists numerous factors that supported the ongoing development of support networks and resources for parents (mainly mothers) who experienced pregnancy loss, including the importance of psychology and counseling, Elizabeth Kubler-Ross's work on death and dying, and of course *Roe v. Wade* and the emergence of abortion as a major topic of discussion and emotional and religious investment.[24] She specifically notes that fetal imaging puts increased emotional pressure on American women, echoing arguments related to *mizuko kuyō* in Hardacre's work (which I discussed in the introduction to this book).

One result of all this fermentation regarding pregnancy loss is the emergence of a new American literary genre: the post–pregnancy loss manual, often further divided into post-abortion or post-miscarriage manuals. An example is the work that opens this chapter—*You're Not Alone: Healing through God's Grace after Abortion*—wherein born-again Christian Jennifer O'Neill describes her abortions and the traumatic effect they had on her life, and recommends that similarly damaged readers heal by taking Jesus Christ as their personal lord and savior before performing their own post-abortion rituals. Naturally enough, these manuals are a prime source for *mizuko kuyō* information, even when they are penned by conservative Christians or secular feminists.[25] In their manual *The Healing Choice: Your Guide to Emotional Recovery after an Abortion*, pro-choice doctors Candace De Puy and Dana Dovitch equate *mizuko kuyō* with the Catholic sacrament of reconciliation, and offer it as a template for American women to create their own "cleansing" post-abortion rituals.[26] In some cases, these manuals are distributed by the wider networks or organizations studied by Layne that specialize in post–pregnancy loss support. Exhale, an unaffiliated but basically pro-choice organization that runs a counseling hotline and Internet site, directs women to Goat-in-the-Road Zendo, an American Zen Buddhist temple providing regular water baby ceremonies that was discussed in chapter 2.[27]

Mention of Goat-in-the-Road's water baby ceremonies brings us to another significant factor in the spread of knowledge about *mizuko kuyō* to non-Buddhist American circles: the role of American Buddhists themselves in promoting the ritual to others. As noted in the previous chapter, the American Zen groups performing water baby ceremonies have in many cases allowed non-Buddhists to participate in these ceremonies—sometimes the ceremonies have even been prompted specifically by the requests of non-Buddhists. Because of the high percentage of health and psychology professionals in convert Zen groups, as well as the feminist stance of most of these communities, Zen teachers who advocate for the ritual are often aware of the pain involved in pregnancy loss and are already plugged into local or national networks that offer support to women (and men) who have experienced abortion, miscarriage, or a similar crisis.[28] Thus, these teachers and their students sometimes place information about *mizuko kuyō* and Jizō in the newsletters and journals of post-abortion or similar organizations, speak at conferences and workshops, and minister to non-Buddhists who seek out their services—services and pastoral counseling these non-Buddhists often feel they cannot receive in their primary religious traditions. Consider Kim Kluger-Bell's widely popular *Unspeakable Losses: Healing from Miscarriage, Abortion, and Other Pregnancy Losses*:

> It was a rainy day and everyone had to cram together in a small meeting room instead of being able to wander freely through the gardens,

finding a private corner in which to work. We were all together in
that overheated room, so many of us that when my husband and
I had arrived there were no seats left and we had to sit on the floor
in the oddly silent room. Having gotten lost on the way to the Zen
Center—it was our first visit here—we arrived at the end of the
priest's instructions for preparing the tiny red bib we were to place
around the neck of the Jizo statue of our choice in the ceremony that
would follow.

All I knew was that this Jizo ceremony was for anyone who had
lost a baby through abortion, miscarriage, or death after birth, and
that it was intended to honor both those who had died and those who
were still living. The flyer had advised us to bring a small piece of red
cloth, scissors, a needle and some red thread.[29]

Kluger-Bell goes on to extensively describe the ritual and relay her positive feelings toward it as a helpful solution to the general silence about pregnancy loss in
American culture. Her encounter with Buddhists in America through the water
baby ritual is essentially the fulcrum on which her entire book is balanced.

My interest here is primarily on the non-Buddhist channels through
which Americans receive information about *mizuko kuyō*. But we should not
overlook the fact that many non-Buddhists do in fact read Buddhist materials with some regularity. Fifty percent of the two hundred thousand people
who read *Tricycle: The Buddhist Review* are non-Buddhist; the magazine has repeatedly discussed abortion and *mizuko kuyō*, including an article by William
LaFleur and another by *Tricycle* founding editor Helen Tworkov that set off
a flurry of letters to the editor, some of them from non-Buddhists. Likewise,
Jan Bays's *Jizō Bodhisattva: Modern Healing and Traditional Buddhist Practice*
appears to have attracted attention outside of American Buddhist circles.[30] In
some cases, these readers may be—to use Thomas Tweed's label—"night-
stand Buddhists": Americans who subscribe to another religion or none at all
but who nonetheless read Buddhist materials and incorporate them into their
personal practices from time to time.[31] In other cases, the individuals involved
seem to have so tenuous a connection to Buddhism that they fall outside even
this liberal definition.

One final category of sources deserves to be mentioned. Non-Buddhist
American interest in *mizuko kuyō* is not confined solely to essays and books—at
times, Japanese Buddhist abortion rituals appear in artistic endeavors as well.
Wendy MacLeod's play *The Water Children* debuted in New York City in 1999 to
positive reviews from the *New York Times, New York Magazine,* and the *Village
Voice.* Written in the wake of MacLeod's reading about *mizuko kuyō* in *Harper's
Magazine* and an encounter with William LaFleur at an on-campus speaking

engagement, the play explores the ambivalent feelings of a pro-choice actress hired to play a regretful mother in a pro-life commercial. Megan, the protagonist, meets many different characters from the landscape of the American abortion wars, and when she finds herself unexpectedly pregnant, she wonders whether to keep it or abort as she did years earlier. Her dilemma is finally resolved when she visits Japan and performs an informal *mizuko kuyō* at a temple. The spirit of her aborted child appears and says he'd like to be born this time, giving the unmarried Megan the confidence to go ahead and become a mother. The audience learns not only about the practice and philosophy of *mizuko kuyō* but is told that Megan's aborted child didn't resent his "return" to the spirit world.[32]

The Water Children has been performed in San Francisco, Denver, Los Angeles, and many other cities in the nine years since its debut, introducing theatergoers in various parts of the country to *mizuko kuyō*. Another way in which a play like *The Water Children* informs a wider audience is through reviews. In each town where the play is performed, reviews appear in local newspapers, thus allowing the concept of *mizuko* to reach a far larger number of people than those who actually attend a performance.

Novelists too have served to disseminate information about *mizuko kuyō*, with the ritual or concept sometimes playing an important role in the plot development. In Wendy Harris's modern fantasy novel *Inventing Memory*, the young protagonist, Wendy, is upset after her abortion, especially by the attitudes of pro-life picketers at the clinic she visits. But she is able to participate in a healing ritual after a friend describes the practice of public grieving for water babies in Japan.[33] In *The Professor's Daughter*, Emily Raboteau (daughter of African-American religious history scholar Al Raboteau) spins a thinly veiled tale based on her relationship with her famous father and her biracial heritage. At a party, the protagonist learns of *mizuko kuyō* and relates it to a prayer offered by her mother at the time of her brother's death.[34] And in his bestselling *Memoirs of a Geisha*, Arthur Golden describes a character's trip to perform rites for aborted fetuses before three tiny statues of Jizō.[35]

Visual artists as well have found inspiration in *mizuko* Jizō shrines, and art exhibits displaying variations on the idea have appeared in a number of American cities. For example, as the *New York Times* art critic Holland Cotter noted in 2003:

> The combination of devotion and commerce [that *mizuko* Jizōs] represent is the theme of Yoko Inoue's "Liquidation," an installation that turns Five Myles into a kind of Jizo shrine. In this case, most of the figures are abstract, made from disposable plastic water containers adorned with hand-knitted caps and bibs inscribed with sutras. They

are set against a projected video that alternates shots of thousands of Mizuko monuments in tiers at Japanese shrines, with others of individual figures set by the sea as if keeping watch or awaiting passage.[36]

This idea had already been tried, in a different form, the previous year by two art students at Washington University in St. Louis (fig. 5.3). Rachel Ray-Hamaie and Ruth Reese constructed a "Mizuko Shrine" out of hay bales, mud, and other materials, and invited the public to spend the next five weeks "grieving, mourning, and healing." As with the garments put on Jizō statues in American water baby ceremonies, the "Mizuko Shrine" was designed to "biodegrade and return to the earth."[37]

There are still other sources of information about these Japanese Buddhist rituals for non-Buddhist America. Information also appears in many miscellaneous places, such as works on ritual, ethics, language, healing, or death: for example, FuneralWire—"Your Leading Source for Deathcare Industry News"—distributed a *Daily Yomburi* article about *mizuko kuyō* in 2002.[38] And, of course, there are the channels that flow beyond the scholar's gaze—the conversations with Buddhist family members, the encounters in clinics and

FIGURE 5.3. "Mizuko Shrine" art installation created in 2002 by Rachel Ray-Hamaie and Ruth Reese at the Tyson Research Center of Washington University in St. Louis (Photograph by Rachel Ray-Hamaie, used with permission).

churches, the neighbor who wonders about the brightly bibbed statue in the local temple's backyard. Together these recognized and unrecognized vectors are adding a new element to the American debates over abortion, miscarriage, and religion.

Pro-life Rhetorical Appropriations of *Mizuko Kuyō*[39]

In 1992, evangelical minister John MacArthur Jr. delivered a blistering sermon at his nondenominational Grace Community Church in Panorama City, California, against "humanists," "atheists," and "feminists" who, "under the control of Satan," had engineered *Roe v. Wade* and turned America into a country of "mass murderers":

> This nation, which certainly prides itself on its humanitarianism, is in a murderous cycle of violence that makes the Nazi Holocaust look mild by comparison. Nearly 2 million babies are aborted every year in America.... It is estimated that perhaps as many as 75 million babies will be murdered this year around the world—75 million! That's probably conservative. It's more than all the deaths in all the wars, in all the history of the world. This kind of murder is shocking and I don't want to be too shocking, but I want to tell you how it is done, and I hope I don't offend anyone. The processes of abortion are somewhat frightening and bizarre.[40]

Despite his disclaimer, some of MacArthur's audience at the popular megachurch may well have been offended by the graphic description of tearing, sucking, dismembering, crushing, and puncturing that followed, and the subsequent horror stories of human-animal hybrid experiments and garbage bags of fetal material on the streets of New York City.

And then, MacArthur took a perhaps unexpected turn, moving from his jeremiad against America to report on a very different culture.

> Japan has been very aggressive in the abortion field for a number of years, and in Japan there is severe trauma on the part of Japanese women because there have been millions and millions of abortions that have occurred there.... The women have been traumatized by these abortions, in terms of their own emotional life, and so the Buddhists have erected temples for the express purpose of dealing with the issue of abortion. These are temples which memorialized what are called "water babies" (this is a term for an aborted child)....

In order to secure peace for their departed souls, these women come to these places. And they are now aware of the fact in their own conscience (at least they assume this to be true *without biblical revelation*) that these little aborted "water babies" have a soul, and they have got to do something for the departed soul; so the Buddhists, in their religion, have erected temples where the departed souls of "water babies" can be attended to by penitent mothers. For somewhere between $340 and $640 a grieving mother can purchase a small stone Buddha. And somehow purchasing this small stone Buddha not only feeds the business enterprise but relieves some of the anxiety and, apparently, does something for the departed soul of the baby.

In one temple alone, tens of thousands of these have been sold; the grounds have become a commercial attraction where visitors pay to come and take pictures of women who are there agonizing over their departed "water babies." Priests will offer prayers at that place for "water babies" at $120 per baby and $40 for each additional baby that you have aborted. That is just one illustration from one country of the trauma that has occurred in the lives of these women.[41]

MacArthur's sermon continued, laying out in intimate detail the symptoms of psychological trauma and sociological effects that allegedly follow in the wake of abortion, before proceeding to a long series of biblical scriptures designed to hammer home the evil of abortion.

Ironically, this appropriation of Buddhism for the consumption of Christian audiences originates in a "culture war" over ultimate sources of moral authority in American society—a war in which MacArthur's side locates authority strictly in traditional sources, most especially the Bible. The concept of culture war originates perhaps in the late-nineteenth-century German idea of *kulturkampf,* but in the present context it refers to the struggles between orthodox and progressive forces in American society during the second half of the twentieth century and into the twenty-first. "Culture war" has become a fundamental aspect of contemporary America, with many commentators depicting the conflict in slightly different ways. Perhaps the best examination of this phenomenon is presented by James Davison Hunter, a professor of sociology and religious studies at the University of Virginia, in his 1991 book *Culture Wars: The Struggle to Define America.* Hunter describes a divided American society wherein new alignments of conservatives (drawing especially from the one-time enemies of fundamentalist and evangelical Protestantism, traditionalist Catholicism, Orthodox Judaism, and Mormonism) are actively engaged in rhetorical, political, and legal battle with broad coalitions of progressives (liberal

Christians and Jews, secularists, and many identity groups such as homosexuals).[42] As he explains:

> Because this is a culture war, the nub of political disagreement today on the range of issues debated—whether abortion, child care, funding for the arts, affirmative action and quotas, gay rights, values in public education, or multiculturalism—can be traced ultimately and finally to the matter of moral authority. By moral authority I mean the basis by which people determine whether something is good or bad, right or wrong, acceptable or unacceptable, and so on.... It is the commitment to different and opposing bases of moral authority and the world views that derive from them that creates the deep cleavages between antagonists in the contemporary culture war.[43]

For Hunter, the orthodox side of this culture war is defined by where it derives its moral authority from—transcendent supernatural agencies and/or intrinsic moral laws, most frequently defined as God's commandments as revealed in sacred scripture—and to what concomitant moral/social commitments it is most attached: "Based upon this general understanding of moral authority are certain non-negotiable moral 'truths.' Among the most relevant for the present purposes are that the world, and all of the life within it, was created by God, and that human life begins at conception and, from that point on, it is sacred."[44] The progressivists, meanwhile, tend to locate moral authority in personal experience, individual conscience, and rational empiricism. When historic faiths are referenced they are typically "resymbolized" to meet the spirit of a largely secularized, privatized age.[45] As these two viewpoints on moral authority meet they clash in the public and private spheres over a wide range of social and political issues. Abortion tops Hunter's list of issues, and for good reason—arguably more than any other single issue, abortion has been a flashpoint for the struggles over American culture and a site of intense, all-or-nothing moral reasoning for both conservatives and progressives. Whether a political candidate is pro-life or pro-choice is the essential litmus test in many races, and the issue affects government and culture on every level from local town councils to Supreme Court nominations.

The Reverend John MacArthur Jr., whose sermon quotes began this section, is a seasoned veteran of the American culture war. He has made guest appearances on *Larry King Live*, hosts a weekly syndicated radio program broadcast by thousands of stations on six continents, and is the author of such bestselling books as *Why One Way? Defending an Exclusive Claim in an Inclusive World* and *Fool's Gold: Discerning Truth in an Age of Error*.[46] The question that naturally arises in the present context is this: Given his fundamental commitment to the Bible as the sole source of transcendent moral authority, why would an evangelical Christian minister offer his flock an extensive description of Buddhist practices? What work is done for his side of the culture war by educating other Christians about *mizuko kuyō*? And, taken further, why is MacArthur's sermon only one among a large number of American Christian pro-life books, articles, sermons, and other media that have brought information about *mizuko* and Jizō to the attention of fellow believers. Why do these opponents of Buddhism care?

One major reason that some American Christians are prompted to discuss *mizuko kuyō* is the ideologically charged concept of post-abortion syndrome.[47] This syndrome is not a psychological or medical condition recognized by the American Psychiatric Association or the American Medical Association, but its existence is near-gospel truth in pro-life circles. Abortion, they suggest, is a traumatic experience that can physically and psychologically damage the mother (and, in some interpretations, the father, siblings, other relations, neighbors, and abortion providers and nurses—and perhaps even the soul of the aborted fetus),[48] akin in many ways to post-traumatic stress disorder, which is caused by violent conflict, assault, or accidents. It is in the discussion of post-abortion syndrome that *mizuko kuyō* most frequently appears in non-Buddhist materials, such as this passage by John Wilke, a Catholic and cofounder of the National Right to Life committee, and his wife, Barbara Wilke:

> How about an example from a non-Christian culture? In Japan,
> where abortion has been legal and accepted for over four decades,
> a common custom is to conduct Mizuko Kuyo services in honor of
> the god Jizo. This god has been made the patron saint of infants who
> died of starvation, abortion, or infanticide. Small baby statues, in his
> honor, are bought and dressed. Then, in a Buddhist Temple, rites of
> sorrow and reconciliation are carried out.[49]

One of the foremost promoters of the notion that women who have undergone abortion are subject to this "syndrome" is David Reardon of the Elliot Institute, whose writings and frequent appearances on television and radio programs have publicized and legitimized the concept.[50] According to Reardon's article "The Complexity and Distortions of Post-Abortion Research," the cognitive dissonance engendered in an aborting woman between the physiological changes she experiences during pregnancy and society's contention that she is merely removing "a blob of tissue" results in "psychological defense mechanisms of denial and repression [that are] massively in effect by the time she leaves the clinic." These lead in time to symptoms such as depression, suicidal thoughts, impaired work efficiency, weight loss, insomnia, alcoholism, psychosomatic pains, family problems, sexual difficulties, and feelings of worthlessness. Women and men may have haunting mental images of their aborted fetuses in pain or crying for help, and may communicate in some way with these imagined children.[51]

The similarity to Japanese concepts of *mizuko tatari* (spirit attack by aborted ghosts) is striking. All of these symptoms occur regularly in the rhetoric of Buddhist promoters of *mizuko kuyō*. Furthermore, Reardon says that seemingly inexplicable distress that women display decades after an abortion may be post-abortion syndrome surfacing; this is reminiscent of those Japanese who say that virtually any ill luck or depression may have sprung from an abortion that the woman had many years earlier. The similarity continues even further: just as some Japanese *mizuko kuyō* entrepreneurs claim that undiagnosable symptoms or bad luck may be caused by the wandering *mizuko* of total strangers, some American commentators theorize that people who have never had an abortion may nonetheless experience post-abortion syndrome simply because they live in a culture that so devalues fetal life. Thus abortion's negative effects become an all-encompassing interpretive rubric for some people in both Japan and the United States, providing a cipher with which all distressing situations may be decoded to reveal their origins in the wrong behavior of women.

Given these extreme similarities, it is possible that the American pro-life concept of post-abortion syndrome was derived, in part or in whole, from exposure to Japanese Buddhist *mizuko kuyō* rhetoric. It is difficult to prove or disprove such a speculation, and it may simply be a case of "convergent evolution" in the attitudes of both countries. But whether or not post-abortion syndrome derives in some degree from Japanese antecedents, we can certainly state that what in Japan is culturally understood as the actual intervention of angered spirits, has in America been presented as a psychological reaction to trauma. In fact, American Christians interpret *tatari*-like symptoms in a manner extremely close to that of the American Zen Buddhists described in chapters 2–4. Neither liberal Buddhist nor conservative Christian Americans resort to the traditional Buddhist explanation of interference by ghosts. Instead, they both prefer to see bad feelings and possible physical effects in the aftermath of abortion as an essentially psychological, individualistic phenomenon outside the realm of the supernatural. If anything, this reaction could be more surprising among the Christians than the convert Buddhists: these same sources that advance a psychological interpretation of post-abortion syndrome are also replete with references to an angry God who pours out his wrath on sinners. Yet while dire religious consequences are predicted for women who abort and men who aid them, God is rarely deemed responsible for the actual afflictions that pro-life Christians claim abound in the wake of abortion.[52]

Mizuko kuyō provides conservative Christians with ammunition for their battle to promote the concept of post-abortion syndrome. Consider this quote from Catholic writer Joan Frawley Desmond, writing in *First Things*:

> Jizo began to attract followers in the 1970s, after a decade of steadily rising abortion rates. The cult defies simple explanations, and Westerners should not shrug off this memorial service as a peculiar, if haunting, foreign custom. Its importance lies in its revelation of the damaging consequences of abortion. *Despite the lack of moral guidance*, Japanese parents want to admit wrongdoing.[53]

In *mizuko kuyō*, American Christians have found a practice that seems to support their assumptions about abortion's injurious effects. The logic put forward in this argument goes as follows: if post-abortion syndrome is a universal phenomenon, then abortion must be *naturally* traumatizing, without need for a supernatural explanation or connection to a specific set of values or culture. *Even without biblical revelation*, a benighted Buddhist woman in pagan Japan knows in her gut that abortion is wrong. Abhorrence of abortion is natural—that is to say, it is automatic and undeniable. It is not a product of a particular worldview, but of human nature. Those who do not share in this abhorrence must therefore be acting against their own humanity, perhaps because of evil influences or excessive greed, lust, pride, or narcissism.

This serves more than one ideological purpose. First, it bolsters the argument that post-abortion syndrome exists as a real mental disorder. Second, it weakens the counterarguments of opponents by characterizing this syndrome as a cross-cultural phenomenon that arises naturally—thus, it is not something unique to Americans, Christians, or abortion opponents. Third, it reimagines women as natural mothers, who (should) feel automatic shame and despair when they go against their ordained role. Here again is a parallel to *mizuko kuyō* as it operates in some sectors of Japanese culture, where it is pushed by right-wing politicians and religious figures who feel women have generally stepped outside their prescribed positions. Bringing up *mizuko kuyō* allows angry pro-life activists to chastise sinful women who have had abortions and yet know in their hearts, inescapably, that they've done wrong. This dynamic is clear, for instance, in the works of Anthony Zimmerman, an American missionary priest who has served in Japan for many years:

> The ideology of "choice" which rationalizes abortion in America blocks out social acceptance of mourning for the deceased child. A less rigid rationale in Japan facilitates the expression of grief by parents for their hapless little ones; the ritual Mizuko Kuyo (literally

"water-child ceremony") is not only an elixir that aids the psychic healing of the parents, especially the mother, but doubles as a lucrative windfall for obliging temples. In the USA, a rigid dogma which canonizes "choice" may encourage its adherents to march into abortuaries with heads held high in disdain for motherhood. "Choice" encourages the young woman to suppress her motherly instinct to grieve over the loss of her child; she must be strong. She incarnates manly symbols of power and control, submerging womanly instincts of nurturing and altruism. Years may pass before she relaxes her guard, to become herself again.[54]

Fourth, references to *mizuko kuyō* support antiabortion activists' claims that post-abortion feelings of guilt and depression are religious concerns, indirectly bolstering Christian authority on the issue. This may be played out, as in the case of MacArthur's sermon, with a subsequent appeal for women who have had an abortion to come forward and seek forgiveness from God through the church. The overall effect of introducing a post-abortion "syndrome" into the debate is to further associate abortion with violence and antisocial behavior, and to cast abortion rights proponents as acting against the best interests of women. By declaring that abortion leads to trauma and misfortune for abortive mothers, Christian and other pro-life activists can condemn women who have had abortions and yet simultaneously present themselves as the true supporters of women's health and well-being.

Reardon himself employs descriptions of *mizuko kuyō* in this manner. For instance, to illustrate that women may experience severe symptoms on the anniversary of their abortions, he relates an incident in which a grieving Japanese student was referred to him. The young woman, he said, was each month wracked by guilt on the day coinciding with the day of her procedure. He learned from her that "it is common in Japan to request memorial services for their children whom they believe they have 'sent from dark to dark.' At Buddhist temples parents rent stone statues of children for a year during which time prayers are offered for the babies to the god Jizu."[55] Similarly, Marvin Olasky, editor of the evangelical *World Magazine*—at 250,000 subscribers the world's largest Christian weekly news periodical and America's fourth largest weekly news periodical—editorialized about *mizuko kuyō* on the thirtieth anniversary of *Roe v. Wade*:

> Thirty years ago, they commonly dehumanized unborn children
> and made abortion seem easy: 15 minutes to feel "like a brand-new
> woman," the Omaha World-Herald propagandized.... That was conventional liberal talk in those days. Now, even feminists admit that

abortion is sorrowful, and that the conflict about it will not go away because of the gut guilt that abortion intrinsically yields. They want to mourn abortion but continue it, much as the Japanese do.

Aborting mothers in Japan typically make or buy mizuko Jizo, small statues of babies. They dress the statues in bibs and knitted caps, and leave next to the statues bottles of milk, baby rattles, and furry toys. You can find stacks of mizuko Jizos in cemeteries and also in special temples where they are housed, with mourning parents paying hundreds of dollars per year to have a small statue bathed and dressed, with incense burned and prayers recited.

One survey showed 86 percent of Japanese women and 76 percent of men saying they felt guilty upon having an abortion or pressuring their partners to have one. In this country [i.e., the United States], abortion advocates have generally sneered at the reality of post-abortion syndrome. Maybe now they will accept it and call for government provision of "grief-recovery specialists."[56]

In some cases, pro-life writers bring up *mizuko kuyō* in the context of actual debates with pro-choice opponents, or place information about *mizuko kuyō* in forums where pro-choice or undecided readers could conceivably learn about the ritual and be pushed toward an antiabortion position. But it is noteworthy that in other cases, *mizuko kuyō* is discussed in settings where readers other than already-convinced pro-life Christians are extremely unlikely. The interest in *mizuko kuyō*, therefore, is not confined to simply strategic arguments meant to win others to their own side. The implication is that even many politically conservative, theologically fundamentalist American Christians are on some level further convinced of the correctness of their position by reference to the ideas and practices of Japanese Buddhists. They seem to imply that it is not always enough to hear that Christians oppose abortion and that Americans experience post-abortion grief, or that the Bible condemns taking the life of the unborn. Although these writers and readers frequently profess that there is no light in religions that do not have a basis in the Bible and a conscious commitment to Jesus Christ, in practice they are in fact finding further support for pro-life positions by learning about Buddhism.

Pro-life Christians also can use the phenomenon of *mizuko kuyō* as a prod to radicalize seemingly complacent fellow Christians. An example of this strategic employment of information about Japanese ritual practices appears in a *Life Advocate Magazine* column by evangelical Baptist and vigorous pro-life activist Paul deBarrie. After describing *mizuko kuyō* and using it as a club to rhetorically bash Planned Parenthood, deBarrie begins to lash out at his real target: fellow pro-life Christians who seem lukewarm in their activism:

> The misery of the Japanese women—*who have no moral teaching against abortion*—is palpable....
>
> It doesn't even require a particularly astute listener to hear the wailing grief-stricken mothers in Japan.
>
> Here in America, we have our annual Washington, D.C., march, many local activist groups...and we have no real concerted cry of grief heard throughout the land.
>
> These are women—even members of our churches—who have murdered their own infants and we hear nothing of it save an occasional muffled noise out from under the misnomer of "victim of abortion."
>
> Little comes from the Church on this matter. Pastors are afraid of offending a murderous mom for fear she will leave instead of speaking out for fear of being accountable for her blood. Even when a woman does repent she is often treated as a victim instead of a perpetrator....I suspect that deeper down, the reason there is no confrontation of this sin is that there remains so much of it still in the camp. After all, we can't have little Suzy embarrass her father the pastor or elder by being pregnant outside of wedlock. And we just can't have another child—that would be bad stewardship!
>
> Going to the Church on this is like the woman with marital problems going to her divorced friend for advice.... Japan is so much better off.[57]

American Catholics too use *mizuko kuyō* in this way: for instance, a columnist for the *Superior Catholic Herald* (drawing on Olasky's *World* editorial for *mizuko kuyō* information) embeds a description of the mourning expressed in the Japanese ritual in his attack on poor leadership from church authorities on the abortion issue. "We note that *even in a country that is not imbued with Christian principles*, a profound sense of loss and guilt accompanies the unnatural act of abortion which, somehow, must be recognized, mourned and hopefully forgiven by the child whose life was so brutally ended.... [Yet] we are in a strange position as Catholics in America of getting moral leadership on abortion from our Congress and president than from our bishops and priests."[58]

While in MacArthur and Olasky's depictions "even" heathens such as the Japanese felt remorse at their killing, here the Japanese are in some ways rhetorically elevated above Christians; as deBarrie and Ackeret see it, these non-Christians are willing to dramatically and publicly admit their grief and guilt and seek repentance, while ostensibly pro-life American Christians routinize their political activism, harbor murderers in their midst without comment, and keep silent on the issue for fear of offending their flocks. What began as the rhetorical appropriation of *mizuko kuyō* to attack pro-choice positions becomes the employment of Japanese Buddhism to attack other pro-life supporters.

Pro-Choice Rhetorical Appropriations of *Mizuko Kuyō*

The pro-life faction is not the only side to call upon *mizuko kuyō* in the battle over abortion in America. Information about *mizuko*, Jizō, and Japanese Buddhist rituals appears in a number of prominent pro-choice venues. As might be imagined, these commentators refer to *mizuko kuyō* because they believe that, contrary to the opinions of their pro-life opponents, the phenomenon actually supports their demand for legal access to abortion. Considering the strength that anti-abortion advocates feel *mizuko kuyō* lends their cause, what are the advantages that pro-choice advocates discern in raising the issue?

Dissemination of information about *mizuko kuyō* can sometimes be used by feminists as an inoculation against the argument for post-abortion syndrome. An interesting case is that of abortion providers who discuss *mizuko kuyō* with their clients. For instance, Peg Johnston, the director of the Southern Tier Women's Services clinic (in Binghamton, NY) tells women about the Japanese phenomenon *before* the abortion is carried out. Her motivations are partially political, since she specifically contextualizes it as an attempt to diminish the stigma of abortion and offer a counterpoint to widespread antiabortion rhetoric. An article in *Ms.* magazine cited this practice with tacit approval, intimating that proactive acknowledgment that abortion is a serious and emotionally straining experience can prevent unspoken feelings from developing into hysteria later on.[59] Johnston also authored a "Pregnancy Options Workbook," used by abortion clinics across the country, which describes the practice of *mizuko kuyō* and its Japanese background.[60] Patients are encouraged to read the workbook—which describes conflicted feelings as normal and manageable through ritual and other means—to help deal with any negative emotions either before or after the abortion.

An extended discussion of Japanese Buddhist practices in relation to abortion appears in Daniel Maguire's *Sacred Choices: The Right to Contraception and Abortion in Ten World Religions.* Many of the motivations and strategies at work in other pro-choice articles on *mizuko kuyō* are clearly on display in this book. Maguire first describes Buddhism as a peaceful, admirable religion with a deep commitment to ethics. After a discussion of basic Buddhist ideas and some attention to attitudes toward abortion, he draws on William LaFleur's *Liquid Life* to assert that *mizuko kuyō* shows "how a contemporary Japanese woman could accept Buddhism with its First Precept against killing, have an abortion, and still consider herself a Buddhist in good standing."[61] Maguire emphasizes the love of children in Japan and how the Japanese nonetheless are enabled by Buddhism to deal with unwanted pregnancies in a practical manner:

> Japan has always strongly valued children. Francois Caron, who lived in Japan in the early seventeenth century, made this observation: "Children are carefully and tenderly brought up; their parents strike them seldom or never, and though they cry whole nights together, they endeavor to still them with patience; judging that infants have no understanding, but that it grows with them as they grow in years, and therefore they are to be encouraged with indulgences and examples."
>
> LaFleur sees all of this as "evidence that there is no necessary correlation between the allowance of abortion and the quality—or even the overall tenor—of family life in a given society.... Apparently it is possible for a society to practice abortion and still have what is generally called a 'strong' conception of the family." Additional proof may be found inversely in those modern right-wing resisters to abortion rights who, with all their talk of *family values*, display no great concern for born children, their schools, their families, or their welfare. There are lessons here. Do no equate the use of abortion with cruelty or resistance to it with gentleness. It's just not that simple....
>
> Even today, we can see that Japanese Buddhists do not take abortions lightly. They do not forget the aborted fetus, which they see, in LaFleur's words "not so much as being 'terminated' as being put on 'hold,' asked to bide its time in some other world."[62]

Maguire then talks about the process of *mizuko kuyō* and the "sweet savior-figure" Jizō. He concludes that "There is nothing coldhearted about the care of the *mizuko*."[63]

Maguire discusses a range of other cultures and their attitudes toward abortion in his book. Yet it is the Japanese Buddhist case that he seems to find most intriguing. *Sacred Choices* was followed in 2003 by the similarly titled *Sacred Rights: The Case for Contraception and Abortion in World Religions*, an anthology edited by Maguire with almost entirely new material. There was one part of his own earlier book that he couldn't resist republishing in *Sacred Rights*, however: he includes an appendix titled "Editor's Note on Japanese Buddhism," wherein he excerpts the material that specifically relates to *mizuko kuyō*.[64] In this he follows the lead of other American pro-choice advocates—to the extent that material about non-Western cultures appears in pro-choice books or Web sites, *mizuko kuyō* seems to be by far the most commonly referenced religious practice. Pro-Choice Connection (www.prochoiceconnection.com), for instance, includes an entire separate page titled "Mizuko Kuyo," which describes the ritual in detail and the logic behind it.[65]

As with the employment of rhetoric about *mizuko kuyō* in pro-life sources, its appearance in pro-choice arguments serves multiple ideological agendas. First, by showing that foreign cultures contextualize and ritualize the issues of abortion differently, pro-choice advocates demonstrate that American attitudes and discussions are not "natural"—that is to say, they are contingent approaches based on the limited and historically determined ideas of just one culture, not automatic human reactions to abortion. Other peoples don't necessarily assume that abortion angers God or goes against religion, and therefore, this line of argumentation suggests, when pro-life partisans make these claims they are merely trying to impose their personal ideas on everyone else. Second, the case of *mizuko kuyō* demonstrates that people who have abortions or support the legal right to do so are not hardhearted monsters or child-haters. Before and after an abortion these Buddhists care about their fetuses, and they seek to provide some care for them in the afterlife or apologize for necessary acts. Pro-choice advocates thus use gestures toward *mizuko kuyō* in an attempt to re-produce themselves as caring, concerned human beings who are wrestling honestly with difficult situations. *They* are the *real* family-values people, it turns out. Third, *mizuko kuyō* enables pro-choice partisans to claim the mantle of religion. The default assumption in America seems to be that pro-life positions are religiously motivated, whereas pro-choice positions are possibly antireligious. With *mizuko kuyō*, pro-choice advocates believe they have found an example of religious people who can support abortion rights without any hypocrisy. Fourth, the idea of *mizuko* offers a new way of discussing the status of the fetus: abortion doesn't kill a full human person, but only a "person-in-process," who clearly has lower ontological status than the mother. And fifth, another novelty of *mizuko kuyō* is that it offers a new way of imagining what occurs in the act of abortion itself: instead of a termination, with a heavy sense of finality, abortion can now be represented as a pause in a possibly ongoing process to be continued later.

The case being advanced here by pro-choice advocates presents the following argument: American Christian hostility to abortion is an unusual phenomenon. Sadness after abortion *can* be dealt with religiously and need not be seen as a major psychological trauma. *Even such a child-centered culture as Buddhist Japan* knows that women need to have access to legal abortion. Absolute opposition to reproductive rights is unnatural—that is to say, it only occurs when someone is indoctrinated by religious fanatics.

Appropriations beyond the Abortion Debate

Let us turn our attention for a moment to other American battlegrounds where non-Buddhists are discussing *mizuko kuyō*. While abortion is undeniably the most contentious issue in the wrangling over "creating a culture of life," there are other important areas of cultural conflict, such as harvesting of human embryonic stem cells, human cloning, and genetic manipulation. At least since 2000, *mizuko kuyō* has begun to emerge as a point of discussion in relation to these issues. These discussions are particularly interesting because they typically take place in academic and medical forums, among doctors, researchers, and bioethicists who rarely resort to specifically religious arguments to win points in what are essentially secular and scientific environments. Just as it seemed at first strange that born-again Christians would widely discuss Buddhist post-abortion rituals, it may be unexpected to find geneticists and their colleagues examining ideas of ghosts and cosmic bodhisattva saviors for orientation about how to conduct their experiments. Nevertheless these scientists play a role in the Americanization of Buddhism as they disseminate, debate, and act on information about *mizuko kuyō*.

The first important appearance of *mizuko kuyō* in these debates seems to be Dorothy Wertz's article "The Cult of Jizō" in an early 2000 issue of *Gene Letter*, a periodical for professionals working in the field of human genetics. Wertz provides a description of *mizuko* Jizō, the offerings made to these figures, and temples with tens of thousands of statues, drawing on LaFleur's *Liquid Life*. Then, extrapolating from the logic of the concept of *mizuko* as unformed spirits who can be sent back to the pre-mortal world and brought to term at some future point, she makes a rather remarkable observation:

> Mizuko are always seeking to return to life; some people believe that they try to find their original families. So preserving fetal cells and later cloning them to provide an identical—butcured—body would provide an ideal welcome for a mizuko seeking its family.[66]

It seems unlikely that any Buddhist monk had such a scenario in mind when the practice of *mizuko kuyō* was being developed in Japan. Here *mizuko kuyō* has been used to support the idea of preserving fetal cells following an abortion for reasons of genetic abnormalities; later, when a cure for the genetic conditions has been developed and the preserved cells can be manipulated so that they would grow into a healthy child, they could be cloned and grown into a living human being, presumably the same human being who would have resulted from the original pregnancy, who would be grateful for its "resurrection." This is indeed the science fiction laboratory equivalent of Japanese Buddhist *mizuko kuyō*: returning a pregnancy to a state of stasis so that later it can be retrieved in better conditions.

The following year, a more protracted debate began in *The Hastings Center Report*, one of the primary forums for sustained attention to bioethics and emergent laboratory technologies in America. The discussion was opened by Michael Meyer and Lawrence Nelson in their article "Respecting What We Destroy: Reflections on Human Embryo Research."[67] For Meyer and Nelson, *mizuko kuyō* provides a compelling example that people are able to show respect and compassion for lives that they are nonetheless compelled to destroy. "Such acts as *tikkun*, as well as the practice of *mizuko kuyō*, are manifestations of genuine respect for the aborted fetus, even if that respect was by itself not enough to lead a woman to forgo the abortion."[68] Researchers who destroy human embryos to gain stem cells for further medical experiments therefore are not necessarily callous or disrespectful toward human life in the abstract or toward the living embryos and cells in their possession.

This argument was less than convincing to some readers. In a later issue, Daniel Callahan, a fellow at the Hastings Center, fired back:

> Since when is it good ethical methodology to root around in anthropology files to find cultures that do what we want to do? Does the fact that a culture simply does or believes something give its behavior automatic moral standing? If so, that's news to me.[69]

Cynthia Cohen, of the Kennedy Institute for Ethics at Georgetown University, was also ambivalent about this argument. Citing LaFleur and her own encounters with *mizuko kuyō* in Japan, Cohen asserts that the practice indicates that Japanese Buddhists attribute far greater moral status to pregnancies than Meyer and Nelson admit:

> As the example of *mizuko kuyo* suggests, it is difficult, even across cultures, to escape the nagging realization that a human embryo is a human being in process. Although I do not pretend to have a final answer to the question of the weight of its moral status, I venture to say that because it is a potential human being, it has more than weak moral status. I dare add that many others agree and are consequently reluctant to see it destroyed. It therefore behooves us agnostics to recommend that first attempts at stem cell research

should use adult stem cells to avoid the destruction of potential human beings.[70]

Turning the tables, Cohen thinks *mizuko kuyō* actually supports the argument against using human embryos for experimentation. As with the pro-life and pro-choice debates over *mizuko kuyō's* significance, the ritual can be made to support either side in these further bioethical discussions.

A final note on this subject: while the professional researchers abstractly debate the ethics of their experiments, some of their student assistants may be struggling with these issues in a far more visceral way. One indication comes from the online journal of a University of Washington undergraduate who, having grown human bone cells as part of class lab work, was left conflicted about what to do with them at the end of the experiment. Following this train of thought led to reading about *mizuko kuyō* and the idea of perhaps creating a Buddhist-influenced ritual for people working in laboratories. "What would the ritual look like? Is it ethical to perform religious rituals over tissue and genetic material of someone belonging to a different faith? Is there an ethical way to incorporate more respectfully religious action in a research clinic environment, and is it necessary in the first place?"[71] Clearly, not all thoughtful consideration of these subjects takes place at the top of the biomedical industry's hierarchy.

Naming an Overlooked Phenomenon: Buddhist Appropriators

In the first section of this chapter, I criticized the historiographical turn in studies of American Buddhism that has shifted attention from how Buddhism arrives here to wrangling over what types of Buddhists there are in America. Converts, ethnics, sympathizers, night-stand Buddhists, and many other creatures have become the basic characters of scholarly studies on Buddhism in North America. In this section I intend to add yet another exotic animal to our menagerie, but one of a very different type—one that I hope will help expand the possibilities of research on Buddhism in America, as well as on religions with a stronger and longer presence in the historiographical annals, such as Christianity and Judaism.

I have already noted the terms "Buddhist opponent" and "Buddhist interpreter," which were coined by Thomas Tweed but were not given much attention by him or by subsequent researchers. Here is the sum of his discussion:

> Some other non-Buddhists, whom I have not discussed here, play an important role, too, in the story: *Buddhist opponents,* such as evangelical Protestants who dismiss Buddhism as a dangerous "cult" or try to

convert followers in Asia; and *"Buddhist interpreters,"* journalists, film makers, scholars, poets, painters, and novelists who represent the tradition for American audiences.[72]

Neither term fits very well for many of the people covered in the present chapter. Some are most certainly opponents of Buddhism; yet they figure in this story not as enemies seeking to displace Buddhism but as observers eager to employ Buddhism for their own ends. They certainly don't fall under Tweed's category of "Buddhist sympathizers," people with a certain affinity for elements of Buddhism but no wish to actually convert or become full practitioners of the religion. Neuhaus, O'Neill, and other conservative Christians stretch the bounds of "sympathy" for Buddhism well beyond reason. Meanwhile, the definition of Buddhist interpreters offered above seems to split into two broad camps: first, a professional class that disseminates information on Buddhism primarily to increase public knowledge of human culture (journalists, scholars, some filmmakers); and second, a professional class that draws on selected Buddhist tropes for creative inspiration (poets, painters, novelists, other filmmakers). Playwright Wendy MacLeod, for instance, whose play *The Water Children* used *mizuko kuyō* to resolve the main character's dilemma, would be considered one of these interpreters. Many others, though, probably should not be included here. John Wilke and David Reardon are not simply journalists or poets—they spread information about Buddhism specifically to advance political and religious agendas.

Rather than try to uncomfortably cram the people encountered in this chapter into ill-fitting typologies, I prefer to refer to them as "Buddhist appropriators." A Buddhist appropriator is not a type of Buddhist. The term, as I use it, refers to non-Buddhists who employ elements of Buddhism for their own purposes. Thus pro-life minister John MacArthur and pro-choice author Daniel Maguire are both Buddhist appropriators: they bring up *mizuko kuyō* in their discussions not as Buddhist apologists, opponents, or sympathizers, but to use it to score points in a debate that otherwise has little if anything to do with Buddhism. In the process, such Buddhist appropriators add to the general pool of knowledge (and, not uncommonly, misunderstanding) of Buddhism in America, and partially alter the terms on which the culture war will be fought.

Adding the term "Buddhist appropriator" to the lexicon of religious studies allows us to acknowledge a particular type of non-Buddhist as players in the larger discourse on Buddhism in America. This has obvious utility for scholars whose primary research interests are American Buddhist phenomena. But the term can also benefit scholars who concentrate on other religious groups, such as American Catholics or evangelicals. Seeing their subjects as Buddhist appropriators helps to bring into focus the fact that even conservative groups exist within a milieu of religious diversity, and they take things from outside groups without necessarily desiring to forge ongoing relationships with these others. It also exposes some of the effects of globalization on local religious communities: because there are Catholic priests ministering in Japan, midwestern Catholic newsletters end up carrying information about Buddhist post-abortion rites. It is hard to maintain the stereotype of provincial Christian fundamentalists when you encounter one sermonizing about *mizuko kuyō*.

Furthermore, the notion of appropriators may be expanded to include non-Buddhist phenomena. Many of these Buddhist appropriators are also Jewish appropriators, for instance, readily referencing Jewish ideas or traditions if they seem to support their cause. Note the reference to *"tikkun"* in Michael Meyer and Lawrence Nelson's article on human embryos. They may even be shamanistic, polytheistic, or animistic appropriators, drawing on the local religious/cultural beliefs and practices of various ethnic groups for fodder. For a quick example of this latter type, consider this passage from Catholic philosophy professor Peter Kreeft's *How to Win the Culture War: A Christian Battle Plan for a Society in Crisis*:

> I know a doctor who spent two years in the Congo winning the confidence of a dying tribe who would not trust outsiders (black or white) and who were dying because of their bad diet. He was a dietician, and he saved their lives. Once they knew this, they trusted him totally and asked him all sorts of questions about life in the West. They believed all the things he told them, like flying to the moon and destroying whole cities with one bomb, but there were two things they literally could not believe. One was that in the West there are atheists—people who believe in no gods at all ("Are these people blind and deaf? Have they never seen a leaf or heard a waterfall?") The other was that in one nation alone (America), over a million mothers each year pay doctors to kill their babies before they are born. Their reaction to this was to giggle, which was their embarrassed way of trying to be polite, assuming it was a joke. They simply had no holding place in their minds for this concept, and they expected every day that the doctor would tell them the point of the joke.
>
> And it is we who call these people "primitive." The irony is monstrous.[73]

As with John MacArthur's extensive description of *mizuko kuyō* in his sermon, here Kreeft appropriates the attitudes and beliefs of a foreign religious and cultural system to score points against his domestic opponents. Even the polytheistic peoples we call "primitive" know better than American atheists and pro-choice advocates about religion and morality, he alleges. This employment of a Congolese ethnic group's beliefs is not meant to honor them or suggest that American Christians should learn from them—it is purely a rhetorical tool for making people who oppose the author's agenda seem "blind," "deaf," and "monstrous." Increasing contact between different cultures and religions, and even learning from outside sources and willingness to discuss the ideas of others, does not necessarily lead in a straightforward way to tolerance and pluralism. MacArthur's evangelical congregation and Kreeft's Christian readers operate in a somewhat diverse environment where conservative Christian leaders actively expose them to non-Christian ideas and practices. But it is difficult to argue that actual pluralism, in the sense of appreciation for other ways of thinking and acting, is being achieved here when the framework of appropriation so seamlessly plugs these new religions into preexisting structures of thought and value.

Many American Buddhists are themselves Christian appropriators, frequently making use of Christian language or concepts when they serve to illustrate points of doctrine. And finally, we should not confine appropriations of Buddhism to non-Buddhist religious commentators. Some of the people in this chapter are not explicitly religious (some are openly agnostic), yet they resort to references to Buddhism and other religions when it suits their purposes. Perhaps we need to talk of "religious appropriators," people who employ discussion of religion to make points in arguments that are not necessarily considered religious matters, or where the commentator's own motivations are not religious in character. Certainly this would seem to be a common phenomenon in the contemporary United States, hardly confined to the use of *mizuko kuyō* in discussions of abortion or human cloning.

Conclusion: Liquid Lives and American Arguments

Repeatedly, William LaFleur has surfaced in this narrative as an important source for non-Buddhist knowledge of *mizuko kuyō*. From Catholic priests to visual artists, Americans with a wide variety of occupations, religions, and political views have learned about Japanese Buddhist abortion concepts from his 1992 book. In fact, his intentions in writing *Liquid Life: Abortion and Buddhism in Japan* included the possibility of influencing the American debate over abortion. "If some of the ideas presented here could be used as a heuristic tool for looking at—and trying to solve—our own abortion dilemma, I would be doubly pleased," he writes in his introduction.[74] LaFleur's main concern is not with whether abortion is moral or whether it should be legal, and his book is not strongly pro-life or pro-choice. He is focused on another problem altogether, which perhaps—he hopes—knowledge of *mizuko kuyō* could help us resolve: the corrosive effect of the abortion dispute on American society as a whole.

> The debate about learning from Japan ought also to include a careful, balanced, open look at how abortion is dealt with there. For Americans to join in that debate might prove to be very profitable—especially since, as now seems to be the case, discussions of abortion in the United States threaten to remain dead-locked, divisive, or both. One of the salient features of the Japanese approach [i.e., *mizuko kuyō*] appears to be that it has enabled society to avoid the kind of social division and disruptions we have been absorbed in for decades now. To the extent that it contributes to social solidarity rather than to fracturedness, the Japanese approach is eminently pragmatic.[75]

The information presented in this chapter may argue against any apparent potential of *mizuko kuyō* to alleviate the cultural war over abortion. In the wake of exposure to the idea of *mizuko kuyō*—in no small part because of LaFleur's influence—both pro-life and pro-choice Buddhist appropriators resort to discussions of the ritual because they feel it helps them strengthen the weaknesses of their own sides and undermine the positions of their opponents.

And as with the pro-life and pro-choice debates over *mizuko kuyō's* significance, the ritual can be made to support either side in a number of other bioethical discussions on such issues as cloning and gene therapy. This mutability of *mizuko kuyō's* meaning in American discussions is not simply because the ritual comes from a foreign culture and therefore is designed to meet the needs of a different situation. It also arises because the multifaceted ritual can be abstracted in multiple ways, such that different observers may find reflected in the ritual differing elements that appear to support their biases about abortion and biomedical issues. Water baby rituals turn out to be so fluid that they can be marshaled to support opposing positions on a wide range of (sometimes only tenuously associated) subjects, and once introduced into the discussion they may be used to attack others who share one's own general perspective or even reinterpreted against the original appropriator. This extreme fluidity may be too strong for *mizuko kuyō* to form a foundation for LaFleur's desired common ground: since *mizuko kuyō* can be channeled into support of any number of partisan positions, it seems to lack the ability to fundamentally sway opponents. It does change the nature of the debate by diversifying the number and type of religious and cultural resources drawn upon in the American culture wars. This is a significant development that deserves attention. But nonetheless, at least on the level of political discussion, knowledge of Japanese Buddhism doesn't seem to change *minds*. Rather, *mizuko kuyō* becomes another site for argumentation and self-justification, not a lever that actually moves significant numbers of people to one side or another of these debates. Jizō, who functions as the bodhisattva patron of firefighters, so far has shown little capacity to extinguish the raging flames of the American abortion debate.

But there is another aspect of the non-Buddhist encounter with *mizuko kuyō* that needs to be considered. On the level of *discussion*, at least, *mizuko kuyō* is easily used as yet another weapon in the abortion cultural war. With the level of antagonism so high, neither side seems prepared to back down in the arena of debate and attempt to reach some accord. But the pragmatic approach that LaFleur desires—which he sees as a formerly widespread element of American thought that has now been largely abandoned—does appear to make some headway in another aspect of American life. On the level of *action*, of ritual, there is evidence that *mizuko kuyō* is slowly altering the way some Americans on both sides of the debate relate to abortion and religion. It is this second area of appropriation—ritual—that is the concern of the next chapter.

6

"Thank You GetupGrrl for Giving Me My Mizuko"

Therapeutic Appropriations of Mizuko Kuyō by Non-Buddhist Americans

The only cure
I know
is a good ceremony,
that's what she said.

—Leslie Marmon Silko, *Ceremony*

In early 1925, Gloria Swanson was the most famous and popular woman on earth. Already a veteran star of the silver screen at age twenty-five, the dark-haired American actress had worked with such stars and starmakers as Charlie Chaplin, Rudolph Valentino, and Cecile B. De Mille, and she was in Paris preparing to marry the Marquis de la Falaise. It should have been the crowning moment of a triumphant life. But as Swanson explains on the first page of her 519-page autobiography, she was secretly in the grip of terror and despair.

Gloria Swanson, the million-dollar-girl, was pregnant. If the news reached Hollywood, defensive under the scrutinizing eye of the oppressive Hays Office, her career was over. Although unplanned, she wanted to bear the Marquis' baby—yet she also felt an obligation to her fans to fulfill their dreams for her. And, as she made clear, there was all the money to be made if she just didn't let this little bump in the road derail her. Torn by the situation, she imagined the fetus speaking to her plaintively, begging not to be flushed into the cold sewers. She saw the face of death in the fog, stalking her. Telling no one but the few people she needed to arrange the procedure, she quietly obtained an abortion. Immediately she contracted blood poisoning and fell into a near-fatal fever that lingered for weeks, as she thrashed in the sheets with nightmares of her dead child. She knew her illness was a punishment. Eventually, Swanson recovered and moved on to even greater stardom, succeeding not only as an actress but as a fashion designer, artist, and advocate for women. Decade by decade, she was gazed at by hundreds of millions, none of whom knew that sadness and a desire for some sort of forgiveness gnawed at her.

Finally, unexpectedly, she found her redemption. On the last page of her international bestseller, after all the triumphs and the ever-lingering effects of the tragedy that opened the book, Swanson visited Japan:

> The greatest regret of my life has always been that I didn't have my baby, Henri's child, in 1925. Nothing in the whole world is worth a baby, I realized as soon as it was too late, and I never stopped blaming myself. Then in 1979 Bill and I traveled to Japan, and at a Buddhist temple at a place called Kyo San, or Honorable Mountain, our guide and a Buddhist monk led us up through the most timeless, peaceful landscape I have ever seen, asleep or awake: a mountain forest of pathways lacing the area, and ancient graves everywhere. At one point I noticed a tiny stone figure near the massive roots of one of the cedars. Then another. Then I realized that there were hundreds. With little cloth bibs around them.
>
> "What are these?" I asked.
>
> "Babies," the guide said. He crouched down for a closer look at one stone. "Fifteen hundred twenty-five. This baby's life was ended before he was born."
>
> Then he and the monk must have seen how deeply moved I was, for they showed me how to pay respect in that place. They gave me a dipper of water and indicated that I should pour it over the tiny stone figure. Then I burned the incense the monk gave me and left some grains of rice.
>
> As we stood up, I was crying fresh tears out of a guilt I had carried for fifty-four years. The guide and the monk exchanged some words, and then the guide said to me, "We all choose our parents. We choose everything. No blame."
>
> I believed him. The message came to me too directly for me to disbelieve it. I believe it to this day. In fact, I tried to convey a bit of that message on the first-day cover I designed for the United Nations. And since that day on the Honorable Mountain I look at my children and their children and their children with respect and awe as well as love.[1]

Swanson closes by saying that now "things are getting clearer." Fame, fortune, power, love, four husbands, and the cultural and religious riches of America failed to heal that lifelong self-inflicted wound. But in an impromptu *mizuko kuyō* atop a dreamlike mountain in Japan, Swanson found the release she sought.

In the previous chapter, I described non-Buddhist Americans who rhetorically appropriate *mizuko kuyō* to bolster their arguments over abortion and other contentious bioethical issues. Most often, such appropriations were used to critique ideological opponents. But there are other appropriations of *mizuko kuyō* that deserve attention. For some American Christians and others, Jizō's role in *mizuko kuyō* offers a compelling new vision of religious response to the difficult question of abortion, as well as other wrenching pregnancy losses such as miscarriage or stillbirth. At times, where God seems unapproachable or forbidding, Jizō is being marshaled to offer solace to women after pregnancy losses, intentional or otherwise. Beyond the simple rhetorical employment of *mizuko* in the contentious American culture wars, there is the emergence of another kind of phenomenon: some non-Buddhist Americans, including pro-life Christians, are participating in *mizuko kuyō* rituals themselves as a way to heal after a pregnancy loss.

On this final leg of our exploration of Jizō's perambulations through non-Buddhist America we find that—despite all the wrestling over whether *mizuko kuyō* is a pro-life or pro-choice ritual—some tentative common ground is achieved between the two sides. The appropriations covered in this chapter are therapeutic ones.[2] If the appropriations of chapter five were most often designed to wound—to score points or draw rhetorical blood in the wars over abortion and other issues—those investigated here are intended to heal. And in healing a wounded nation, these appropriators offer the most unexpected glimpses of how Buddhism is Americanized by non-Buddhists operating outside of Buddhist venues.

"The Japanese Approach Is More Sensitive": Japan as Better Off Than America

Let us begin with Gary Chamberlain, one of the most perceptive interpreters of *mizuko kuyō* for a non-Buddhist audience, writing in the Jesuit journal *America*:

> As the bus neared Purple Cloud Temple, two long miles by train and bus from Tokyo, loud-speakers were already blaring in the early-morning sunshine. From the bits of Japanese I know, I could make out words like "sorrow," "sadness," "water child" and others, which

told me I had arrived at a unique Buddhist temple devoted exclusively to prayers and rituals for aborted fetuses. But beyond the sounds of chants, music and rhythmic phrases, I was overwhelmed by the sight before me. On every side of the mountains surrounding the temple, small statues of the god Jizo, special protector of children, stretched out as far as the eye could see....

I had come to this spot nestled in the mountains as part of my own work on abortion and family planning in Japan and the response of the Roman Catholic Church....Today these rituals serve at least two purposes. They provide an outlet and expression of personal loss, and they provide a ritualized, public policy that replaces our Western reliance upon law to resolve our anguish about abortion. I believe that *such rituals* not only can teach us a great deal about how to deal with abortion but also, *if adopted by Christian communities, can absorb the divisions and tensions created by the political climate surrounding abortion in the United States.*[3]

What America needs to heal the deep divide over abortion, Chamberlain suggests, is Christianized *mizuko kuyō*. This statement from a Catholic in a Jesuit weekly may seem startling, yet variants on this theme are surprisingly common. In fact, Chamberlain's sentiments are echoed from many directions. Already in 1989, Anthony Zimmerman, an American Catholic priest serving in Nagoya, had made a similar suggestion:

We who are Catholic—we are strangely silent about reparation for the injustice done to our children whom we aborted, and to God whose commandment we broke. Mothers keep the pain in their hearts, without opportunity to express it in prayer, and in making offerings. Is it right?...*Maybe we Catholics should look past the superstition, and learn from the Japanese* to do a little penance for our sins in killing the preborn. When will we have a corner in our churches to honor the "water children?" *When will priests offer Masses for the water children of the city, state, and nation,* accepting offerings in a box which protects confidentiality; offerings which would be used to help pro-life causes and to finance birth costs for unwed mothers, and adoption costs for their children?[4]

Even the American Life League, a virulently pro-life Catholic group opposed to abortion and contraception in all situations, saw a positive connection between Japanese Buddhist rituals and the American abortion debate:

Japanese women at least have a religious mechanism for dealing with their guilt and remorse. Buddhist memorial services for their aborted babies which are referred to as "water children sent from dark to dark" have become a booming business in Japan.... *We in the United States have begun to imitate the Japanese with grave plots and memorial services for the preborn*, despite the fanatical resistance of such anti-religious groups as the American Civil Liberties Union and the National Organization for Women, who have actually taken pro-lifers to court for daring to attempt to bury the sad little bodies of aborted preborn babies.[5]

These feelings are not confined to Catholics. There are also voiced by Protestants, Jews, neopagans, Unitarian Universalists, agnostics, atheists, and others. They represent pro-choice, pro-life, and undecided viewpoints. Though the sources are varied, the lament is the same: the United States is worse off than Japan because Japanese Buddhists have recourse to *mizuko kuyō*, whereas American Christians and others have no widespread post-pregnancy loss rituals.

Let's listen in for a moment on these voices before analyzing them further. We hear Mormon legal scholar Lynn Wardle characterizing *mizuko kuyō* as "remarkably honest and healthy."[6]

The Japanese practice of abortion allows for mourning and grieving. Acknowledgment of responsibility is socially encouraged in Japan. The result—open ritual grieving for abortion—is beneficially and compassionately healing with respect to the feelings of the woman and is also very honest by recognizing that a child's life has been sacrificed. The American approach is to deny responsibility, suppress guilt, and repress mourning. Guilt or grief is a sign of weakness. Feminists shouts of "no apology" and "no shame" and the legal principle that abortion is a fundamental constitutional right, intimidate American women and obstruct their grieving.... *The Japanese approach is more sensitive to non-economic, intangible dimensions of life, especially bonds and relationships, and is more holistic.*[7]

From the opposite direction, pro-choice writer Wren Farris declared in *Vision Magazine*:

The culture of Jizo in Japan may have vital insights to lend to our own country as we contend with an anti-woman governmental system and a culture of secrecy and shame around abortion.... *Japanese women, on the other hand, have the great opportunity to share their grief, participating in culturally accepted rituals with their families and communities.*... So what could an American version of Jizo look like? What would it feel like to acknowledge and mourn our losses instead

of feeling forced to hide them?... Perhaps it is time for women in
America to develop a set of personally and culturally empowering practices, or deeper understandings surrounding reproductive
choice....

Finding ways to counterbalance and break the ideology of secrecy
around abortion that exists in our country may be the next step in the
centuries-long reclamation of true equality from within society for
women.... Gratitude to the women and men who tend Jizo; may we
take strength from their willingness to openly grieve.[8]

Another voice is that of Zachery Braverman, an American Jew living in Japan:

Jizo is the patron saint of, among other things, lost children. One
meaning of lost children is aborted children, as well as those who
died in childbirth.... *In Japan, abortion is not politicized as it is in the
States. It's just a fact of life.* That means that there is a place within the
society for things like this, where women can go to make an offering to a spirit that didn't—for whatever reason—make it into this
world. Thus the women have a place to seek comfort, the memory of
the unborn child is respected, and healing can happen. *I don't think
the polarization of the issue in the States allows for such sentiments to be
expressed semi-publicly like this, which is too bad.* It negates the possibility of comfort where there should be some.[9]

Like Chamberlain, each of these writers recognizes that the United States
has reached some sort of deadlock, which is hurting the nation as a whole,
and women and their families involved with abortion in particular. At a loss as
to how to move the conversation forward and find a healthier way, a solution
suddenly seems to materialize when the idea of *mizuko kuyō* is encountered.
Nearly all non-Buddhist observers concede that *mizuko kuyō* offers some degree
of genuine post-abortion healing, and this concession often comes with a tinge
of jealousy. Collectively, these many non-Buddhist commentators on *mizuko
kuyō* seem to be making the following statement: the Japanese aren't paralyzed
by the issue of abortion—it hasn't rent their social fabric and balkanized the
country into angry groups that are viciously and mutually suspicious. Their
women are allowed to grieve for abortions and heal, while ours suffer in shame
and silence. Apparently the key is a Buddhist memorial ritual for fetuses. So if
it works for them, might it work for us too?

It is interesting to note that some of the voices expressing the most dismay at the American situation and the greatest respect for Japan's lack of strife
are conservative Christians. There is a tendency for some commentators to

assume an easy relationship between conservative Christianity and knee-jerk American patriotism. But the discussion of *mizuko kuyō* in these circles shows significant dissatisfaction with American culture and admiration for aspects of very foreign cultures. One lesson from attention to these appropriations of Buddhism is that although the United States often figures as the savior of the world in fundamentalist discourse, it can just as easily appear as the Antichrist when American politics or society seem to stray from a strongly conservative Christian vision of what they should be.[10]

There are several important points to take from these American musings on *mizuko kuyō*. First, there is a desire by many on both sides of the abortion debate for less rancor and greater social unity. Naturally, this wish for social unity is sometimes connected with the desire that one's own side win outright, eliminating the battle by eliminating the opposition. But there are also significant instances of simple dismay at the battle itself. Even among those who are actively involved in polarizing American religion and politics, there is often a counterdesire for greater social harmony. In fact, opponents often enter the fray in the name of social harmony: many pro-life Christians and Jews see social disharmony as a result of murder of pre-born babies and devaluation of women's roles as mothers, while many pro-choice advocates (religious or otherwise) believe social disharmony arises from suppression of women's reproductive rights and the intrusion of fundamentalist religion into the secularized public sphere. In their attempts to achieve social unity, the two sides cause further breakdown in the social fabric. This is simply one of the basic ironies of the culture wars. Another irony is that each side tends to react to this degradation of the public discourse by blaming the other, increasing the divide yet further.

But these ironic twists do not remove the underlying desire for a united America. Even as they blame and at times demonize one another, opponents on both sides express frequent desire for a more polite, unified, and compassionate society. Furthermore, the dyed-in-the-wool culture warriors are a clear minority of the American population as a whole. As political science professor Morris P. Fiorina explains in *Culture War?*, most Americans are in fact moderates on the issue of abortion. This great moderate middle has few voices in the highly polarized public debate over abortion, which is typically monopolized by people who are more extreme to one side or the other than the average citizen:

> The evidence is clear that the broad American public is not polarized on the specifics of the abortion issue. They believe that abortion should be legal but that it is reasonable to restrict it in various ways.... Overwhelming majorities regard rape, birth defects, and threats to the mother's life and health as sufficient justifications for

abortion, while clear majorities regard personal convenience and gender selection as insufficient.... In sum, public opinion on abortion does not support militants on either side of the issue. Pro-choice activists who play an important role in the Democratic Party argue that any infringement on a woman's right to choose is unacceptable, even if that means the occasional abortion of a healthy, near-term fetus. Such people probably comprise less than 10 percent of the population. Pro-life activists who play an important role in the Republican Party argue that any abortion is unacceptable, even if that means the occasional death of a woman. Such people certainly comprise less than 10 percent of the population. The great majority of the American citizenry rejects extreme positions and could be content with compromise laws, but such compromises are hard to achieve given the current state of American electoral politics.[11]

Despite the dominance of public discourse (and the political process) by the voices of the extremes, some of these moderates do publicly articulate a desire for less rancor, and some culture warriors, even while personally desiring a more radical stance, are aware of this moderate tendency and are willing to discuss compromises that are more faithful to the majority's wishes.

Mizuko kuyō enters this situation as a potential way of healing the rift between pro-life and pro-choice Americans. As Americans gaze at Japan, many are startled to encounter a society that simultaneously has a high abortion rate, little social strife over abortion, and apparently high levels of religious acknowledgment of abortion. In the previous chapter, the competing interests of the appropriators caused them to make opposite assessments of *mizuko kuyō's* meaning: pro-life advocates saw it as a pro-life ritual, whereas pro-choice advocates framed it as supporting abortion rights. Both rhetorically appropriated *mizuko kuyō*, and in the process the ritual was used to push the two sides further apart. But on the issue of greater social harmony, the desires of the two sides converge, and therefore they tend to agree that *mizuko kuyō* opens up a space where one side can tentatively reach out toward the other in the hope of using *mizuko kuyō* to turn down the heat in the American debate.

Different commentators see different levels of potential in *mizuko kuyō* for America. For some, it is simply an example of a nation where legal abortion doesn't dramatically damage society. This resembles the pro-choice appropriation that seeks to employ *mizuko kuyō* to prove that there is something unusual about America and its angry abortion battle. If some other country can get along despite the presence of abortion, perhaps we can too, whether or not we support the practice. For others, *mizuko kuyō* offers a more specific clue as to *how* to achieve the desired social harmony. Some analyze the situation and declare that it is the religious angle that matters: if we could take some responsibility by humbly and religiously acknowledging abortion's sinful and/or regrettable nature, then we would be on our way to a less rancorous situation, even if we did not necessarily criminalize abortion itself. This is close to the stance taken by Naomi Wolf in her widely discussed 1995 essay:

> How could one live with a conscious view that abortion is an evil and still be pro-choice? Through acts of redemption, or what the Jew-ish mystical tradition calls *tikkun*; or "mending." Laurence Tribe, in *Abortion: The Clash of Absolutes*, notes that "Memorial services for the souls of aborted fetuses are fairly common in contemporary Japan," where abortions are both legal and readily available. Shinto doctrine holds that women should make offerings to the fetus to help it rest in peace; Buddhists once erected statues of the spirit guardian of children to honor aborted fetuses (called "water children" or "unsee-ing children").[12]

Wolf assimilates Japanese *mizuko kuyō* practices to her own Jewish perspective, trying to suggest a path between the two polarized options available to Ameri-can women around abortion: the Scylla of pro-choice feminism that defends the procedure but refuses to allow religious language into the debate, and the Charybdis of pro-life conservatism that acknowledges people's spiritual side but demands the abrogation of reproductive rights. Yet other commentators take their analysis another step and conclude that it is specifically the *ritual* context of abortion in Japan that provides the answer: because the Japanese avoid "rights talk" and focus on ritual solutions to social problems, "mother and fetus" or "religion and women" are never hypothesized as opposing com-batants.

For those whose analysis doesn't proceed past the simple observation of Japan as a less polarized society, *mizuko kuyō* remains a ritual that is merely rhetorically appropriated. These people raise the issue of *mizuko kuyō* to en-vision a better America, but for various reasons—opposition to Buddhism, lack of interest in ritual, the sense that America is too different a culture from Japan to utilize the same solution, and so on—they do not go further. But for those who see Japan as a model that can actually be emulated to some degree, *mizuko kuyō* becomes a resource that can potentially be copied and used in North America to heal a troubled society. Thus, Chamberlain and others call for *mizuko kuyō*-type rituals in American Christianity as a method of dealing with the fact of abortion that doesn't contribute to the creation of harsh public wrangling over the procedure. Staunch pro-life and pro-choice partisans may not be able to agree on the issues, but, these commentators suggest, they could potentially participate side by side in shared ritual that expresses regret over abortion without explicitly condemning or valorizing those who support it. And once they sit down together, perhaps a new solution will eventually grow from these first tentative steps.

Healing Pregnancy Losses through *Mizuko Kuyō*, Online and Off

In the passages quoted above, there is another significant issue constantly being raised: the potential of *mizuko kuyō*–type rituals to provide spiritual or psychological healing to individual women who have experienced abortion. It is not only the promoters of the notion of "post-abortion syndrome," described in chapter 5, who feel that such women (and perhaps their families) need healing. Like Wolf, many pro-choice advocates and undecided moderates have expressed the need for some sort of recognition that abortion is a painful event that can give rise to grief, shame, and depression.

Of course, not all pregnancy losses are caused by abortion. A second group calling for help with their losses is women and their partners dealing with miscarriage. In many cases, these writers resent what they see as the abortion debate's oppressive polarization of pregnancy loss issues, such that miscarriage can't be acknowledged as a source of real grief—to do so would open up the question once again of whether a fetus is a full-fledged person.

> If one publishes a rite in which a stillborn infant of five and a half
> months gestation, or even a fetus miscarried in the first trimester, is
> referred to as a "baby," and perhaps given a name, one seems to have
> settled the question of when an individual human life begins. Is this
> a person or not? The question is central to the problem of whether
> there is a clear promise of eternal life for this little one. But what
> makes it a highly volatile, politicized issue in our society is its relation
> to the abortion debate, and that social situation obscures the choice
> of language with ideology. There are those who ideologically refuse
> to call a stillborn or miscarried fetus a baby, and those who ideologi-
> cally insist that if a woman who has miscarried doesn't use the word
> "baby," she is denying her grief.[13]

At the same time, funerals for miscarried fetuses have not been a prominent part of Christian and Jewish practice, and the lack of such an acknowledgment of loss can leave a woman who has miscarried feeling abandoned by all sides. Not surprisingly, many non-Buddhists consider *mizuko kuyō* a possible solution to this felt lack of ritualization. And there are yet other American voices looking at *mizuko kuyō* and demanding recognition of their losses: parents of stillborn children and of dead infants, and even infertile couples.

Reflecting this interest in the ritual, highly detailed *mizuko kuyō* descriptions appear in many of the most popular post–pregnancy loss manuals, such as *Unspeakable Losses: Healing From Miscarriage, Abortion, and Other Pregnancy Loss*; *The Healing Choice: Your Guide to Emotional Recovery After an Abortion*; and *Finding Hope When a Child Dies: What Other Cultures Can Teach Us*—as well as in more generalized publications, such as *Grieving for Dummies*.[14] Web sites and the literature of their associated offline organizations devoted to miscarriage and abortion support frequently carry in-depth information on *mizuko kuyō*, including Post Abortion Stress Syndrome, Pro-Choice Connection, Exhale, Life After Abortion, and Earth Island Angels.[15] Online communities for pregnancy and parenting, such as MotheringDotCommune and BabyCenter, very frequently include forums for discussion of pregnancy loss, and *mizuko kuyō* is raised by non-Buddhists at these sites time and again.[16] And the ritual is carefully described and explicitly promoted in many non-Buddhist publications for female spirituality, such as *Return to Spirit* and *Keys to the Open Gate: A Woman's Spirituality Sourcebook*.[17]

For many American women, simply reading that the Japanese memorialize their lost pregnancies brings amazement, gratitude, and, in some cases, claims of healing—the more mediated equivalent of the "*mizuko* arrest," described in the previous chapter, of Americans when first encountering rows of *mizuko* Jizō at Japanese temples. One place to observe this dynamic is in online forums where women gather to support one another in the wake of pregnancy losses. These sites have become a major online phenomenon in recent years—the most popular ones get tens of thousands of unique visitors each day, and there are hundreds of smaller forums where women cluster to find comfort in the quasi-anonymous world of virtual community.[18] Here they can express those feelings that Chamberlain and others complain have no comfortable place in American society.[19] Voiceless and frustrated in real life, online the almost-mother of a fetus that has been aborted, miscarried, or lost at birth can cry out and receive near instant recognition from hundreds of other women dealing with similar losses. And again and again, these women share the concept of *mizuko kuyō* with one another.

Religion in cyberspace is a relatively new phenomenon, but since the turn of the millennium it has attracted increasing scholarly notice. One of the primary interpretive lenses that has been applied to this phenomenon is "religion online" versus "online religion," a typology first coined by Christopher Helland.[20] Briefly, the distinction is mainly between preexisting religious organizations that create

Web sites designed to spread their message (religion online), and new virtual communities dedicated to exploring the specific potential of cyberspace as a spiritual source itself (online religion). Understandably, the preliminary work investigating religion online has tended to focus on sites and groups specifically created for religious purposes, whether it be mainstream religions beginning to develop an online presence (Buddhists, evangelicals, and so on—i.e., religion online), or creative new spiritual uses of the Internet (religion in Second Life, the House of Netjer, and so on—i.e., online religion). Furthermore, the preponderance of sociologists among the early researchers has intensified the focus on "communities" and "identity formation," two traditional concerns of this major discipline. The result is that most energy is put into exploring how specific groups with religious orientations intersect with online technology.

All of this is important work, but it also tends to overlook other significant aspects of religion online. One of these is the recognition that religious interactions take place outside explicitly religious forums. The hypertextual basis of online communication enables conversation partners in unrelated forums to bring in religious information whenever the discussion provides an opportunity, and without necessarily derailing or rerouting the main conversation. Furthermore, when exposed to new religious ideas a participant can instantly open a new browser window and seek further information that may be unavailable or relatively inaccessible offline.

This is an overlooked aspect of religion on the Internet that *mizuko kuyō* helps to bring into focus. While many religious sites carry information about *mizuko kuyō*, the parenting and other bulletin boards and blogs that are the main focus in this section fall outside the normal parameters of either religion online or online religion. Most often, they are "secular" sites that are unaffiliated with any particular religious tradition and are not devoted to explicitly religious subjects. That they become sites of religious encounter and exchange arises directly from the activities of their users, not the intent of their creators. In their quest for answers, Web surfers are not only shaped by the virtual spaces they inhabit but actively "terraform" secular Web sites to create communities of meaning.

The number of women in these online forums who are actually Buddhist seems to be tiny, but through the channels described in the previous chapter, these non-Buddhists have encountered *mizuko kuyō* concepts and pondered them in their hearts. When new women come along seeking some sort of solace, discussion of Jizō and water babies readily emerges. Likewise, Web diaries (blogs) that offer information on *mizuko kuyō* rapidly attract the attention of commentators:

> Thank You GetupGrrl for Giving Me My Mizuko: For those of you
> who have provided so many encouraging words and stories to me

regarding my past miscarriages and my attempt to get pregnant
again—I offer you getupgrrl's latest entry [link to post about *mizuko
kuyō*].... She gave me a place, and a way, to mourn my loss. If you
read the entry—be sure to also read the comments, which ended
up being a place for women to post their own stories of loss. It's an
amazing thing going on there. It was nice to be a part of it. Although
I could have done without the floodgate of tears I seemed to be unable to control while reading....

Samantha: i thought it was a particularly beautiful entry—those
Japanese have got it right. And the part about her mother crying?
Definitely caused some tears. Much love to YOU, Zoot!!

Mary: Oh, my. I just read through each and every story and comment and I am at a loss. I posted my own comment—an apology, of
sorts, for being a rotten, impatient ingrate. If I ever complain about
either of my kids again I want someone to tell me to just shut the
fuck up. I'm so glad she shared the concept of mizuko. It's obviously
helping a lot of people. I'm sorry for your loss, Zoot.[21]

The people in this latest example are discussing a post at the blog Chez
Miscarriage, which describes the concept of *mizuko kuyō*, based on Peggy
Orenstein's 2002 *New York Times* tale of performing one in Tokyo. The
author complains "We have no such rituals in our culture. I know of no
church or synagogue that invites women to mark the passing of a mizuko.
I know of no formal rite, no specific prayer, no community acknowledgement. Unlike in Asia, where Jizō temples offer women a tangible place to
take their grief, I know of no public space in this country devoted to the
topic of miscarriage or infertility."[22] Her description of *mizuko kuyō* and
lament over Americans' lack of something similar set off a flurry of activity. Within a week of posting this entry, 150 comments were left in reply.
Because they provide such a rich collection of voices that offline are often
subaltern, and because the sentiments expressed in this forum are closely
representative of those expressed at many other blogs and bulletin boards,
extended quotations seem to be justified here. What follows are messages
left by many different commentators over the course of a few days; for ease
of reading, they have been broken into sections based on when they were
posted:

"Today Grrl spoke for all of us. Today she just described totally how
we feel. Something that most people who haven't been through
something like this dont understand. This is her entry She had me
crying and wanting to scream this words to e..." "Grrl, thank you

for that lovely post. I remember reading that NYT article awhile back and thinking how lovely it was to have a word, and some traditions, to surround such a lonely loss." "I've never posted anywhere before but this post hit me hard. I am glad to have this word Mizuko. I have often wished there was a word for me, the woman I am now after these losses." "I do find comfort in the idea of mizuko, I have never heard of it before, but if I had I would have sought out a temple, without a doubt. Its a comforting thought to think that my children went and found another path. I hope that their new path is wonderful." "Peggy Orenstein's article about mizuko was one of the things that helped through the next while. For that one (the others were very early), we had a ceremony with close friends and family. We planted a tree in memory of our son, read prayers and passages from the journal we kept for him...As part of the ceremony, we then filled a memory box, saying that in a way, our memory box is like a Jizo statue, in that it contains our material remembrances of our son and our love for him." "I wish we had Buddist temple that honored our losses. Imagine it filled with women of all shapes, sizes, nationalities...we would have a name, we would exist." "If anyone is interested in Buddhist ceremonies for lost children, there are a couple of Zen centers in Northern California who offer them." "Mizuko...yes...this is what has been missing in my mourning process. I wish all of our losses could be honored so openly."

"What a gift you have for putting into words what we all feel and what a gift of healing you've given me...now, I feel I can name this pain and acknowledge my water babies. You've given me a sense of peace. I wish them well in the lives they'll have to come and remember them always in my heart."

"Thank you, grrl, because your writing's really what got me through. I love the concept of mizuko. There really does need to be some acknowledgement that yes, these children were here, yes, they were real, and yes, they were loved." "My pastor often says a prayer for 'those known only to God.' I've always thought it was about mizuko." "I have four Mizuko's, all lost within the last six years..."

"I remember the NYTimes article she writes about as if I read it yesterday and it was over 2-years ago. The cultures that formalize the loss of an unborn, whether sadly intentional (it is NEVER an easy choice for a woman) or sadly 'natural,' understand the sense of deep loss. I also remember the article because I love to think of our little boy as water and part of a continuum."[23]

These are only a small portion of the discussions of *mizuko kuyō* I have encountered in online grief forums and blogs by people who have experienced pregnancy loss.

What is it about *mizuko kuyō* that appeals to all of these people? There are basically three separate but interconnected demands—all related to ideas of healing—that are being expressed in these discussions of *mizuko kuyō* by non-Buddhist Americans who have experienced pregnancy loss. They are the desire for a voice, the desire for public recognition of their pain, and the desire for a plan of action in the wake of traumatic pregnancy loss. These wishes are mirrored in many of the offline publications on *mizuko kuyō* as well. For each of these desires, *mizuko kuyō* provides a site for expressing criticism of American religion and society, and a potential solution to American inadequacies. I will now explore each in turn.

Finding a Voice

In the wake of abortion or another pregnancy loss, a major concern for many women seems to be the inability to talk about the experience and their feelings. When a family member or friend dies, people have recourse to funerals, memorial services, and other religious resources that provide a context and language for the loss. But this often does not hold true for losses that occur prior to birth. Recognition of these losses seems not to have been a common part of American religious history, especially in the case of abortion. Because abortion is condemned by many religious groups, women often have nowhere to turn in their hour of need. For instance, the Vatican considers abortion a grievous sin that automatically leads to excommunication (*latae sententiae*) whether or not it is reported to a church official: the acts of receiving or carrying out an abortion result in immediate supernatural severance of the ties between believer and church.[24] Doctrines such as this not only reduce the ability of women to ritually deal with their pain but also may rob them of the possibility of even talking about their situations, effectively enforcing a code of silence around the issue. Miscarriage and stillbirth are not as stigmatized as abortion, yet they too frequently slip into an uncomfortable interstitial realm where the normal rites and concepts surrounding loss seem inadequate or unavailable.

In her feminist study of pregnancy loss in America, Linda Layne highlights the importance attached by American women to regaining the ability to speak as a step in dealing with abortion and miscarriage: "Pregnancy-loss support groups are fundamentally designed to break this silence. Through their meetings they carve out a space in which it is permissible to speak, and with the claim that pregnancy loss is a legitimate source of grief, they define loss as an acceptable topic of conversation outside support-group meetings."[25] Layne locates pregnancy loss support groups—of which the online forums are a special subtype—within the wider landscape of American self-help groups. As discussed in chapter 3, what Eva Moskowitz calls the "therapeutic gospel" provides the major philosophical grounding for these groups.[26] The Buddhist women in that chapter tightly associate therapy and religion in their production of Americanized water baby ceremonies; the non-Buddhist women under discussion here likewise combine the two into an often seamless whole, as will be discussed further below.

Sukie Miller, in her post–child loss manual, articulates the feelings of many women on this issue:

> The fact that there is no name for the one who has lost a child is of enormous consequence: the nameless live in a kind of limbo. They still exist, but in a new stratosphere where their namelessness effectively isolates them from the rest of the world.
>
> When we don't name things, they remain out of reach. I have never known a parent or anyone else who has lost a child not to describe a period of feeling out of touch, beyond the reach of anyone else's comfort or understanding. And it's true. You can't engage on any deep level with someone whose name you don't know.... Those things about which we cannot speak or will not speak do not simply disappear because we don't discuss them. In fact, they gain some of their power over us *because* we don't have language to vent them. They remain crouching in the shadows of our lives, unpredictable, a locus of rage, of despair, of fear, looking for an opportunity to be heard.[27]

Here the unarticulated feelings that arise in the wake of a young child's loss (Miller explicitly connects these to pregnancy losses as well) become transformed into a kind of menacing spirit nearly identical to the threatening *mizuko* described in the introduction. Language then becomes the key to rendering these fluid and ungraspable lost children tangible:

> Language is in every way an antidote to our fears and anxieties and general paralysis on the subject of death and dying. Language allows us to describe what happens, what is going through our minds, what we feel and have felt...With language what was amorphous takes shape. Whatever the subject, language brings it to life, and this is true even when the subject is death....With language not only can we name what we couldn't name before, but we may also be able to see

what we couldn't see before. With language whole worlds open up to us. In some places that access may extend to the world where our deceased children reside.[28]

The central thesis of Miller's manual is that Western societies lack sufficient terms and rituals to deal with child and pregnancy losses, and therefore we must turn to non-Western cultures to buttress our own. The case of the unborn receives particular attention in her book:

> If the death of a child we love is a subject about which we do not speak because of insufficient language, we have even fewer words with which to talk about the death of the unborn. What was it that we carried and lost? We're shy about calling it a baby until it is born, and for many people the word *fetus* sticks in the throat.... We don't describe the emotional aspects because without language, we can't express them— besides, our culture rarely acknowledges that there are any emotional aspects to miscarriage.... Among all the cultures I have researched on this subject, Japan seems to have the most developed language, in our broad sense of the word, for the phenomenon of death before life.[29]

Miller then embarks on several pages of extensive description of *mizuko kuyō* and Jizō's place in Japanese religion. For her, the word *mizuko* provides that missing language. Learning about Jizō and *mizuko* allows a grieving mother to face up to her loss and reestablish a connection with the child who never came to term. It allows her to acknowledge the value of that lost baby and imagine the child moving on to the next step in its journey. All of this might result in healing—a healing that, Miller claims, Western society currently doesn't provide a means for.

Does merely having a vocabulary with which to discuss issues provide healing? The answer to that question lies outside the scope of this study. Nor do I feel qualified by my training in religious studies to pontificate about a subject on which even psychiatrists and clinical psychologists cannot agree. But there is certainly evidence that some non-Buddhist Americans claim a strong benefit simply from having been exposed to the idea of *mizuko*. Look again at some of the online quotes provided in the previous section: "Grrl, thank you for that lovely post. I remember reading that NYT article awhile back and thinking how lovely it was to have a word, and some traditions, to surround such a lonely loss." "I've never posted anywhere before but this post hit me hard. I am glad to have this word Mizuko. I have often wished there was a word for me, the woman I am now after these losses." "What a gift you have for putting into words what we all feel and what a gift of healing you've given me...now, I feel I can name this pain and acknowledge my water babies. You've given me a sense of peace. I wish them well in the lives they'll have to come and remember them always in my heart."

The linguistic theories of anthropologists Edward Sapir and Benjamin Whorf provide one possible lens through which to view this phenomenon. Sapir-Whorf linguistics points out the tight relationship between thought, language, and culture. Two aspects of their work are particularly relevant: linguistic determinism and linguistic relativity. Linguistic determinism suggests that language shapes thought; some proponents go so far as to say that without access to a word for a phenomenon, that phenomenon literally cannot be thought about. Linguistic relativity suggests that language shapes worldview; for some, this means that different cultures inhabit different worlds because of the separate language-related ways in which they map their environments.[30] It isn't necessary to subscribe to the strongest versions of these theories to see how they might shed light on the situation of American women who wish to mourn their aborted or miscarried fetuses. Lacking an adequate English term for fetuses/babies that never come to full term, they have difficulty communicating their feelings about their losses. The average person reading about *mizuko kuyō* in a post–pregnancy loss manual or online forum probably will not go on to perform a *mizuko kuyō* ceremony. But if comments like those above are an accurate indication, Jizō's healing work is accomplished on some level, to some extent, when women merely learn about the idea of *mizuko*. This Buddhist practice seems to give them a lexicon and a concept with which to think about what has happened to them. Their religious imagination is expanded and the possibilities of what religion might do to help them or others increase. As scholar of American religion Colleen McDannell has noted:

> Religious practice, however, is more than merely lived. Religious
> practice is also imagined. In dreams, visions, and fictional accounts,
> people participate in worlds that are not a part of everyday life. These
> special worlds can eventually become as real as everyday life, or they
> can remain speculative fantasies. Just as through rituals people learn
> and construct religious worldviews, so they build religious environ-
> ments through vision and imagination.[31]

Sharing information about *mizuko kuyō* becomes a site where non-Buddhist women can form supportive networks, whether for a moment or lasting friendships that sometimes continue for years and extend into the offline world.[32] Reading about *mizuko kuyō* provokes grief, tears, and catharsis. The ritual performance itself is almost secondary—it is the *existence* of such a ritual which gives many of these women the strength to carry on.

Miller and other Americans who share her viewpoint may be categorized as "Buddhist appropriators." Few if any of these women will become Buddhists through their interaction with *mizuko kuyō* concepts. It may be possible to read them as Buddhist *sympathizers* of a sort according to Thomas Tweed's definition. But I would contend that the category is stretched too far by the people examined in this chapter. Sympathizers do not explicitly identify as Buddhists, but they do have a sustained engagement with some aspect of the religion, such as a regular meditation practice, frequent reading of Buddhist books or magazines, or ongoing participation in online Buddhist forums. Meanwhile, the women and men under discussion here are not only explicitly non-Buddhist, but their interactions with Buddhism are temporary and strategic. Buddhism appears at just the right moment to help them deal with a traumatic or vexing issue, either through actual participation in a water baby ceremony or simply through learning about and reflecting on *mizuko kuyō*. After the issue is resolved, Buddhism is left behind again, perhaps with fond memories but rarely with any lasting attachments. In other words, Buddhism is momentarily appropriated, used for a specific end, and then abandoned once more.[33]

Even these fleeting encounters and brief appropriations can leave indelible marks, however. While the religion as a whole is left behind, words and concepts may be permanently added to the religious consciousness of non-Buddhists by these appropriations. Beyond the relief expressed in the quotes above, note too the way some women now forthrightly declare that they are the mothers of *mizuko*, not simply babies, children, or fetuses: "I have four Mizuko's, all lost within the last six years ..."

If a Woman Talks about *Mizuko Kuyō* and No One Is Around, Does Healing Happen?

A closely related, but not identical, desire expressed by many of the non-Buddhists who discuss *mizuko kuyō* is for recognition of their grief and loss. Gaining a language for speaking about pregnancy loss allows people to give shape to their thoughts and voice to their feelings, and sometimes that is enough. But for many, a second step is apparently required: someone else must hear their voices. There is a need or desire for public acceptance of their grief and loss. Without it, a feeling persists that their pain and suffering are not valued by society, and that they have no right to mourn or feel depressed. There is friction between how others see them and how they are actually feeling. If they feel shame around the loss, such as many women feel in the wake of abortion, there is a desire for recognition of their shame, regret, and pain. If they feel robbed of their anticipated status as mothers, as many women do when miscarriage or stillbirth occurs, there is a need to be seen as having been pregnant, as being a mother-of-sorts. Indeed, these two trends are hardly confined to one or the other type of loss: in these accounts, many women who have had an abortion desire to retain some status as mothers, and women who have experienced miscarriage may feel great shame.

The lack of language compounds this problem but doesn't wholly encompass it. As described in a popular textbook on human development:

> The Japanese word *mizuko* means "water child." Japanese Buddhists believe that life flows into an organism gradually, like water, and a mizuko is somewhere on the continuum of life and death (Orenstein, 2002). In English, by contrast, there is not a word for a miscarried or aborted fetus, nor any ritual of mourning. Families, friends, and health professionals tend to avoid talking about such losses, because they are considered insignificant compared to the loss of a child (Van, 2001).[34]

For the women involved, however, the loss may feel very significant indeed. Cries for acknowledgment of these losses echo through the manuals, books, and forums that discuss pregnancy loss. After discussing *mizuko kuyō* as a comforting approach on pregnancy and loss that regrettably has no American analogue, one woman went on to say:

> *Perhaps writing about my miscarriage is a way for me to demand recognition from others because it means my suffering is real.* When we suffer and grieve, we need to talk about it because we must reclaim what has happened to us. It is important to remember the details: the happiness I felt when the pregnancy test came back positive, the absolute despair I felt two months later, and the anguish I will always feel. I must make my experiences real because, ultimately, I must learn how to live with it. I will never forget the child I lost, and I no longer want to. I simply need to find a way to live with loss. Having the space to speak freely about it is the first step.[35]

Exactly who these women wish would acknowledge their situation varies considerably and is often vague. Some specifically want their boyfriend's or husband's attention; others want attention from additional family members (especially parents); some want recognition from "society"; many indicate they desire some sort of religious acknowledgment, usually phrased as recognition from their minister or church; but most often there is no specific object from which they seek recognition. They simply want *someone* to hear their story and acknowledge the legitimacy of their grief. Online forums often seem to work well in this regard: invariably, posts that call for recognition receive numerous comments from readers offering support and encouragement.

So, step one in the process is appropriating Japanese Buddhist concepts to produce an adequate vocabulary around pregnancy loss, while step two is then actually speaking in a public (online or off) space about one's own experiences and how *mizuko kuyō* relates to one's feelings. Speaking out in this way attracts sympathetic responders who provide some level of recognition, and in doing so, often leave their own stories in search of their own recognition and healing. *Mizuko*, Jizō, and Japanese rituals for the unborn are particularly compelling topics in these discussions and seem to elicit more replies than many discussions that do not reference these Buddhist concepts. And these testimonials often describe how, after initially receiving the recognition they sought online, women frequently felt emboldened to raise the topic with family, friends, and others offline.[36]

Seeking a Ritual

A major theme that appears again and again in discussions of pain around abortion and other pregnancy losses is the lack of rituals in American society. When a pregnancy loss of any type occurs, it seems that a large number of Americans feel culturally unprepared and bereft of indigenous religious resources to help them deal with their pain. Pregnancy loss precipitates a tremendous feeling of powerlessness (among other negative emotions) and the American response seems to be an overwhelming desire to regain power by some sort of activity, along with a frustration that there seems to be nothing available to do. It is here that rituals like *mizuko kuyō* appear to offer a society with little history of ritualization of pregnancy loss a way to actively deal with grief.[37]

This attitude is expressed clearly in Sukie Miller's post–child and –pregnancy loss manual *Finding Hope When a Child Dies: What Other Cultures Can Teach Us*:

> What defines ritual and distinguishes it from other big life events is that ritual can remove us for a little while from the everyday world to the world of the spirit, from the mundane world to the sacred one.
>
> For many people in many places in the world, ritual is actually *part* of the everyday world. Throughout Japan, Jizo figures representing the ritual for the unborn are visible in private homes and public places....

In the West we treat rituals differently.... We may enjoy our rituals, but they don't necessarily connect us with the world where the spirit lives.

But in places where ritual is natural to the people, where it is steeped in the tradition of the people, where its power to move us from the mundane world to the world of the spirit is well understood, it has great healing properties. And for families who have lost a child, rituals to help that child on her journey to the next world and, later, rituals to keep her happy in that world are the answer to "What can I do to help my child?"... How fortunate are those cultures that incorporate such helping rituals as the Yoruba have for their twins, the Japanese have for their unborn, and the Hindus have for their children who die violently.... These rituals contain a certain wisdom that bears thinking about, and perhaps there is a way for us to translate them for our own lives—maybe through our churches and temples and communities and traditions that are authentic to us.[38]

As Miller sees it, rituals like *mizuko kuyō* offer their participants a way to *do something* for the deceased child or fetus, and in gaining that ability to take action, performing such rituals empowers those who feel powerless in the face of loss.

Ritual theorist Ronald Grimes discusses *mizuko kuyō* in his book *Deeply Into the Bone: Re-Inventing Rites of Passage.* While noting Kim Kluger-Bell's participation in an American Zen water baby ceremony (cited earlier in the previous chapter), he suspects that "Jizo is probably too removed from the experiences of North American women for statues of him to be effective."[39] Perhaps; perhaps not. It may be that Jizō will indeed prove too foreign a figure for many American women seeking a focus for pregnancy loss grief. But so far the indications are that Jizō and *mizuko kuyō* have tremendous appeal to many non-Buddhist Americans, if for no other reason than that Jizō has few if any competitors for the attention of grieving post-abortion/-miscarriage women. As the Jizō movement described in chapter 2 continues to expand and promote veneration of the bodhisattva in America, Jizō has the potential to become a crossover figure, perhaps as an ecumenical figure worshipped across religious boundaries, or perhaps assimilated to another figure (such as St. Jude) in a syncretistic mode similar to Vodou or Santería.[40] Such speculations may not be too farfetched; such a phenomenon can arise naturally when figures and symbols from one religious system are used to explain those of another, as in this passage from a participant in a forum on grieving lost children:

I found that in the Buddhist faith, they have a bodhisattva called Jizo and there are large Jizo gardens throughout Japan and other parts of the world—a couple of them in the US—where bereaved families are welcome anytime. *Jizo is a little like Saint Christopher in Western Systems.* Jizo is a protector and guardian of bereaved parents, pregnant women, children, travelers. Jizo is called upon in everyday life, acknowledging that any transition can be exciting, but also dangerous, and may call forth grief.[41]

The beginnings of such transreligious appreciation of Kuan-yin bodhisattva are already apparent due to the related Kuan-yin movement described in chapter 2, and such appropriations of the Buddhist "goddess of mercy" may pave the way for additional Buddhist figures such as Jizō.

There is considerable evidence that after encountering *mizuko kuyō*, either directly or through the descriptions of others, non-Buddhist American women are actually performing their own pregnancy loss rituals.[42] As discussed above, American Jew Peggy Orenstein's 2002 *New York Times* article "Mourning My Miscarriage," describing her performance of a *mizuko kuyō* at a Tokyo temple, was widely discussed and is approvingly cited by dozens of articles and Web sites dealing with pregnancy loss. The article even appears as a resource for women in the companion Web site for the latest edition of the classic feminist workbook *Our Bodies, Ourselves.* The blog Flying Standby chronicles the travels of a young midwestern couple who flew to Tokyo in 2006, in part so they could perform a *mizuko kuyō* for their miscarried child.[43] This followed in the wake of their attempt to find a Zen temple in Cleveland to perform a water baby ceremony; neither of them is Buddhist (fig. 6.1).[44]

Flying to Japan to perform *mizuko kuyō* is a dramatic act and an uncommon one. Much more frequent are private ceremonies carried out at home by non-Buddhists after encountering the concept of *mizuko kuyō* through one of the resources described in chapter 5. Many pregnancy loss bulletin boards contain messages from women who announce their intention to participate in, or their previous participation in, *mizuko kuyō*-derived rituals:

> Sunnmama: I lost a pregnancy in November—14 wks pg but the babe was only about 6 wks. A week ago, I came across the remembrance/ritual for me in a book. It is part of the Japanese Buddhist tradition for any being lost prior to birth (thru miscarriage or stillbirth or termination). The family buys a small statue called a Mizuko Jizo, and then the parents hand stitch a small garment for the statue from red fabric: a hat, or a bib, or (my choice) a cape. The parents can spend time adding as much detail to the garment as they please. Traditionally, this would go on an altar in a temple, but we are not actually Buddhist so will simply be paying homage this tradition in our own home and our own way. Since

FIGURE 6.1. *Mizuko* Jizō at Zōjōji, including one adopted by an American couple who traveled to Tokyo after the woman suffered a miscarriage.

> dh is a potter/sculptor, he is going to make the statue for us [smiley face icon with hearts]. Then I will handstitch the garment. Making this small tribute to our lost baby with our own hands will be healing for us, I believe. Anyway, I wanted to add this ritual as it has been helpful for us. Maybe it will help someone else, as well. Hugs to all those mourning losses [smiley face icon hugging another smiley face]…
>
> BCmamaof5: Oh! I LOVE that idea. That is so beautiful. I think I'll ask a potter friend of mine to make something like that. Thank you for sharing.[45]

Post-abortion and other pregnancy loss support specialists are now emerging both on a professional level and as informal healers ministering to communities of women. Many of these specialists tell their clients to perform *mizuko kuyō*, or they offer it themselves as independent ritualists.[46] In other cases, post–pregnancy loss rituals are merely one part of a larger, eclectic range of services provided by unaffiliated ritual specialists. For example, Santa Monica–based "bodywork" practitioner Sarah Harper has set up various altars on her retreats. One is a Jizō altar for children who have died at any stage, including prebirth.[47] There seems to be an echo of the independent spiritualists described by Helen Hardacre, who promote and perform *mizuko kuyō* in Japan outside of a traditional Buddhist framework. Perhaps it is not going too far to suggest that therapists and "healers" (many of whom display a clear debt to psychology and the "therapeutic gospel") in America occupy a niche served by spiritualists and similar ritualists in Japan. This is in addition to the participation of non-Buddhist women in water baby ceremonies at various American Zen temples already discussed in chapter 4. Also, it seems that some of the other post–pregnancy loss rituals that have emerged in the last twenty-five years that do not draw on Buddhism explicitly have in some way been stimulated by *mizuko kuyō*. For example, charismatic Catholic Jesuit priests Matthew Linn and Dennis Linn have written extensively about their healing ministry that includes prayer and laying on of hands for post-abortion women (and visualized healing of the aborted fetuses). They cite *mizuko kuyō* practices in their book *Healing the Greatest Hurt*, seeming to indicate that the Japanese practice has influenced or possibly even stimulated their own.

To summarize, through the evidence presented in this and previous chapters, it is clear that unknown numbers of *non-Buddhist* Americans are now participating in *mizuko kuyō*. Some are participating in water baby ceremonies at convert Zen centers in the United States. Others are participating in *mizuko kuyō* at temples in Japan. Some are participating through the aegis of a therapist or a nondenominational "healer."[48] And many are performing their own private *mizuko kuyō* rites at home, either alone or with those closest to them, such as spouse, parents, and friends.

Furthermore, there is evidence that participation in *mizuko kuyō* rituals by non-Buddhist Americans goes back at least to the 1970s, and seems to have increased considerably over time, especially from the mid-1990s onward. This increase seems tied to changes within American Zen Buddhism I described in chapters 2–4 (especially the expanding availability of the ritual at more sites), greater circulation of information on *mizuko kuyō* through key publications—both academic and nonacademic—in the 1990s, and the emergence of post–pregnancy loss grief as a significant object of psychotherapeutic attention in the 1990s. Finally, with more American Zen priests intending to offer water baby rituals at their temples, growing interest in the ritual by independent ritualists, and the expanding number of Internet-enabled households, self-publishing programs (such as blogs), and pregnancy/pregnancy-loss dedicated Web sites, it seems reasonable to predict that *mizuko kuyō* will become a topic of even wider discussion and greater participation by non-Buddhist Americans in the future. This increase in the visibility of the issue of religious ritualization of pregnancy loss may stimulate the creation of new pregnancy loss rituals in non-Buddhist religions and greater promotion of those that already exist. Thus part of the process of Americanization of Buddhism may be how component parts are extracted and lose all overt Buddhist ties, becoming acculturated by being fully absorbed into Christianity and other mainstream traditions.

Despite this growing participation in American *mizuko kuyō*, there is often considerable ambiguity in the sources about how exactly the ritual provides healing. This ambiguity appears to arise in some cases because the writer has not thoroughly thought through the logic of healing and ritual. The relationship between religion, ritual, and healing is likewise often obscure in these sources. Sometimes religion seems simply to be a default arena within which ritual occurs—ritual is needed, the writer perceives ritual as usually taking place in religious settings, so religion is needed. There is perhaps a sort of spiritual pragmatism here, something a little different from ideological pluralism. Americans seem to be seeking pregnancy loss rituals and will take them wherever they find them. Since Buddhism offers such rituals they are easily picked up for discussion and possible participation. That these rituals originate in Buddhism seems to be of no real consequence: if Hinduism, say, or Judaism offered such resources, they might well be appropriated at approximately the same rate.

Alternately, it is possible to ask what it is about Buddhism that makes it seem available for appropriation by non-Buddhists. While a certain number of people would certainly appropriate rituals from any source, others might be slower to take rituals from religions that seem too inaccessible, extreme, or otherwise negative in some way. There is a sense in these sources that Buddhism as a religious tradition is open to outsiders and can be partially or selectively participated in without full adherence or conversion. Many commentators explicitly frame Buddhism in terms of open-armed compassion rather than boundary-drawing dogma, and as driven by ritual and practice rather than doctrine or rule. Appropriators present *mizuko kuyō* divorced from a wider Buddhist worldview of no-God, no-self, endless past lives driven by karma, the four noble truths and eightfold path, and so on. The role of the priest as the usual ritual actor—so clearly demonstrated by the survey of Japanese-American temples in chapter 1—is omitted, such that lay non-Buddhists can perform *mizuko kuyō*, and fetal spirit attacks are rarely mentioned as a concept, let alone an actual possibility. All of this renders *mizuko kuyō* more accessible to a new audience. While stressing that it is Japan that acts as a model for America, many appropriators simultaneously depict Buddhism as a universal system that is not linked to any one ethnicity or country. Thus, although post–pregnancy loss rituals or beliefs in other cultures are sometimes noted alongside *mizuko kuyō*, it is the Buddhist ritual that is then most frequently recommended as a template for Americans to emulate. It is relevant to note that Buddhism appears to enjoy a positive reputation among non-Buddhist Americans. As sociologists of American religion Robert Wuthnow and Wendy Cadge report, 55 percent of the American populace has had some form of contact with Buddhists, and 82 percent of those who have been exposed to Buddhists rated these experiences as positive.[49]

Considering further the nature of the alleged healing in the performance of these rituals, one may ask who is being healed: the mother or the child? Nearly all the sources I have encountered, both pro-life and pro-choice, which advocate *mizuko kuyō*-type rituals are clear that the ritual is to be performed for the benefit of the mother.[50] It is she who is in pain and needs healing, a healing that is apparently accomplished by surfacing suppressed or silenced emotional trauma and releasing it through the mechanism of ritual action. This conceptualization closely mirrors that of psychotherapy, wherein unconscious or suppressed feeling and compulsions are brought to light and worked out, through dialogue with the therapist or other means. The possible feelings or plight of the aborted or miscarried fetus are rarely mentioned as justifications for the ritual. They do sometimes surface, however, in the accounts of women who have actually performed private *mizuko kuyō*. While all such accounts include personal healing of the mother as a primary motivation, some also express the desire to conduct the ritual as a way to do something for the child. Most often, this is framed as acknowledgment: by apologizing or publicly declaring that the lost child is/was real, some post–pregnancy loss mothers appear to believe they benefit the fetus. The metaphysics of such benefits are rarely explicit, and the impression is strong that the women themselves do not hold systematic theological opinions about what is happening in the ritual. It does seem, though, that the Japanese idea of actually transferring merit to the *mizuko* or calling on Jizō for direct intervention—such that the *mizuko* is sprung from suffering imprisonment and sent on to a better place—is usually absent. Rather, the benefits conferred are vague, such as "honoring" the lost one, "saying goodbye," and so on.[51]

Conclusion

In his discussion of "tactics"—practices that run against the grain of dominant modes in a society—French social theorist Michel de Certeau noted that "other regions give us back what our culture has excluded from its discourse."[52] There is an ironic form of Orientalism taking place in these therapeutic appropriations of *mizuko kuyō*. Classical Orientalism identified the "mystic East" with superstition, sensualism, and degraded practices such as idol worship.[53] This construction allowed the West to seem rational, refined, organized, and a bastion of pure religion; and, not incidentally, helped justify the military and economic exploitation of Asia. But with the appropriation of *mizuko kuyō*, a second kind of Orientalism provides America with precisely what it is believed to be missing: compassionate spirituality, nonjudgmental savior figures, and ceremonial practices for an angry, divided, bereaved society lacking in healing ritual. The supposed weaknesses of a foreign region in the previous era are now its strengths, at least in the imaginations of some Americans convinced that their country (and often themselves) are in need of help. The process comes full circle as the earlier characterization of Asian cultures as "feminine"—originally a negative value judgment—becomes a positive valuation that provides Western women with gender-related rituals that their own lopsided masculine culture can't offer.

In the conclusion to the previous chapter, I examined William LaFleur's contention that Americans might learn a more pragmatic approach to abortion issues from the Japanese. Knowledge of *mizuko kuyō* appears to have little ability to sway hardened partisans of the abortion cultural war away from their polarized views. Rather, they typically appropriate the ritual in ways that reflect positively on their own side and negatively on their opponents. Nevertheless, as this chapter demonstrates, there are some who wish to use *mizuko kuyō* as a balm rather than a weapon. The key is whether the appropriator is focused on abortion per se or on the effects of the battle over abortion. Neither side budges on abortion—it remains a fundamental right or a horrible tragedy—but both pro-life and pro-choice advocates desire a less fractured society and a more mannered political process. Some, therefore, look to ritual actions as an arena that offers a different way to approach the subject, one that could potentially include participants from both sides. These range from "Christianized *mizuko kuyō*" to simple funerals for the unborn, but all share a common stimulus in exposure to the practice of *mizuko kuyō*.

We should be clear on what is not being adopted by these Buddhist appropriators: a Buddhist worldview. Few American cultural warriors seem willing to accept the Japanese Buddhist understanding of the unborn as life-in-development, neither fully a person nor simply tissue. Though multiple commentators discuss the Buddhist perspective of life flowing progressively into the fetus and the idea that a *mizuko* can be returned to the world of the spirits to be retrieved later, few seem to seriously reorient their worldview so as to accommodate this conceptualization of pregnancy. For pro-life Christians, the aborted or miscarried fetus remains a person from the moment of conception, and intentional or other terminations of the pregnancy typically send the soul of the fetus to heaven to be with God. For pro-choice Christians, Jews, and others, there is often some ambiguity about when precisely the fetus becomes a person or acquires a soul, but it is still typically thought of as occurring around a particular point of time, rather than in gradual stages. Those who most approximate the Japanese idea of progressive in utero development toward personhood are pro-choice advocates who take a purely secular or scientific approach—for these commentators, the issue is frequently framed in terms of the development of the nervous system and degrees of consciousness. But these are still far from the Buddhist views. The idea of return to a nebulous state of prelife and subsequent rebirth is rarely espoused.

There are only two subsets of Buddhist appropriators wherein some significant adoption of Japanese Buddhist views on pregnancy occurs. The minority of women who are basically unchurched but open to religious ideas occasionally do seem to appropriate not only the ritual but the contextual worldview of reincarnation as well. Lacking a strong commitment to a particular religious tradition, they appear in some cases willing to consider Buddhist views that offer comfort in the wake of pregnancy loss. Another subset are people who are involved in New Age or similar alternative religions or spiritual paths. New Age, neopaganism, and related movements are typically sympathetic to views and practices from a wide range of traditions, and Buddhism features heavily in some of these communities. Since many of these people are already involved in some aspect of Buddhism, such as meditation, they might best be categorized as Buddhist sympathizers rather than non-Buddhists.

So part of LaFleur's vision has—sporadically, in some places—begun to come true: non-Buddhist Americans are appropriating Japanese Buddhist rituals and adapting them to their own uses, and some persons concerned about the casualties of the culture war are exploring whether *mizuko kuyō* could offer a solution. At the same time, another part of that vision is nearly unrealized and seems to show little potential for appropriation: non-Buddhist Americans overall show little interest in adopting the concurrent worldview of life as a developing continuum and as capable of being terminated and restarted with a later pregnancy. This raises the question of what it is that actually leads to the lack of polarization in Japanese society over abortion: Is it because they have rituals of mourning and propitiation for their *mizuko*, or because they hold widely shared views that do not put women and fetuses on equal footing and that frame pregnancy loss as only a temporary obstacle on the road to new life? If the answer is the latter, then *mizuko kuyō* may ultimately prove to be an ineffective treatment for the affliction of abortion-related social malaise.[54]

There is one other aspect of LaFleur's study to be dealt with. In his concluding remarks, LaFleur suggests that Americans might do well to "explore the possibility that rituals such as those for mizuko may have a positive therapeutic function."[55] As I have shown, many Americans have begun to undertake precisely this exploration. And many non-Buddhist women indeed express clear beliefs that participation in *mizuko*-type rituals, or even just exposure to the terminology and idea of such rituals, is healing in some fashion. Given the enthusiasm about *mizuko kuyō* by women who are dealing with pregnancy losses, this form of Buddhist appropriation might continue and expand.

In fact, with the emergence of non-Buddhist participation at American Zen water baby ceremonies and the performance of private *mizuko kuyō* by some women, we could potentially be seeing the restructuring of one strand of American religion along lines similar to Japan. In Japan, Shinto rituals structure many life cycle rituals, but Buddhism is frequented resorted to as the specialist religion for death. This is because Shinto often sees death as polluted and prefers to avoid anything associated with death or dead bodies. In the American situation, large numbers of non-Buddhists cannot or choose not to seek ritual recognition of pregnancy loss in their natal traditions. One outcome could be the emergence of Buddhist rituals—both at temples and in homes—as the commonplace resort for otherwise non-Buddhist women in the wake of pregnancy loss. This ritual compartmentalization would be a new configuration of America's growing religious diversity. Currently, this diversity has created many largely separate communities or subcultures that provide religious services for their own members. But Buddhists may develop an alternative configuration in the ongoing process of Americanization, wherein they market services for clients who belong to outside groups that fail to provide such services. There is an old saying that in Japan one is born Shinto, raised Confucian, and dies Buddhist. Perhaps the future of American religion for some will naturally evolve so that one is born Christian and dies Christian, but, in the case of pregnancy loss, one mourns as a Buddhist.

Postscript

"Where Is Buddhism?"

In fourteenth-century Japan, famed monk Gennō Shinshō helped domesticate the recently arrived school of Zen by exorcising troublesome local spirits. One legend describes the "killing stone" of Mount Nasu, a rock inhabited by an extremely powerful and malevolent ghost who originally arrived from across the ocean. No one could come close to the rock without receiving harm; to touch or even just to glance at the stone could lead to death. But Gennō refused to look away, and he pacified the entity with a Buddhist ritual, eliminating the spirit's frightening aspects. He carved the shapeless rock into a statue of Jizō, which became an object of widespread worship as a protector.[1]

In twenty-first century America, some priests—especially women—are domesticating Zen through engagement with the powerful forces swirling around abortion and other pregnancy losses, forces they see as threatening women's health and happiness. In the process, they are removing the threatening nature of Japanese *mizuko* ideas and offering rituals in an often religiously taboo area. By reshaping the menacing weight of American abortion issues to reveal the nurturing presence of Jizō hidden within the pain, these Zen priests are attempting to transform shame and loss into hope and healing. At the same time, non-Buddhist interpreters are carving the rock of *mizuko kuyō* to reveal very different faces of the ritual, from a rite that shows the universality of post-abortion pain to the utter provinciality of various religious ideas about life and death.

We now come to the end of the twisting journey on which Jizō bodhisattva has guided us from Japan to Asian communities in the New World, on into white convert Buddhist groups, and beyond to the fields of battle in the American culture wars and the shoals of grief over lost pregnancies. In the process we have seen many contested meanings applied to a Buddhist ritual, for a variety of different ends. It divides the Japanese-American Buddhist community over issues of superstition and money at the same time that it brings American pro-choice and pro-life foes together to find a way of reconciliation. It provides an arena for male evangelical ministers to excoriate women who have had abortions and a site for female Buddhist priests to offer solace and healing to Christian women seeking comfort they cannot find elsewhere. It moves American temples closer to Japanese religious norms and is subjected to a process of thorough adaptation. Each is a piece in the puzzle of one Buddhist ritual's process of Americanization.

With *mizuko kuyō* as a lens to view American religious phenomena, many unexpected angles of sight come into focus. From one angle, convert Zen seems rather more like Japanese and Japanese-American Buddhism than expected, with a host of overlooked rituals uncovered and much community attention paid to saviors, spirits, ceremonies, and emotions unrelated to the rigors of formal seated meditation. From another angle, water baby ceremonies most resemble not those of a Japanese or Japanese-American Zen temple but rather those of a new religious movement: only the Risshō Kōsei-kai services include women manufacturing their own offerings, meeting in a group, voicing their hidden feelings over pregnancy loss, sitting in supportive circles, and fully participating in all elements of a ceremony that takes well over an hour.

Again, from one angle Japanese-American Buddhist temples seem to move toward ever-greater acculturation as they use pews, lecterns, English, original American liturgy, and other elements unknown in Japan. Yet from another sightline we see that new arrivals from Japan bring previously absent rituals and perspectives into these temples, which still deal in a thoroughly Japanese material culture—formal main worship halls, votive plaques, wooden tablets, memorial plaques, columbaria, good luck charms—virtually unknown to converts to Zen in America.

Stories from these communities suggest that acculturation of Buddhism (and perhaps other religions as well) in America is a never completed project, a process that continually slides back and forth along a spectrum rather than one that moves confidently forward from a beginning point called "tradition" toward a destination called "American innovation." One reason for this is that transnational ties continually introduce foreign innovations and practices to American religious communities, even those that settled in the United States prior to the twentieth century. These stories also reveal that Americanization is often the product of ignorance rather than conscious adaptation, and that the Buddhist contribution to rituals and ideas in some Zen communities is rivaled or even bested by influences from psychotherapy, feminism, and other elements of white middle-class American culture. This points to potential weaknesses in our typologies. The "ethnic" in the category "ethnic Buddhism" seems justifiable when it refers to how certain practitioners understand themselves: as Buddhist by ethnicity, rather than by individual belief. But when it becomes a racial signifier—as in "ethnic" versus "white" Buddhism—it breaks down, for how can we allege that Japanese ethnic influences are greater in Japanese-American Zen than European-American ethnic influences in convert Zen? What is whiteness if not yet another ethnicity? Convert Zen is not a return to the Buddhism of Shakyamuni (or Dōgen) as some scholars have suggested but yet another flavor of ethnic Buddhism, one created largely by and for Americans of white cultural background.

Looking at *mizuko kuyō* from within and beyond the confines of Buddhist discourse demonstrates important aspects of ritual in the abstract. Ritual studies has increasingly favored the term "performance" in recent years, yet ritual is not only performed: it is also imagined, rhetorically appropriated, and painted in prose with no intention of actual practice.[2] As it turns out, other people's rituals, reading about rituals you never carry out yourself, and discussion of rituals all apparently produce results without the need for ritual enactment. It may be that on the whole for Americans the main effects of *mizuko kuyō* are derived not from transformations alleged to occur in actually experiencing these rituals, but from the high amounts of activity put into their imaginative production and the alternate worldviews they support. Ritual, it seems, is about so much more (and less) than performance.

For scholars of American Buddhism, I believe this study demonstrates the need to pay attention to non-Buddhists, including opponents of Buddhism and those who strategically appropriate Buddhism, in the story of Buddhism's ongoing transmission to America. The development of significant Buddhist communities within the United States has not removed the necessity of attending to how the large non-Buddhist community selectively imports, depicts, and adapts elements of Buddhism. Put another way, American Buddhists are not the only producers of Buddhism for Americans, and it would be unwise to assume that the opinions and practices of non-Buddhists ceased to be an essential part of the story at the end of the nineteenth century.

I also believe this project reveals the need for scholars of American religions outside of Buddhism, especially those who focus on Christianities of the United States, to give attention to Buddhism and other smaller religious groups. The number of Buddhists in America need not be large for Buddhism to make an impact on American Christianity. Just as scholars of Buddhism beyond Asia cannot hope to understand their subjects without knowledge of the ways that non-Buddhist culture directly and indirectly shapes the form of American Buddhism, so too researchers concerned with larger American religious groups cannot afford to overlook how minority traditions influence discussion and practice within the dominant groups. Significantly, we see in this study an example of how the post-Protestant era of American religion holds not only perils for a Christianity that must share the playing field but also opportunities: even fundamentalist and other conservative Christian groups have learned to employ non-Christian religions strategically in the fight to maintain their hold on power. Buddhism is thus for these groups not only a threat but a tool that has been provided by the modern religious diversity of the United States.

In the closing paragraph of the anthology *Critical Terms for the Study of Buddhism*, Marilyn Ivy points toward an insight of significance for this study:

> When former Zen teacher Toni Packer asks her students to listen
> to birds outside the practice hall and imitate their cries, where is
> Buddhism? When the Dalai Lama says, "My religion is kindness,"
> where is Buddhism then? Where is Buddhism in the practice of
> radical attention proffered by contemporary mindfulness meditation
> teachers? Perhaps we should talk about post-Buddhism instead, an
> amalgam of therapy, breath awareness, and mindfulness technique
> suited for the inhabitants of postmodernity. Yet as in "post"-anything,
> the *post* still bears the trace of that which has been superseded: post-
> Buddhism is still post-*Buddhism*.[3]

Japanese-American temples are post-Japan. Zen converts are post-Christian, post-Jewish, or post-secular. American Christians who make offerings to Jizō in their backyards are performing a ritual that has arguably become post-Buddhist. Yet the past of each of these is at least as important as their present, and traces remain that have implications for how each will continue to develop. Thus Ivy provides the counterpoint to Orsi's opening observation in the introduction of how religious elements may become freely circulating signifiers, detached from their specific cultural grounds and available for uses never foreseen in their original context. Orsi's view is right: *mizuko kuyō*'s entrance into each situation brings about alterations in the ritual's form and meaning. But Ivy is correct as well: *mizuko kuyō* also carries the "scent" of Buddhism into new arenas that will be reshaped in subtle or overt ways by this contact with the world of Japanese Buddhist post–pregnancy loss rituals. Crossing over into Asian communities of the New World, convert Zen, or Christian America does not completely dispel the karma of these rituals inherited from Japan, which may ripen with implications for their communities that neither they nor scholars of American religion can predict. For there is a footnote to Gennō's story: some sources claim that the rock continues to emit poisonous vapors even today. When dealing with forces as complex as Buddhism and as potent as life and loss, even the greatest ritualists may find that their powers to adapt and transmute them are only partial and conflicted; and the softly smiling Jizō, patiently waiting within the rock, may yet hide deeper surprises for those who come to it for aid.

Appendix

Convert Zen Centers Performing
Mizuko Kuyō

The centers in list A have performed *mizuko kuyō*-based ceremonies for pregnancy losses multiple times. Those in list B have performed a single ceremony as of February 2008. The leaders listed are those who have most often performed these ceremonies at each center; however, many centers have additional priests who have also acted as water baby ritual leaders, and the individuals mentioned here may not currently be active in providing water baby ceremonies (Robert Aitken, for example, is retired, though he continues to offer some religious instruction). Various centers listed here hail from the Suzuki, Maezumi, Kapleau, Aitken, and other major lineages, and thus are connected to the majority of Japanese-descended Zen temples in America.

List A

Chicago Zen Center (Evanston, IL)—Sevan Ross
Clouds in Water Zen Center (St. Paul, MN)—Judith Ragir
Diamond Sangha (Honolulu, HI)—Robert Aitken
Empty Hand Zen Center (New Rochelle, NY)—Susan Jion Postal
Floating Zendo (San Jose, CA)—Angie Boissevain
Goat-in-the-Road Zendo (Muir Beach, CA)—Yvonne Rand
Great Vow Monastery (Clatskanie, OR)—Jan Chozen Bays
Green Gulch Farm Zen Center [San Francisco Zen Center] (Muir Beach, CA)—Yvonne Rand

Rochester Zen Center (Rochester, NY)—Amala Wrightson
Santa Cruz Zen Center (Santa Cruz, CA)—Katherine Thanas
Vermont Zen Center (Shelburne, VT)—Sunyana Graef
Zen Center of Los Angeles (Los Angeles, CA)—Wendy Egyoku Nakao

List B

Berkeley Buddhist Monastery (Berkeley, CA)—Yvonne Rand
Jikoji Zen Retreat Center (Los Gatos, CA)—Angie Boissevain
Zen Community of Oak Park (Oak Park, IL)—Robert Joshin Althouse
Zen Mountain Monastery (Mt. Tremper, NY)—Jan Chozen Bays

Notes

INTRODUCTION

1. Readers interested in that project may wish to consult Jeff Wilson, "Aesthetics of American Zen: Tradition, Adaptation, and Innovation in the Rochester Zen Center Garden," *Japan Studies Review* 9 (2005): 101–114. The epigraph is from Harvey Whitehouse's *Modes of Religiosity: A Cognitive Theory of Religious Transformation* (Walnut Creek, CA: AltaMira Press, 2004), 4.

2. Robert A. Orsi, *Between Heaven and Earth: The Religious Worlds People Make and the Scholars Who Study Them* (Princeton, NJ: Princeton University Press, 2005), 130.

3. I should clarify how I use the term "ritual" in this book. Rituals are embodied practices that orient practitioners to themselves, other participants, outsiders, and to the sacralized "other" hypothesized by religious believers as being holy (note, though, that in some cases the "other" is actually the deepest level of the "self"—which still functions, nonetheless, as a sacred "entity" beyond the experience of the everyday self). Rituals are primarily performative and expressive in nature—they enact, bring about, or express states of being that are considered important by religious practitioners. The actual gestures, postures, and proceedings of rituals occur within a predetermined format, although the outline may be rough and the ritual may be newly invented, rather than traditional. While rituals are practices, their role in religions goes well beyond mere performance—rituals are also written about and discussed, imagined, and opposed, all of which are themselves important forms of religious activity. In some cases, I speak herein of "ceremonies," a particular form of ritual that is more specifically corporate in nature, with liturgical and frequently musical components, and often mediated by religious clergy.

4. William R. LaFleur, *Liquid Life: Abortion and Buddhism in Japan* (Princeton, NJ: Princeton University Press, 1992); Helen Hardacre, *Marketing the Menacing Fetus in Japan* (Berkeley: University of California Press, 1997).

5. The Sanskrit name for Jizō is Kshitigarbha (Earth Womb/Store).

6. Zhiru Ng, "The Formation and Development of the Dizang Cult in Medieval China," PhD dissertation, University of Arizona, 2000.

7. Hsuan Hua, *The Sutra of the Past Vows of Earth Store Bodhisattva* (New York: Buddhist Text Translation Society, 1974). A sutra is a Buddhist scripture attributed to the historical Buddha. Karma is the impersonal force that arises from moral or immoral actions and leads to corresponding good or ill fortune.

8. Patricia Yamada, "A Friend in Need: The Bodhisattva Jizo," *Japanese Religions* 16 (1991): 83.

9. Hardacre, *Marketing the Menacing Fetus,* 52–54.

10. Meredith Underwood, "Strategies of Survival: Women, Abortion, and Popular Religion in Contemporary Japan," *Journal of the American Academy of Religion* 67, 4 (1999): 758–766; Elizabeth Harrison, "*Mizuko Kuyō:* the Re-production of the Dead in Contemporary Japan," in *Religion in Japan: Arrows to Heaven and Earth,* ed. P. F. Kornicki and I. J. McMullen 250–266 (Cambridge: Cambridge University Press, 1996).

11. William R. LaFleur, "Buddhism and Abortion: The Way to Memorialize One's Mizuko," in *Religions of Japan in Practice,* ed. George J. Tanabe Jr. (Princeton, NJ: Princeton University Press, 1999), 194 (italics in original).

12. Hardacre, *Marketing the Menacing Fetus,* 81–91; 166.

13. LaFleur, *Buddhism and Abortion,* 194.

14. William LaFleur, a leading scholar of *mizuko kuyō,* believes that the practice dates back much further into the Japanese past. He suggests that historical data is lacking because it was not a formal tradition and tended rather to be spontaneous actions of grieving women, akin to the current practice of dressing Jizo statues. Some Japanese scholars agree, and there are suggestive traces that go back at least to the Edo (1600–1868) period. I find his account plausible, yet the lack of hard evidence makes it difficult to draw a definitive conclusion. On the other hand, Helen Hardacre's study of how *mizuko kuyō* came to occupy the prominent public position it has enjoyed over the past several decades is meticulously documented. Ultimately, the exact origin of *mizuko kuyō* is relatively immaterial for this study. What matters here is that the ritual eventually "went public" in a major way following the legalization of abortion in Japan in 1948, a fact of no real scholarly dispute.

15. Jamie Hubbard, "Embarrassing Superstition, Doctrine, and the Study of New Religious Movements," *Journal of the American Academy of Religion* 66, 1 (1998): 63.

16. Hardacre, *Marketing the Menacing Fetus,* 63–65; 166–167.

17. Ibid., 5–6 (italics in original).

18. Ibid., 78–80. In a twist on Hardacre's allegations, I found that sonograms of fetuses are now left by some Japanese women in places designated for *mizuko kuyō.*

19. Underwood, "Strategies of Survival."

20. Brief of 281 American Historians as Amici Curiae, Supporting Appellees. *Webster v. Reproductive Health Services,* No. 88–605, Supreme Court of the United States, October Term, 1988.

21. Before abortion developed into a major twentieth century religious issue, it was prefigured in some ways by the furor over birth control. Leslie Tentler in her book *Catholics and Contraception* describes how beginning around 1875, but especially accelerating in the 1920s, Catholic priests in America used birth control as a litmus test of differentiation from and superiority to Protestants. This was also the period when modern forms of birth control were being developed and disseminated in the United States. For these Catholic priests, birth control was one of the most monstrous of sins, a crime against God both because it was a direct repudiation of divine will and, for some, because it resulted in the nonbirth of additional Catholics (this nonbirth was even rhetorically transformed into murder by some particularly righteous firebrands). Branded "race suicide," birth control became the paradigmatic reproductive issue for American Catholics, through which the abortion debate would eventually be approached later in the century. It should be mentioned here that abortion too sometimes appeared alongside birth control in the sermons of these mission priests. See Leslie Tentler, *Catholics and Contraception: An American History* (Ithaca, NY: Cornell University Press, 2004).

22. Tom Davis, *Sacred Work: Planned Parenthood and Its Clergy Alliances* (New Brunswick, NJ: Rutgers University Press, 2005).

23. Eva R. Ruben, ed., *The Abortion Controversy: A Documentary History* (Westport, CT: Greenwood, 1994).

24. Christian Smith, *American Evangelicalism: Embattled and Thriving* (Chicago: University of Chicago Press, 1998).

25. Ruben, *Abortion Controversy.*

26. Indeed, many Catholics refused to believe that a woman would willingly choose to have an abortion, preferring instead to represent it as something her father, husband, or boyfriend pressured her into against her natural instincts.

27. See, for instance, the National Memorial for the Unborn, in Chattanooga, TN (www.memorialfortheunborn.org).

28. Emily Bazelton, "Is There a Post-Abortion Syndrome?" *New York Times Magazine*, 21 January 2007.

29. Many of these consultants were interviewed multiple times for this project. Several important interviews were also conducted by e-mail exchange or fax when other methods could not be arranged.

CHAPTER I

1. The epigraph is from Cuevas and Stone's introduction to their edited collection *The Buddhist Dead: Practices, Discourses, Representations* (Honolulu: University of Hawaii Press, 2007), 3.

2. Kanai Shokai (bishop, Los Angeles Nichiren Shu Buddhist Temple), interview by author, 13 February 2007, at Los Angeles Nichiren Shu Buddhist Temple.

3. William Briones (priest, Los Angeles Hompa Hongwanji Buddhist Temple), interview by author, 23 January 2007.

4. In Jōdo Shinshū doctrine, the dead have already passed on to the Pure Land and require no further ritualization. In orthodox Shin thought, therefore, funerals only serve to comfort and instruct those who knew the deceased. See the discussion in *Jodo*

Shinshu: A Guide (p. 137), produced by the Hongwanji International Center, an official wing of the largest Jōdo Shinshū denomination. Naturally, individual Jōdo Shinshū practitioners have their own opinions on these matters. Most non-Shin Buddhist funerals in Japan are designed to benefit the deceased through posthumous ordination and merit transference.

5. Miyoshi Nobuko (priest, Higashi Honganji Buddhist Temple), interview by author, 10 January 2007, at Higashi Honganji Buddhist Temple, Los Angeles.

6. Doctrinal opposition does not always translate into absolute abstention in practice, of course. Helen Hardacre, in *Marketing the Menacing Fetus in Japan*, reports that she uncovered a significant minority of Jōdo Shinshū temples that were willing to perform some version of *mizuko kuyō*. Likewise, though most temples disclaimed it, I did on occasion discover Shin temples in Japan that either acknowledged performing rites for *mizuko* or displayed clear evidence of such rites (such as *tōba* inscribed "*mizuko no rei*"). Some of this is in line with the general Shin attitude of occasionally using *mizuko kuyō* as a "skillful means" of providing correct dogma to petitioners. But some of it is simply a matter of particular priests performing rituals that are officially forbidden, either because they hold views in opposition to those condoned by the head temple or because they seek to bring in money (or both). Perhaps the most fascinating case of Shin encounter with the omnipresence of *mizuko kuyō* in Japan that I uncovered was at the honorary tomb for Shinran (founder of Jōdo Shinshū) on Kōyasan, the great mountaintop Shingon Shū Buddhist complex. Surrounding his tomb were hundreds of *mizuko* Jizō. Two possibilities present themselves as explanations. It may be that some Shin practitioners, aware of their denomination's doctrinal opposition to *mizuko kuyō*, seek out alternative sites to petition their founder for help after terminating a pregnancy. Okunoin, the massive Kōyasan cemetery, is one such site that, although enshrining Shinran, is not under the jurisdiction of Jōdo Shinshū. Alternatively, it may be that non–Jōdo Shinshū practitioners (presumably mainly Shingon Shū followers), have decided that Shinran is a particularly good patron for *mizuko*. There might be some logic to this idea: of all the founders of major Japanese sects, only Shinran was a married monk, with a wife and daughters. His life was therefore caught up in the issues of family, fertility, and everyday lay matters to a degree utterly beyond that of, say, Dōgen, Nichiren, or Kōyasan's own founder, Kūkai.

7. Kira Ryōichi (manager, Sōka Gakkai Kyōto International Culture Center), interview by author, 25 February 2006, at Sōka Gakkai Kyōto International Culture Center.

8. David Machacek and Kerry Mitchell, "Immigrant Buddhists in America," in *Global Citizens: The Soka Gakkai Buddhist Movement in the World*, ed. David Machacek and Bryan Wilson (Oxford: Oxford University Press, 2001), 261. Note that Machacek and Mitchell consider 22 percent to be a rough estimate because their English-language questionnaire surely missed some Japanese-speaking informants.

9. Edward Clark (coordinator, SGI Plaza Visitor's Center), interview by author, 21 February 2007, at SGI Plaza, Santa Monica. Despite his unassuming title, Clark is one of the most important figures in SGI-USA history. A Japanese immigrant who changed his name, Clark was instrumental in bringing Sōka Gakkai to the West and has played an important role in its development over more than four decades. SGI Plaza is the American headquarters of Sōka Gakkai.

10. For a good exploration of this subject by scholar Charles Prebish, who coined the interpretive term "two Buddhisms," see his "Two Buddhisms Reconsidered," *Buddhist Studies Review* 10, 2 (1993): 187–206.

11. See Jeff Wilson, "'There's No Such Thing as Not My Buddhism': Cross-Sectarian Buddhist Hybridity in the American South," paper presented to the Asian North American Religion, Culture, and Society Group at the American Academy of Religion annual meeting, San Antonio, TX, 21 November 2004.

12. Duncan Williams, "Asian-American Buddhism Bibliography," Cambridge, MA: The Pluralism Project, 2004. Available online at http://www.pluralism.org/resources/biblio/as-am_buddhism.php.

13. I do not use diacritics in the names of American temples if the temples themselves do not use them in their official printed materials. Thus, even though Zenshuji Soto Mission technically should be written as Zenshūji Sōtō Mission based on the kanji used for its name, I do not put the macrons over the u or o's because the temple doesn't do so in its English publications.

14. Kojima Shūmyō (priest, Zenshuji Soto Mission), interview by author, 18 January 2007, at Zenshuji Soto Mission, Los Angeles.

15. Sutras are the central holy texts of Buddhism, typically believed to record the sermons of the Buddha.

16. Kojima Shūmyō, interview.

17. This text is also known by the name *Daihi Shu.*

18. Shujō muhen sei gan do, Bon-no mujin sei gan dan, Ho mon muryō sei gan gaku, Butsu do mujō sei gan jo [Beings are numberless; I vow to free them. Delusions are inexhaustible; I vow to end them. Dharma gates are boundless; I vow to enter them. The Buddha way is unsurpassable; I vow to realize it].

19. Kojima Shūmyō interview. *Bosatsu* is the Japanese word for bodhisattva. "O-Jizō-san" is a polite way of referring to Jizō.

20. This motif is known as Roku Jizō, literally "six Jizōs." They symbolize the six realms of existence as well as the six directions, indicating Jizō's roles as the guardian of beings trapped in samsara after the Buddha's death and his stewardship of travelers. Roku Jizō is a very common motif at temples and along roadsides in Japan. At Zenshuji the Roku Jizō have been given the title Omoi Yari Jizō, meaning Sympathy for Others Jizō.

21. Satō Shinryo (priest, Nichiren Shoshu Myohoji Temple of Los Angeles), interview by author, 24 January 2007, at Nichiren Shoshu Myohoji Temple of Los Angeles.

22. Nikken, "Earthly Desires Are in Themselves Enlightenment," Nichiren Shoshu Globalnet, 2003, http://www.nsglobalnet.jp/page/collected_sermons/32.htm.

23. Satō Shinryo (priest, Nichiren Shoshu Myohoji Temple of Los Angeles), telephone interview by author, 23 January 2007.

24. Satō Shinryo, personal interview..

25. A stupa is a multitiered Buddhist memorial monument. Graves in Japan are often built as mini-stupas.

26. The priests at Myohoji write on the *tōba* "Nam Myōhō Renge Kyō [family name] *ke no suishi rei*"—Adoration to the *Lotus Sutra; mizuko* spirit of the [family name] household. While I have written the text here in Roman letters for the benefit of readers, the actual writing on the *tōba* is done in kanji, sometimes with hiragana or katakana

if appropriate. This is true of all the *tōba* and *ihai* discussed in this chapter. For an example, see the *mizuko ihai* of Zenshuji Soto Mission in fig. 1.3.

27. Evening service consists of chanting chapters 2 and 16 of the *Lotus Sutra*, followed by rapid chanting of "Nam Myōhō Renge Kyō" ("Adoration to the *Lotus Sutra*") and silent prayers; this is virtually the same as morning service. All information here is from an interview with Satō Shinryo at Nichiren Shoshu Myohoji Temple of Los Angeles on 24 January 2007 unless otherwise specified.

28. Kanai Shokai, interview.

29. Rev. Kanai usually reuses these, and prefers not to give the *mizuko* a *kaimyō* (posthumous name given to the deceased during Buddhist funeral rites). *Kaimyō* literally means "ordination name"—through the rites of the priests the dead person is transformed into a monk, the better for him to become a Buddha in the afterlife. It seems to have appeared originally in Zen but is now a standard practice in virtually all sects of Japanese Buddhism.

30. At the Los Angeles temple, this chant is done in the style of modern Japanese, rather than in the Chinese style one often finds at Nichiren Shū temples in Japan.

31. Note that Nichiren Shū chants "Namu Myōhō Renge Kyō," by far the more mainstream pronunciation, rather than "Nam Myōhō Renge Kyō" as performed by Sōka Gakkai and Nichiren Shōshū. This extended chanting during *mizuko kuyō* has no set duration but consists of at least a hundred repetitions of the mantra.

32. Tanaka Kōdō (priest, Jodo Shu Buddhist North America Mission [of Los Angeles]), telephone interview by author, 9 February 2007.

33. These tablets are called *kyogi-tōba* at this temple. The wooden tablet has the mantric syllable for Amida Buddha at the top, followed by the family's name and a posthumous ordination name. The parents' names and the date are also inscribed.

34. A common liturgical element, this chant is called *Jūseige* in the more familiar Jōdo Shinshū denomination.

35. Tablets are called *kyogi* at Koyasan. These wooden tablets have a stupa (monument) image with the five mantric syllables of Dainichi Nyorai (Vairocana Buddha) prestamped on the top, below which the priest adds the participant's family name and the word *suishi* (*mizuko*).

36. In order, these are the Fudō Myōō mantra (Nomaku sammanda bazaradan senda makaroshada sowataya un tarata kamman), the Jizō mantra (On kakaka bisammaei sowaka), the Gohōgō mantra (Namu Daishi Henjō Kongō), and the Kōmyō mantra (On abokyā beirosha nō maka bodarā mani handoma jimbara harabaritaya un). Fudō Myōō is a wrathful protector deity and major patron of Japanese tantric Buddhism. The Gohōgō venerates Kōbō Daishi (also known as Kūkai), the founder of Shingon Shū. The Kōmyō mantra (mantra of light) is one of the most common Shingon practices.

37. Miyata Taisen (bishop, Koyasan Buddhist Temple), interview by author, 7 February 2007, at Koyasan Buddhist Temple, Los Angeles. Sai no Kawara is the name of a legendary river in Japanese Buddhist folklore, akin to Styx in ancient Greek myth. Deceased children go to the riverbank of the afterlife but are unable to cross over. They spend their time pitifully building stone stupas that are smashed by wicked demons. But Jizō appears to chase the demons away and shelter the spirits in his robes.

38. Miyata Taisen (bishop, Koyasan Buddhist Temple), interview by author, 8 September 2005, at Koyasan Buddhist Temple, Los Angeles. Rev. Miyata retired after several decades at Koyasan while this book was in production. His successor has told me that *mizuko kuyō* will continue to be performed at the temple. (Note that interviewees are identified in the notes by the title or position they held at the time of the interview. Thus, Rev. Miyata is listed as "bishop," not "former bishop" or "bishop emeritus.")

39. Okuribi is the ritual end to Obon, the main festival of the Japanese religious calendar, when spirits return from the afterlife to visit with their living relatives. Okuribi specifically is the sending of the spirits on to the other realms after they have resided in the cemetery, temple, or home altar for several days. The twenty-fourth day of the month is traditionally considered Jizō's day, and rituals are held in his honor.

40. There is another Japanese denomination of Buddhism present in America that includes tantric practices: Tendai Shū. Although one of the most important schools in Japan, it has had very little formal representation in the United States. A temple was established in Hawaii in 1918 but closed in 1950. Beginning in 1973, Tendai Shū made modest efforts to reestablish an institutional base in the United States, but at present it still has less than a dozen temples. The ones in North America are not Asian-American in orientation, but rather are small groups presided over by Euro-Americans trained in the Tendai tradition. These new Tendai practitioners tend to be attracted either to its tantric practices or the comprehensive nature of Tendai practice, as opposed to Zen, Pure Land, and Nichiren temples that focus more exclusively on particular practices such as *zazen, nembutsu,* or *daimoku* (anonymous member of Tendai Shu New York Betsuin, interview by author, 8 August 2008, at Tenonkyō, Kameoka, Japan). The temples are in most cases not located near large Japanese-American populations, and the priests, though aware of *mizuko kuyō*, are largely reluctant to offer the ritual (Jimyo Lisa Ferworn [priest, Mitsudoji Hidden Path Temple, Kalamazoo, IL], e-mail message to author, 20 October 2005). The four Hawaiian temples, on the other hand, are run by and oriented toward the Japanese-American population and have a larger base of participants. Overall, Tendai Shū, while fitting somewhat within the rough classification of Japanese-American Buddhism, is an anomaly. Tendai Shū has no formal presence in Los Angeles, the primary fieldwork site for this project. Therefore, I do not present a detailed description of American Tendai *mizuko kuyō* practices in this chapter. I do know that prayers for *mizuko* can be obtained at Koganji Jizoin, a Tendai Shū temple not far from the main University of Hawaii campus in Honolulu. These prayers are not called *mizuko kuyō*, as the elderly Japanese-American nun who founded the temple finds that term distasteful, associating it with moneymaking schemes in Japan. Rather, she speaks of them as prayers for the unborn (Jikyo Rose [abbess, Koganji Jizoin], phone interview by author, 12 February 2007). Women from her congregation, which is mostly Japanese-American, come to her for a consultation session. If she determines that a service for an aborted or miscarried pregnancy is appropriate, she will conduct it on their behalf. Even with the information I was able to obtain, my knowledge of Rose's ceremonies is incomplete. Her age made it difficult to understand her at times on the phone, and she was not present when I made a site visit in August 2008. She does not have e-mail, and she declined to fill out most of a faxed questionnaire. A member whom I talked with at

the temple asserted that formal *mizuko kuyō* was not available, and contradicted other information I had which suggested that a *mizuko Jizō* had been present at Koganji as early as 1978. I therefore present these preliminary findings here in an endnote with the recognition that they are less than adequately researched. I leave it to some intrepid Hawaiian researcher to finish this initial research.

41. Japanese-Americans are typically classified as first, second, third, and fourth generation—Isseis, Niseis, Sanseis, and Yonseis, respectively, using the Japanese counting system. New Japanese immigrants, however, are differentiated as Shin Isseis—"new Isseis."

42. At least, this is what was reported by Rev. Mizutani Shōkō in an interview at Rissho Kosei-Kai Buddhist Church of Los Angeles on 15 February 2007. Because of the Risshō Kōsei-kai practice of testimonials and *hōza*, discussed below, Rev. Mizutani has perhaps greater access to laywomen's feelings than does the average priest.

43. Rev. Mizutani accepted a position at the Rissho Kosei-kai in North America center in Irvine while this book was in production. He is now the former minister of the Los Angeles temple, and some things stated in the present tense in the text should technically be seen as past tense. There was not sufficient time available to determine if Rev. Mizutani's successor would continue to perform *mizuko kuyō* or what modifications the new minister might make. But, given that the ritual was initiated and largely run by the laywomen of the temple and has been performed for several years, it is reasonable to expect that it will remain an annual ceremony at the temple and to retain the general form discussed here.

44. They begin with chapter 3 of the *Sutra of Innumerable Meanings*, then go on to chapters 2, 3, 10, 12, 16, 20, 21, 25, and 28 of the *Lotus Sutra*. The sutra chanting concludes with an excerpt from the *Sutra of Meditation on the Bodhisattva Samantabhadra*. None of these chapters is chanted in full—these are selections from each of the chapters listed, performed in the order above. These chants have been done in Japanese during the three *mizuko kuyō* held so far, although Rev. Mizutani indicated that English would also be appropriate. The *Sutra of Innumerable Meanings* is the *Muryōgi Kyō*; the *Sutra of Meditation on the Bodhisattva Samantabhadra* is the *Kanfugen Kyō*.

45. Risshō Kōsei-kai inherited *hōza* from Reiyūkai, another new religious movement. However, their performances of *hōza* differ in significant ways, and *hōza* is a far more common and central practice for Risshō Kōsei-kai (the tremendous growth of Risshō Kōsei-kai is frequently attributed to its promotion of *hōza*, in fact). *Hōza* is even less common in other Japanese movements and denominations.

46. Mizutani Shōkō (priest, Rissho Kosei-Kai Buddhist Church of Los Angeles), interview by author, 15 February 2007, at Rissho Kosei-Kai Buddhist Church of Los Angeles.

47. Home Buddhist altars are usually called *butsudan* in Japan, but Risshō Kōsei-kai uses the term *gohozen*. This is also the term applied to the Buddha statue in the main worship hall. Note that this is not *gohonzon*, a common term used for a venerated object of worship in Japan, although there is obvious overlap in usage.

48. There are two exceptions in my pool of consultants. One is Jikyu Rose, who immigrated to Hawaii after marrying an American man. A lifelong devotee of Jizō, she

decided to seek ordination and trained at the Tendai Shū headquarters on Hieizan in Kyōto. She then returned to Hawaii and built Koganji, which she presides over (this temple is described in greater detail above in note 40). Note that Rose resists applying the appellation *mizuko kuyō* to her ceremonies. The other exception is Yokota Myojo, an elderly Japanese-American nun at Koyasan Buddhist Temple who has sometimes performed *mizuko kuyō* (she is now too old, leaving services to be provided by the temple's three male priests). I interviewed her at Koyasan Buddhist Temple in downtown Los Angeles on 7 February 2007. It is perhaps noteworthy that these two women—an immigrant and a native-born American—are the only two who were not sent as missionaries from Japan.

49. It is not unusual for urban temples in Japan to have similar columbaria on site. The Los Angeles phenomenon of temples having on-site columbaria but not cemeteries does not hold true for all Japanese-American temples. For example, while most North American temples lack cemeteries, the situation is different in Hawaii, where temples were established early enough—in many cases in areas that remain rural to this day—that they were often able to create large outdoor cemeteries in addition to columbaria. Japanese-Hawaiian Buddhism presents a number of variations in the patterns established by my Los Angeles research. With relatively more space to work with, these temples tend to be somewhat closer in form to Japanese ones, retaining elements such as hand-washing stations, for which the mainland temples usually lack adequate space. It is no coincidence, therefore, that the only full *mizuko Jizōdō* (outdoor covered shrines dedicated specifically to the Jizō who saves aborted and miscarried spirits) in America are found in Hawaii, such as at the Hilo Nichiren Mission.

50. This *mizuko Jizō*, one of the few such full-size statues in America, was dedicated in 1982. Although the typical client for *mizuko kuyō* is an outsider, the statue was purchased with money pledged by temple members, as well as some money from the temple general fund. Honoring their own *mizuko* was a main motivation for the temple members in purchasing the statue from Japan, but another was the hope that it would be good for the temple mission. Miyata Taisen, interview.

51. At about fifty or so *mizuko kuyō* per year, Koyasan Buddhist Temple conducts nearly one a week. However, the actual frequency is less than weekly. In some months, there are only one or two such services, whereas in July and August (the traditional months for honoring the dead in Japan) several *mizuko kuyō* are performed each week. Shingon temples in other parts of America also conduct *mizuko kuyō*, though often with less frequency. And the relationship of relative frequency of *mizuko kuyō* performance between Shingon and other temples varies. For example, in Hawaii the Hilo Hooganji Mission (a Shingon temple in the same lineage as the L.A. Koyasan) performs *mizuko kuyō* rarely, only on request. Meanwhile, the nearby Hilo Nichiren Mission (a Nichiren Shū temple) is so involved in *mizuko kuyō* that it has taken the step of creating a separate *mizuko Jizōdō* outside the main hall, a common sight in Japan but extremely rare in America. This is in contrast to the Los Angeles Nichiren temple, which performs only a few *mizuko kuyō* and lacks a *mizuko Jizōdō*. Thus, while in Los Angeles the Shingon denomination is the main provider of *mizuko kuyō*, in Hilo it is Nichiren Shū that plays this role.

52. Actually, Jikyu Rose, discussed in notes 40 and 48 but technically not a subject of this study because she does not consider her ceremonies to be *mizuko kuyō*, did profess an explicit belief in *tatari* (Jikyo Rose, fax correspondence to author, 21 February 2007).

53. For instance, he specifically mentioned the film *Ringu*. Remade in America as *The Ring*, these movies and their sequels center on haunted videotapes and lend themselves readily to an interpretation as *mizuko* allegory. Anyone who watches the haunted videotapes is killed violently by the angry ghost of a murdered girl one week after the viewing. The main character is a young woman, who, along with her son, is targeted by the child ghost. The spirit is vengeful because it has been wronged (shunned, murdered, and improperly memorialized). It dwells in a cold, clammy proxy womb at the bottom of a well, floating in darkness like the *mizuko*. It ventures forth to harm all those it contacts, but especially the young, its symbolic siblings who have the mortal experiences it lacks and are filled with life (and passion as they enter teenage years). The heroine attempts to offer the traditional solution—she descends into the well, mothers the lost child, buries it properly, and restores it to public memory so it can be memorialized in the future. This should appease the spirit and prevent *tatari*, but it fails. In anxiety-filled modern Japan, the old solutions have broken down. The old ways of memorialization no longer apply. Instead, the spirit demands that modern technology, not ancient ritual, be used to spread her memory throughout the world, as each person passes on the tape in order not to be killed. The memory must spread continuously, and there is no real escape—the spirit can *never* be put to rest, only warded off for the moment. The spirit uses the tape as a cry for remembrance, for its plight to be recognized and regretted. It is a kind of *mizuko* from the beginning, conceived in a sea-cave, the descendant of a water goblin. From the orthodox Buddhist viewpoint, the objection that Rev. Tanaka is vocalizing here is that the people are attacked just for watching a video, an action that carries no negative karmic implications and should not serve to justify ill fortune.

54. Kanai Shokai, "Abortion and a Memorial Service for the Unborn Babies," *The Bridge*, no. 31 (Autumn 2000): 3. In this same article, Rev. Kanai implicitly endorses George Bush in that year's presidential election because of his conservative stance on abortion.

55. I did not speak in depth to any laypeople about *mizuko kuyō* during the Japanese-American portion of my research because these temples felt their records of *mizuko kuyō* participants should be kept confidential This limitation to my study is regrettable. Here the realities of gender and race may apply: it might be that a woman researcher or Japanese-American scholar could be granted permission where I was denied. If so, I hope future researchers will step forward and fill in this crucial piece of the puzzle, whose necessary absence here is the most disappointing aspect of this work for me.

56. That the most conservative attitudes toward *mizuko kuyō* should not be found among missionary priests in America is unsurprising. Self-selection means that Buddhist priests with the most nationalistic views are uninclined to move to the United States. Similarly, those with the greatest inclination to make money from *mizuko kuyō* rites are likely to stay in Japan, where they have a far larger client population for the ritual.

57. American women who had the means often went abroad for abortions during this time period. Canada, Great Britain, and Japan seem to have been the most common destinations.

58. This decrease in Jōdo Shinshū affiliation is attributable to two factors. First, current immigration, while of lesser volume, draws from a wider range of Japanese areas, whereas earlier immigration happened to favor traditional Shin strongholds. Second, denominational affiliation has declined somewhat across all groups in Japan.

59. I would go so far as to say that every single Japanese-American temple in the United States is set up in this manner. Certainly I have seen no exception to this apparent rule in my research at dozens of such temples across a wide range of sectarian affiliations in many different American states. Even in that tiny minority of temples whose architecture suggests that they were not originally intended for use with chairs or pews—such as Kohala Koboji Mission in Hawaii—benches are nonetheless used in actual practice.

60. In a traditional Japanese temple, laypeople, priests, and the main altar are usually all on the same level, with only a low fence to separate the laity from the front of the hall. Alternatively, the main altar may be on a very slightly raised level. But in either case the main object of worship itself will sit on a tall pedestal, putting it well above the heads of kneeling or sitting worshippers.

61. There is another adaptation worthy of mention: many of these temples include American flags in their *hondōs*; in Hawaii, they also often have Hawaiian state flags as well.

62. Kojima Shūmyō (priest, Zenshuji Soto Mission), interview with author, 7 February 2007, at Zenshuji Soto Mission, Los Angeles.

CHAPTER 2

1. Jan Chozen Bays, *Jizo Bodhisattva: Modern Healing and Traditional Buddhist Practice* (Boston: Tuttle Publishing, 2001), 1. The epigraph can be found on p. 22 of Thomas A. Tweed's *Crossing and Dwelling: A Theory of Religion* (Cambridge, MA: Harvard University Press, 2006).

2. Bays, *Jizo Bodhisattva*, 2.

3. Ibid., 3.

4. See, for instance, James William Coleman, *The New Buddhism: The Western Transformation of an Ancient Tradition* (Oxford: Oxford University Press, 2001).

5. For a particularly clear discussion of these ideas, see Robert H. Sharf, "The Zen of Japanese Nationalism," *Curators of the Buddha: The Study of Buddhism under Colonialism*, ed. Donald S. Lopez Jr., 107–160 (Chicago: University of Chicago, 1995).

6. See the appendix for a full list of these temples. Note that Berkeley Buddhist Monastery is officially Chan, the Chinese parent tradition of Japanese Zen. However, even if we consider these as separate traditions—which my consultants typically do not—the Berkeley temple is run by a convert American monk and is similar in many ways to the specifically Japanese-derived groups. Furthermore, the actual water baby ceremony performed in Berkeley was carried out by Zen priest Yvonne Rand of San Francisco Zen Center and was not significantly altered from her normal Zen ceremonies to make it somehow "Chan."

7. Sunya Kjolhede (abbess, Windhorse Zen Center), interview by author, 17 June 2006, at Windhorse Zen Center, Alexander, N.C.

8. Tenshin Charles Fletcher (abbot, Yokoji Zen Mountain Center, of Mountain Center, CA), telephone interview by author, 12 January 2007. The center also has a large Jizō statue with a small child at its base peering up in devotion at the bodhisattva, a common *mizuko* motif. Rather than an import from Japan, it was actually carved with a chainsaw by an American woman, using cedar from the center site. Women sometimes hang ribbons for lost pregnancies or babies in the grove that holds the statue, and Fletcher performs a ceremony that contains the same elements of the offering portion of the ritual in true water baby ceremonies: the *Heart Sutra*, *Enmei Juku Kannon Gyō*, and Jizō mantra. However, the center is primarily monastic in orientation and has not held a specific ceremony for lost pregnancies.

9. Sallie Jiko Tisdale (priest, Dharma Rain Zen Center, of Portland, OR), e-mail message to author, 1 October 2006.

10. Other names applied to these ceremonies include "Abortion healing circle," "Ceremony for children who have died," "Ceremony on the death of an unborn child," and the "Jizō ceremony." Not all centers discussed in this chapter actively use the label "water baby ceremony," but most do use the term "water baby" and recognize "water baby ceremony" as an accurate moniker for their rituals. "Water baby ceremony" and "Jizō ceremony" are the most widely used names.

11. Yvonne Rand, "The Buddha's Way and Abortion: Loss, Grief, and Resolution," *Inquiring Mind* (Fall 1993): 21. This article has been widely reprinted in mostly unaltered form in many Buddhist publications, spreading awareness of Buddhist post–pregnancy loss rituals.

12. Ibid. A mudra is a symbolic Buddhist hand gesture, in this case the familiar pose of bringing one's palms together, fingers pointing up, in front of the chest.

13. Yvonne Rand (abbess, Goat in the Road Zendo), telephone interview by author, 24 January 2007.

14. Robert Aitken (teacher, Honolulu Diamond Sangha), e-mail message to author, 18 August 2006.

15. Robert Aitken, e-mail message to author, 5 June 2006.

16. Robert Aitken, e-mail message to author, 24 September 2006. Many Zen teachers have told me that they read Aitken's ceremony with interest when it was published. It was also the subject of a brief but perceptive analysis by William LaFleur in *Liquid Life: Abortion and Buddhism in Japan* (Princeton, NJ: Princeton University Press, 1992), 199–201. Although he seems to assume (incorrectly) that Aitken imported and then modified the ceremony, LaFleur's basic analysis remains useful.

17. Luckily, Aitken's ceremony was published with some useful comments in 1984. He also graciously consented, despite ill health, to an extended e-mail exchange that provided key information. Rand agreed to a phone interview with me, and has published frequently on the water baby ceremony, including extended explanations of her motivations in offering the ceremony and research into its Japanese background.

18. Aitken's ceremony is noticeably different, and Rand writes in "Buddha's Way and Abortion" (21) that she has modified her ceremonies since this earlier period. One significant change is that whereas the ceremonies she conducted before the conference were oriented toward individual mourners, subsequent ceremonies have been communal affairs.

19. Aitken does use the term "water baby" in his book but not "water baby ceremony," which he names "The Diamond Sangha Ceremony on the Death of an Unborn Child." He still does not use the label "water baby ceremony," and he called it the "Ceremony for an Unborn Child" in his correspondence with me (e-mail message, 5 June 2006). Rand's newfound dedication to the ritual is described in Bays 2001: 12.

20. Rand, telephone interview.

21. Rand, "Buddha's Way and Abortion"; "Abortion: A Respectful Meeting Ground," *Buddhism through American Women's Eyes*, Karma Lekshe Tsomo, ed., 85–89 (Ithaca, NY: Snow Lion, 1995).

22. Melody Ermachild Chavis, "A Ceremony for Aborted and Miscarried Children," *Turning Wheel: Journal of the Buddhist Peace Fellowship* (Summer 1990): 28–30.

23. Goat-in-the-Road has moved around somewhat, and Rand sometimes offers her ceremonies at other temples or even non-Buddhist spiritual centers.

24. Empty Hand Zendo has now become Empty Hand Zen Center and is in the process of affiliating with the Sōtō-based San Francisco Zen Center. Postal's background also includes ten years as one of the first Tibetan Nyingma Buddhism practitioners in America and an earlier period with the Gurdjieff Work. (Susan Jion Postal [abbess, Empty Hand Zen Center], telephone interview by author, 23 January 2007.

25. Sunyana Graef (abbess, Vermont Zen Center), e-mail message to author, 25 September 2006.

26. Jan Chozen Bays (abbess, Great Vow Monastery), interview by author, 5 November 2006, at Great Vow Monastery, Clatskanie, OR.

27. Bays 2001: xxvii.

28. Bays, interview.

29. Kojun Hull (priest, Great Vow Monastery), interview, 5 November 2006, at Great Vow Monastery, Clatskanie, OR.

30. Judith Ragir (priest, Clouds in Water Zen Center), telephone interview, 9 July 2008.

31. Per Drougge, "Jizo Bodhisattva," *Zen Bow* 16, 3 (Summer 1994): 30–31; Anonymous member of Rochester Zen Center, interview, 6 November 2005, at her home, Rochester, NY.

32. Kjolhede, interview.

33. "Water Baby Ceremony to Remember," notes, Rochester Zen Center, 1999; Anonymous former member of Rochester Zen Center, interview by author, 2 November 2005, at Starry Nite Café, Rochester, NY.

34. Wrightson does return regularly to the Rochester area for additional training and to practice outside the demands of being a teacher, however.

35. Angie Boissevain (abbess, Floating Zendo), telephone interview by author, 18 January 2007. Boissevain's group was founded by Kobun Chino, a Sōtō Zen teacher associated with the San Francisco Zen Center.

36. Wendy Egyoku Nakao, "Journey to the Earth's Womb: A Healing Council on Abortion," *Water Wheel*, 2000 (unpaginated).

37. Wendy Egyoku Nakao (abbess, Zen Center of Los Angeles), interview by author, 30 June 2006, at the Zen Center of Los Angeles.

38. Sevan Ross (abbot, Chicago Zen Center), interview by author, 9 May 2008, at the Chicago Zen Center, Evanston, IL.

39. Katherine Thanas (abbess, Santa Cruz Zen Center), telephone interview by author, 25 January 2007.

40. The only person who even consulted with a Japanese teacher was Aitken, who asked Yamada for permission to conduct the proto–water baby ceremony he had already developed and thus received information about Shingon, Tendai, and Nichiren—but not Zen—*mizuko kuyō* rituals. Some American ritualists have gone on to discuss *mizuko kuyō* with priests in Japan, but only after they had already begun to perform water baby ceremonies.

41. Possibly arguing against this interpretation, we should note that Maezumi did counsel at least one woman who was considering abortion and apparently provided her with some sort of private ritual, and on another occasion he held a funeral for an unborn child after a miscarriage. This ceremony was apparently based on adult funerals, not *mizuko* rituals, and these were both one-time events, not intended as vehicles for teaching rituals to Zen Center students (Nakao, interview.)

42. Sevan Ross (abbot, Chicago Zen Center), interview by author, 14 March 2006, at the Chicago Zen Center, Evanston, IL.

43. Boissevain, telephone interview. *Oryoki* is a ritualized form of eating employed in some Zen monasteries. The AZTA's listserve is an email chat group. Shasta Abbey is a convert Sōtō Zen monastery in Shasta, CA. Sōjiji is one of the two main Sōtō Zen monastic training headquarters in Japan. When Boissevain says her friend is "transmitted," she means she has received dharma transmission, i.e. is sanctioned to teach as a full member of the lineage.

44. Kojima Shūmyō (priest, Zenshuji Soto Mission priest), interview by author, 18 January 2007, at Zenshuji Soto Mission, Los Angeles.

45. Here again I am specifically referring to those who practice the full water baby ceremony, rather than the proto–water baby ceremony designed by Robert Aitken. Aitken would not fit this description, as he is older and, though not Japanese, was a foundational figure for the first generation of convert Zen (although we can note that none of these other water baby ceremony proponents is a direct disciple of his). He too did not receive the ritual directly from his teachers and invented his ritual in part based on his own intuition, not Japanese precedent.

46. Anonymous member of Rochester Zen Center, interview by author, 2 November 2005, at the Rochester Zen Center.

47. Wendy Egyoku Nakao (abbess, Zen Center of Los Angeles), interview by author, 22 January 2007, at the Zen Center of Los Angeles.

48. Rachel K. Jones et al., "Abortion in the United States: Incidence and Access to Services, 2005," *Perspective on Sexual and Reproductive Health* 40, 1 (March 2008): 6–16. The primary reason for the decline can be tied to demographics: since 1990, the baby boomers have begun to experience menopause, meaning that the largest single cohort of Americans is moving out of its child-bearing years. The number 1.61 million is a rounded figure from 1,608,600; 1.21 million is rounded from 1,206,200, the number recorded for 2005 (the last year analyzed by the Guttmacher Institute in the

study cited here, which provides the most recent available data). Alternative figures are available from the Centers for Disease Control and Prevention. However, that agency's current public records do not go past 2004, and they omit areas of the country that did not disclose their figures. For 2004, they listed 839,226 abortions, but California, New Hampshire, and West Virginia did not report, which largely accounts for the difference between this number and the Guttmacher Institute's findings. The CDC numbers are nonetheless helpful in that they support the observation that abortion rates have declined since 1990 and that the procedure nonetheless remains one of the most common surgeries for pre-menopausal women in America. See Straus et al., *Abortion Surveillance—United States, 2004* (Atlanta: Centers for Disease Control and Prevention, 2007). Available online at www.cdc.gov/mmwr/preview/mmwrhtml/ss5609a1.htm.

49. Nakao, interview, 22 January 2007.

50. Bays, interview.

51. Although they are centered on devotion to a particular figure, I call these phenomena "bodhisattva movements," as in "the Jizō *movement*," rather than "the Jizō *cult*." The primary reason for this decision is that devotion to Jizō, for instance, is widespread but also diffuse—there are no groups specifically dedicated to worshipping Jizō and no temples founded to offer devotions to this figure. Rather, the Jizō movement is made up of individuals across a range of groups and of those belonging to no group in particular, and it takes place within Buddhist institutions and other sites in which loyalties do not lie solely with Jizō. Devotion to Jizō augments preexisting practices and does not create sustainable new communities. The same is true of Kuan-yin. A secondary reason is that although Jizō is called upon for general guidance, support, and inspiration, the bodhisattva is not usually petitioned for physical or material ends, such as pregnancy, easy childbirth, healthy children, alleviation of specific physical problems (blindness, back pain, incontinence, etc), success in school, or other practical benefits associated with bodhisattva cults in Asia. I should stress, however, that these are only broad trends, as there is some exception to this general rule with the water baby ceremony.

52. Taigen Dan Leighton, *Bodhisattva Archetypes: Classic Buddhist Guides to Awakening and Their Modern Expression* (New York: Penguin Arkana, 1998). This popular book was reprinted by Wisdom Publications in 2003 under the title *Faces of Compassion: Bodhisattva Archetypes and Their Modern Expression*. Leighton mentions *mizuko kuyō* a number of times and discusses the phenomenon at greater length in the chapter on Jizō. See Leighton, *Bodhisattva Archetypes*, 217–219.

53. Leighton's work on bodhisattvas was often referenced by my consultants and is drawn upon by many figures in the Kuan-yin and Jizō movements that I describe.

54. For more information on the Kuan-yin movement, see my article "'Deeply Female and Universally Human:' The Rise of Kuan-yin Worship in America," *Journal of Contemporary Religion*, vol. 3, no. 3 (October 2008): 285–306.

55. Kuan-yin is only one possible spelling of the bodhisattva's name and is in fact somewhat archaic. Other spellings include Kwan Yin, Kwan-yin, Kwanyin, Kuan Yin, Kuanyin, Kuan-shih-yin, Quanyin, and Guanyin. Additionally, in Japan this same incarnation of Avalokiteshvara is known as Kannon, Kanzeon, or Kanjizai; in Korea, as Kwan Um; and in Vietnam, as Quan Am. All of these versions can be found in American

convert writings on the bodhisattva. However, I have chosen to term the new devotion the "Kuan-yin movement" because it is this spelling that is most frequently used by Americans. I am not arguing for the use of this spelling by Sinologists but rather suggesting its adoption in relation to a specific stream of thought and practice in American convert Buddhism.

56. It is not my wish to argue that such qualities or analogous figures are in fact absent in non-Buddhist religions. I am simply reporting the attitudes and feelings of American Buddhists, who largely believe Kuan-yin to be uniquely relevant in these respects. On the matter of Avalokiteshvara's flexible compassion being a female trait, as often alleged by American consultants, it is worth noting that in the chapter of the *Lotus Sutra* that most embodies this idea the bodhisattva is considered *male*. The willingness to help others in any situation was a trait of this bodhisattva before it was transformed into a female in China—in fact, the male-into-female transformation was likely a manifestation of this adaptability—but American Buddhists consistently derive her compassionate mutability from the fact of her femaleness, reversing the arrow of history. The definitive work on this history is Chun-fang Yu's *Kuan-yin: The Chinese Transformation of Avalokitesvara* (New York: Columbia University Press, 2000).

57. Sandy Boucher, *Discovering Kwan Yin, Buddhist Goddess of Compassion* (Boston: Beacon Press, 1999), 1.

58. Martin Palmer, Jay Ramsay, and Man-Ho Kwok, *Kuan Yin: Myths and Revelations of the Chinese Goddess of Compassion* (London: Thorsons, 1995); Christina Feldman, *Compassion: Listening to the Cries of the World* (Berkeley, CA: Rodmell Press, 2005). Feldman's book received wide exposure through excerpts in *Shambhala Sun* and *The Best Buddhist Writing of 2006*. A partial list of New Age titles includes Quanyin (through Dan Klatt), *Experience Unconditional Love This Year* (Sedona, AZ: Cellular Publishing, 1999); Penelope Genter, *Returning Home: A Workbook for Following Your Path to Ascension—Channeled Lessons from Mother Mary, Merlin, and Quan Yin* (Cedar Crest, NM: MMB Publishing, 2002); Hope Bradford and Lena Lees, *The Living Word of Kuan Yin: The Teachings and Prophecies of the Goddess of Compassion and Mercy* (Charleston, SC: BookSurge, 2006); and dozens of more general books on goddesses and female spirituality.

59. Wendy Cadge, *Heartwood: The First Generation of Theravada Buddhism in America* (Chicago: University of Chicago Press, 2004), 62. Similarly, in my fieldwork in Richmond, VA, many Vipassana practitioners told me that they had Kuan-yin statues on their home altars.

60. Kimberly Snow, *In Buddha's Kitchen: Cooking, Being Cooked, and Other Adventures in a Meditation Center* (Boston: Shambhala, 2003), 78–82.

61. This is not an original American adaptation. Images of *mizuko* Kannon are common in contemporary Japan, though outnumbered by images of *mizuko* Jizō.

62. At present, no convert Zen temple performs a water baby ceremony dedicated solely to Kuan-yin rather than Jizō. But because her popularity is significantly greater than that of Jizō, it is conceivable that the Kuan-yin movement may eventually co-opt the water baby ceremony and begin to present post–pregnancy loss rituals that exclude Jizō entirely.

63. Zenworks is in fact alternatively known as Gentle Jizōs. Jan Chozen Bays (abbess, Great Vow Monastery), interview by author, 20 January 2007, at Great Vow Monastery, Clatskanie, OR.

64. Bays, interview.

65. Ibid.

66. The Zen Community of Oak Park, for instance, displays not only panels and pictures but even kimonos covered in Jizō images that were created for the Jizōs for Peace project.

67. Stamen Trejner (priest, Chicago Zen Center), interview by author, 9 May 2008, at Chicago Zen Center.

CHAPTER 3

1. I also attended the January 2007 ceremony. The epigraph from Young's *Post-colonialism* (Oxford: Oxford University Press, 2003) appears on page 138 of that book.

2. Bays employs a partial script for the ceremonies, which I have access to, making the reconstruction of quotes a more viable project.

3. The Bodhisattva of Compassion is Kannon (Kuan-yin). Prajna is a type of especially penetrating insight that leads to Buddhahood.

4. American Zen Buddhists refer to this as a "dharma name," called *kaimyō* ("precept name") in Japan. As discussed in chapter 1, such names are typically given to the deceased in Japan, converting them into a sort of posthumous monk. The unborn and young children did not receive such names in premodern times, but now *kaimyō* can be purchased as part of *mizuko kuyō* at many temples.

5. Some centers also chant the four bodhisattva vows to close their rituals. This is a disputed practice in the water baby ceremony because some ritual leaders feel it is too strongly Buddhist and thus excludes non-Buddhist participants. Here is an interesting case of Buddhists changing their own liturgy specifically to adapt to the needs of outsiders.

6. The exception is Clouds in Water Zen Center. A $40 donation is asked from center members; $45 from nonmembers. Note, however, that this is considerably less than the approximately $100 donation that is expected at Zenshuji and other Japanese-American temples described in chapter 1. Clouds in Water typically asks for donations at events, so this request is not unique to their water baby ceremonies, but rather is in line with general center policies.

7. Sevan Ross (abbot, Chicago Zen Center), interview by author, 14 March 2006, Chicago Zen Center, Evanston, IL.

8. For an extensive discussion of the place of money in Japanese religion, see Ian Reader and George J. Tanabe Jr., *Practically Religious: Worldly Benefits and the Common Religion of Japan* (Honolulu: University of Hawaii Press, 1998).

9. Jan Chozen Bays (abbess, Great Vow Monastery), interview by author, 5 November 2006, at Great Vow Monastery, Clatskanie, OR. The Zen Center of Los Angeles also restricts its water baby ceremonies to temple members.

10. Yvonne Rand, "The Buddha's Way and Abortion: Loss, Grief, and Resolution," *Inquiring Mind* (Fall 1993): 21.

11. Sunya Kjolhede (abbess, Windhorse Zen Center), interview by author, 17 June 2006, at Windhorse Zen Center, Alexander, NC.

12. Amala Wrightson (priest, Rochester Zen Center), interview by author, 29 December 2002, at Rochester Zen Center.

13. Robert H. Sharf, "Sanbōkyōdan: Zen and the Way of the New Religions," *Japanese Journal of Religious Studies* 22, 3–4: 417–419.

14. In actual practice, Jizō statues are frequently present in the room during sewing. But they are nonetheless not the focus of concern during this stage, as demonstrated by the physical postures of participants, which are oriented inward toward a circle of fellow mourners rather than toward the statues. In fact, one of the main reasons that statues are present during this stage is simply so that sewers can take measurements for the bibs and other clothing they are manufacturing. It is not uncommon for a woman to approach a Jizō, examine its size and shape, and then proceed to sit down with her back to it while she sews a bib or hat.

15. There is, however, the practice of *hōza* found in Risshō Kōsei-kai, described in chapter 1. In the postscript I will consider the meaning of this apparent convergence between a Japanese Buddhist new religious movement and convert American Zen.

16. Wendy Egyoku Nakao (abbess, Zen Center of Los Angeles), interview by author, 30 June 2006, at the Zen Center of Los Angeles.

17. This does not mean that Japanese women never sew hats or other items at home and then leave them on Jizō statues. But this is a far cry from actually manufacturing offerings on site as part of the process of a ritual.

18. Melody Ermachild, "A Ceremony for Aborted and Miscarried Children," *Buddhist Peace Fellowship Newsletter* (Summer 1990): 28.

19. Stephanie Kaza, "Becoming a Real Person," *Buddhist-Christian Studies*, 20 (2005): 49. Monks too sometimes wear *rakusus* in place of their formal robes.

20. Diane E. Riggs, "*Fukudenkai*: Sewing the Buddha's Robe in Contemporary Japanese Buddhist Practice," *Japanese Journal of Religious Studies* 31, 2 (2004): 323. I thank Professor Richard Jaffe for pointing me to this excellent resource.

21. Many of the observations about *jukkai* here and below come from fieldwork and conversations conducted at Zen centers around the country since 1997, particularly at Richmond Zen Group, in Virginia, and Chapel Hill Zen Center, in North Carolina.

22. Hozan Alan Senauke, "A Long and Winding Road: Sōtō Zen Training in America," *Teaching Theology and Religion* 9, 2 (2006): 129.

23. Amala Wrightson (priest, Rochester Zen Center), interview by author, 29 December 2002, at Rochester Zen Center.

24. During fieldwork in Japan I never saw anyone cry during *mizuko kuyō*. The most common attitude seemed to be a calm seriousness. Priests agreed that emotions were not typically expressed overtly during the ceremonies, though there are sometimes exceptions. I do not mean by this to imply that Japanese women and men do not feel strong emotions during *mizuko kuyō*, only that such emotions, if present, are infrequently given expression through weeping, and no particular avenue for their expression is sought through *mizuko kuyō*—its regular format includes no segment devoted to such expression. Other evidence, such as interviews with lay participants, messages

written on *ema*, and the occurrence of weeping in Japanese-American *mizuko kuyō*, do suggest that some participants feel a range of strong emotions.

25. T. Griffith Foulk, "About Soto Zen Liturgy," *Soto School Scriptures for Daily Services and Practice* (Tokyo: Sotoshu Shumucho, 2001), 153.

26. Reader and Tanabe include a particularly interesting discussion by the former head of the Sōtō Zen sect on the magical efficacy of the *Heart Sutra*. See Reader and Tanabe, *Practically Religious*, 76.

27. R. J. Zwi. Werblowsky, "*Mizuko Kuyō*: Notulae on the Most Important 'New Religion' of Japan," *Japanese Journal of Religious Studies* 18, 4 (1991): 301.

28. Lisa Hunter (pseudonym for member of Rochester Zen Center), interview by author, 3 November 2005, at Rochester Zen Center.

29. Amala Wrightson (priest, Rochester Zen Center), interview by author, 29 December 2002, at Rochester Zen Center.

30. Robert DeCaroli, *Haunting the Buddha: Indian Popular Religions and the Formation of Buddhism* (Oxford: Oxford University Press, 2004), 18.

31. See Duncan Ryūken Williams, *The Other Side of Zen: A Social History of Soto Zen Buddhism in Tokugawa Japan* (Princeton, NJ: Princeton University Press, 2005).

32. William M. Bodiford, "The Enlightenment of Kami and Ghosts: Spirit Ordinations in Sōtō Zen," in *Chan Buddhism in Ritual Context,* ed. Bernard Faure, 250–265 (London: RoutledgeCurzon, 2003),.

33. Rand, "Buddha's Way and Abortion," 21.

34. See Helen Hardacre, *Marketing the Menacing Fetus in Japan* (Berkeley: University of California Press, 1997), for discussion of such priests (for example, Hashimoto Tetsuma of Shiunzan) and the general misogynistic attitude of *mizuko kuyō*.

35. Every convert consultant I interviewed affirmed a pro-choice attitude and supported women's equality and a liberal political orientation. Some rejected the label of "liberal" but did so in the context of rejecting political and other labels generally; even these consultants acknowledged their agreeing with "liberal" issues more frequently than "conservative" ones as understood in mainstream American politics.

36. Ryushin Creedon (priest, Great Vow Monastery), interview by author, 5 November 2006, Great Vow Monastery, Clatskanie, OR. *Cintamani* jewels are wish-fulfilling gemstones often held by Jizō figures. It is interesting that Creedon imagines Jizō to be blue. This may be a crossover from the lapis-colored Yakushi Nyorai—the so-called Medicine Buddha—or perhaps even an iconographic assimilation of Krishna from Hindu mythology.

37. Jan Chozen Bays, *Jizo Bodhisattva: Modern Healing and Traditional Buddhist Practice* (Boston, MA: Tuttle, 2002), 224–228.

38. Nakao, interview.

39. Bays, *Jizo Bodhisattva*, 215.

40. Nakao, interview.

41. Wrightson, interview. William LaFleur also noted the importance of the lack of fear and participant orientation in his brief analysis of Aitken's proto–water baby ceremony. See LaFleur, *Liquid Life: Abortion and Buddhism in Japan* (Princeton, NJ: Princeton University Press, 1992), 191–201.

42. Great Vow Monastery remembrance book, unpaginated. This is a memorial book in which water baby ceremony participants write the names, ages, and causes of death of those they are remembering. I have a copy of this book containing every water baby ceremony performed by the Zen Community of Oregon from 1994 to 2007. I also have a copy of a similar memorial book employed by Rochester Zen Center, in which water baby ceremony participants write messages to their *mizuko*. Along with messages written on offerings left in the Jizō garden of Great Vow Monastery, these books have provided an important source of insight into how participants understand the ceremonies, what sort of losses they seek ritual help for, and other significant questions for this project.

43. Eva Moskowitz, *In Therapy We Trust: America's Obsession with Self-Fulfillment* (Baltimore: Johns Hopkins University Press, 2001), 2–3.

44. Ibid., 6–7, 23.

45. Anonymous Great Vow Monastery member, interview by author, 5 November 2006, at Great Vow Monastery, Clatskanie, OR.

46. "Healing Circle for Abortion," Zen Center of Los Angeles, undated, unpaginated. This is the script for water baby ceremonies performed at the Zen Center of Los Angeles. I was able to obtain copies of the actual scripts used for these ceremonies from approximately half of the convert Zen centers that perform them. Joan Halifax, a long-time Zen practitioner, explicitly connects the root of these circles to Native American traditions in her short book *A Buddhist Life in America: Simplicity in the Complex* (New York: Paulist Press, 1998), 27.

47. James William Coleman, *The New Buddhism: The Western Transformation of an Ancient Tradition* (Oxford: Oxford University Press, 2001), 218.

48. Robert Joshin Althouse (abbot, Zen Community of Oak Park), interview by author, 13 March 2006, at Zen Community of Oak Park, Oak Park, IL.

CHAPTER 4

1. Shitou Xiqian and *Cantongqi*, respectively, in Chinese. See Shunryu Suzuki, *Branching Streams Flow in the Darkness: Zen Talks on the Sandokai* (Berkeley: University of California Press, 2001), 10. The epigraph, from G. Victor Sōgen Hori's "Japanese Zen in America: Americanizing the Face in the Mirror," can be found on page 55 of *The Faces of Buddhism in America*, ed. Charles S. Prebish and Kenneth K. Tanaka (Berkeley: University of California Press, 1998).

2. I am not arguing that convert American Zen should be classified as a new religious movement. Though it certainly is informed by minority Japanese reform and revitalization movements (such as Sanbōkyōdan) and substantially altered by the needs of a new cultural environment and a clientele with religious motivations very different from those of most Japanese Zen practitioners, convert Zen is nonetheless not a full-fledged new sect. Rather, it is a new development within the stream of Zen Buddhism, one which maintains significant institutional ties to established Zen organizations in Japan. What I am suggesting is that this venerable tradition nonetheless takes on significant aspects of new religious movements in many circumstances and that

viewing convert Zen through this prism is more fruitful than considering it simply a continuation of Japanese Zen trends and customs. Zen used to be approached this way during the emergence of new religious movements studies in the 1970s as a discipline within religious studies.One good example from this time period is Jacob Needleman and George Baker's 1978 anthology *Understanding the New Religions*, wherein Zen gets plenty of coverage alongside the Unification Church (Moonies), Scientology, and similar groups. But the tendency to draw from new religious movements theory has decreased over time, in part, perhaps, from a desire on the part of scholars (often themselves personally involved in Buddhism to some degree) to distance their subjects from the "disreputable cults" that new religious movements scholars specialized in. The implicit argument is that Zen is not an appropriate object for theory within this area because it has such a venerable Asian pedigree. But this argument obscures an important development within Zen. Though it certainly was a distortion in earlier scholarship to designate Zen as a new religious movement, overcorrection can hide the ways that twentieth- and twenty-first-century Zen communities in America sometimes operate similarly to new religious movements (and thus may be illumined by recognition of this resemblance).

3. Or, for that matter, the classical baggage Buddhism—Jōdo Shinshū—which also declines to conduct true *mizuko kuyō* rites.

4. The amount of ink that has been spilled in the last ten or so years over how to typologize American Buddhism is nothing short of remarkable. The best overview of this scholarly debate is Paul David Numrich's "Two Buddhisms Further Reconsidered," published in *Contemporary Buddhism* in 2003 (4, 1: 55–78). Despite my misgivings about it, I am forced to agree with the logic of Numrich's argument that the fundamental split between Asian-American cultural Buddhists and (mainly) Euro-American convert Buddhists will remain a powerful and important heuristic tool for years to come. Though this two-part typology has the potential to actually reinforce stereotypes and racial boundaries in unfortunate ways, it is reflective of actual differences that arise in the main part from power disparities between Asian communities in America and the dominant, historically racist white majority. Until the legacy of this historical racism has passed, American Buddhism's divide will likely remain an influential factor in community organization and orientation.

5. Duncan Ryūken Williams, *The Other Side of Zen: A Social History of Soto Zen Buddhism in Tokugawa Japan* (Princeton, NJ: Princeton University Press, 2005), 3.

6. Ibid., 4. *Kōans* are brief anecdotes of supposed encounters between past Zen masters, often used as meditation devices; Dōgen was the thirteenth-century founder of Sōtō Zen in Japan. For a quick but excellent record of some of the most important publications that have forced a reevaluation of the actual prevalence of ritual in Zen, see Williams, *Other Side of Zen*, 133 n. 2. Like Williams's work, this study is heavily indebted to the work of such scholars as Bodiford, Faure, Buswell, and Foulk, as well as Williams himself.

7. For a detailed assessment of contemporary Zen practices, see T. Griffith Foulk, "Ritual in Japanese Zen Buddhism," in *Zen Ritual*, ed. Steven Heine and Dale Wright, 21–82 (Oxford: Oxford University Press, 2008).

8. Regina McMaster (pseudonym, member of Rochester Zen Center), interview by author, 6 November 2005, at her home in Rochester, NY. It is worth noting that nearly all these early ceremonies and celebrations mentioned come from outside Zen Buddhism. Most are standard American holidays given a Zen gloss.

9. Paula K. R. Arai, "Women and Dōgen: Rituals Actualizing Empowerment and Healing," *Zen Ritual: Studies of Zen Buddhist Theory in Practice*, ed. Steven Heine and Dale S. Wright (Oxford: Oxford University Press, 2008), 192.

10. Sydney Ahlstrom, ed., *Theology in America: The Major Protestant Voices from Puritanism to Neo-Orthodoxy* (Indianapolis: Bobbs-Merrill, 1967), 25–26.

11. Readers may wish to refer again to note 3 of the introduction, wherein I discuss the terms "ritual" and "ceremony."

12. This perspective is not native to the Asian tradition itself, as T. Griffith Foulk points out: "Westerners interested in Zen, by the same token, are often attracted to 'practices' of seated meditation (*zazen*), manual labor, and doctrinal study but uncomfortable with the 'rituals' of offerings, prayers, and prostrations made before images on altars. There is nothing to prevent people from making distinctions of this sort, but it is important to recognize that they are fundamentally alien to the East Asian Buddhist tradition of which Zen is part" (Foulk, "Ritual in Japanese Zen Buddhism," 23).

13. Segaki is an autumnal ritual that centers on helping hungry or wandering ghosts. American Zen communities often assimilate it into Halloween, and as with their treatment of the water baby ceremony, sometimes hungry ghosts are identified as aspects of the practitioner rather than actual entities—perhaps a somewhat less flattering reinterpretation than the assertion that the enlightened bodhisattva Jizō is your own self!

14. The growth of Buddhist studies as an academic field has contributed to this increased knowledge—many of the people with whom I spoke had read William LaFleur's *Liquid Life*, for instance.

15. Reconstructionist ideas in American Buddhism are hardly limited to convert Zen. Jōdo Shinshū in the last two decades, for instance, has experienced a notable shift away from some of the quasi-Protestant elements originally adopted as survival strategies in a racist culture. Buddhist "churches" are renaming themselves as "temples," the "bishop" now calls himself the "*Sōchō*," and the critical term *shinjin*, once ubiquitously translated as "faith," is now often left untranslated because there is a growing feeling that no English term (especially one with Christian baggage) can hope to encompass the nuances of the original. Yet these attempts to present a more fully Buddhist façade for the denomination come not through an influx of foreign Japanese influence, but rather during a time of Asian-American assimilation into the mainstream and dramatic decline in Japanese-language speakers within the American Jōdo Shinshū community.

16. Incidentally, it is very difficult to distinguish "liberal" and "conservative" groups in such a situation. Is an American abbot who resists importing normal Japanese rituals because they've never been done at his center a liberal who is changing a Japan-based tradition, or a conservative who clings to the forms that have been standard at his temple for a generation?

17. Wendy Cadge, *Heartwood: The First Generation of Theravada Buddhism in America* (Chicago: University of Chicago Press, 2004), 197.

18. Perhaps the paradigmatic case was that of Richard Baker's infidelity and exploitation of students at San Francisco Zen Center. One useful study of this situation is Michael Downing's *Shoes outside the Door: Desire, Devotion, and Excess at San Francisco Zen Center* (Washington, D.C.: Counterpoint, 2001).

19. See Catherine Bell, *Ritual: Perspectives and Dimensions* (Oxford: Oxford University Press, 1997), 257–258, 263–265. American Protestantism too has seen a major return to ritual practices during this period. See Randall Balmer and Lauren F. Winner. *Protestantism in America* (New York: Columbia University Press, 2002), 200–202.

20. Sarah M. Pike, *New Age and Neopagan Religions in America* (New York: Columbia University Press, 2004), 98.

21. Paula K. R. Arai, "Women and Dōgen: Rituals Actualizing Empowerment and Healing," in *Zen Ritual*, ed. Steven Heine and Dale Wright (Oxford: Oxford University Press, 2008), 194.

22. Kojun Hull (priest, Great Vow Monastery), interview by author, 5 November 2006, at Great Vow Monastery, Clatskanie, OR.

23. Sevan Ross (abbot, Chicago Zen Center abbot), interview by author, 14 March 2006, at Chicago Zen Center, Evanston, IL.

24. Robert Joshin Althouse (abbot, Zen Community of Oak Park), interview by author, 13 March 2006, at Zen Community of Oak Park, Oak Park, IL.

25. Thomas A. Tweed, *Crossing and Dwelling: A Theory of Religion* (Cambridge, MA: Harvard University Press, 2006), 98.

26. Norma Crest (pseudonym for Great Vow Monastery member), interview by author, 5 November 2006, at Great Vow Monastery, Clatskanie, OR.

27. Sunya Kjolhede (abbess, Windhorse Zen Center), interview by author, 17 June 2006, at Windhorse Zen Center, Alexander, NC.

28. Lisa Hunter (pseudonym for Rochester Zen Center member), interview by author, 3 November 2005, at Rochester Zen Center.

29. Anonymous member of Rochester Zen Center, interview by author, 2 November 2005, Rochester Zen Center.

30. Rochester Zen Center water baby memorial book, unpaginated.

31. Sevan Ross (abbot, Chicago Zen Center), interview by author, 14 March 2006, Chicago Zen Center, Evanston, IL.

32. Althouse, interview.

CHAPTER 5

1. Jennifer O'Neill, *You're Not Alone: Healing through God's Grace after Abortion* (Deerfield Beach, FL: Health Communications, 2005), 142. The epigraph, from Robert Orsi's essay "Everyday Miracles: The Study of Lived Religion," is on page 8 of *Lived Religion in America: Toward a History of Practice*, ed. David D. Hall (Princeton, NJ: Princeton University Press, 1997).

2. O'Neill, *You're Not Alone*, 142–143, emphasis added.

3. Ibid., 143.

4. Were I to include the many scholarly works by Americans on *mizuko kuyō* or abortion in Japan and re-publications of nonscholarly articles in new venues, this count

would run into the many hundreds. Some of the American sources that mention *mizuko kuyō* are included in this book's bibliography, but many are not. For a much fuller, though still not quite complete, list, see the bibliography of my dissertation. Jeff Wilson, "Mourning the Unborn Dead: American Uses of Japanese Buddhist Post-Abortion Rituals." Ph.D. dissertation, University of North Carolina at Chapel Hill, 2007.

5. See, for instance, Thomas Tweed's *The American Encounter with Buddhism, 1844–1912: Victorian Culture and the Limits of Dissent* (Chapel Hill: University of North Carolina Press, 2000); and Richard Seager's *The World's Parliament of Religions: The East/West Encounter, Chicago, 1893* (Bloomington: Indiana University Press, 1995).

6. I do not wish to suggest that these are wholly unconnected concerns. For instance, Nattier's threefold typology of import, export, and baggage Buddhists is explicitly based on interpreting types of Buddhists according to the channels through which they receive their connection to Buddhism. Nonetheless, the conversation has largely moved to dissecting ever finer distinctions within the acknowledged Buddhist communities of America, leaving relatively little room for studies of the continuing and changing roles that non-Buddhists play in disseminating information about, and shaping attitudes toward, Buddhism in America.

7. See Nattier's "Who Is a Buddhist? Charting the Landscape of Buddhist America," in *The Faces of Buddhism in America*, eds. Charles S. Prebish and Kenneth K. Tanaka, 183–195 (Berkeley: University of California Press, 1998).

8. Thomas Tweed, "Night-Stand Buddhists and Other Creatures: Sympathizers, Adherents, and the Study of Religion," in *American Buddhism: Methods and Findings in Recent Scholarship*, eds. Duncan Ryuken Williams and Christopher S. Queen, 71–90 (Richmond, UK: Curzon, 1999).

9. Beth Reiber and Janie Spencer, *Frommer's Japan* (Hoboken, NJ: Wiley Publishing, 2004), 7.

10. Many temples that primarily cater to tourists perform *mizuko kuyō*, such as the popular Kyōto temples Sanjūsangendō and Kiyomizudera.

11. Works by American tourists who encounter *mizuko kuyō* unexpectedly in Japan include Lutheran minister Ruth Gabrielson's "A Prayer for the Water Children" in the Advent 1992 issue of *Aeropagus* (pp. 47–50); J. Patrick Conroy's essay "Cultural Differences . . . or Honesty?" in the April 2003 issue of the *Cincinnati Right to Life* newsletter (p. 2); and Rabbi Ellen Lippmann's sermon "What About the Woman?" delivered to Kolot Chayeinu in Brooklyn on April 23, 2004.

12. Thomas P. O'Connor, "Consoling the Infants: For Whose Sake," *Japan Christian Quarterly* 50 (Fall 1984): 206.

13. Ibid., 208, 213–214. Another example of responses by American missionary priests in Japan to *mizuko kuyō* are the frequent appearances of the ritual in the writings of Anthony Zimmerman, such as "Grieving the Unborn in Japan" in the February 1996 issue of the *Catholic World Report* and "Memorial Services for Aborted Children in Japan" in the April 1989 issue of *All About Issues* magazine (both available online). On the other hand, non-American priests sometimes describe *mizuko kuyō* to outsiders in American Catholic periodicals, as does John Nariai in "The Prolife Struggle in Japan" (*New Oxford Review*, March 1997): 23–24, 29; and Michael Molloy in "The Healing of

Mizuko Jizo" (*Columban Mission,* May 2005): 16–18. As a side note, it is interesting how closely this perspective resembles that of Jōdo Shinshū. Substitute some of the referents (Amida for God, etc.), and this paragraph would read like a typical Shin explanation for that Buddhist school's rejection of *mizuko kuyō*.

14. Sheryl WuDunn, "In Japan, a Ritual of Mourning for Abortions," *New York Times,* 25 January 1996. Other articles on *mizuko kuyō* in major periodicals include "Dispelling an Abortion's Bad Karma" in the March 1993 issue of *Harper's* magazine (p. 23); and "Beliefs," by Peter Steinfels, in the 15 August 1992 edition of the *New York Times.* Sometimes *mizuko kuyō* is included in American articles that are not solely about the ceremony—a good example is the photos and captions of *mizuko* Jizōs in "Japanese Women" in the April 1990 issue of *National Geographic* (Deborah Fallows, pp. 53–84).

15. Martha Shirk, "Temples Show Japan's Ambivalence toward Abortion," *St. Louis Post-Dispatch,* 18 March 1997. Other articles on *mizuko kuyō* in more locally prominent news outlets include Jay Sakashita's "Buddhist Rite Gives Solace for Abortions" in the *Honolulu Star-Bulletin* of 26 May 2001. Sakashita notes that readers can request *mizuko kuyō* at a number of Buddhist temples in Hawaii, one of the few instances of awareness of the ritual in Japanese-American communities.

16. Elizabeth Harrison, "Women's Responses to Child Loss in Japan: The Case of Mizuko Kuyō," *Journal of Feminist Studies in Religion* (Fall 1995): 67–94, and "Strands of Complexity: The Emergence of *Mizuko Kuyō* in Postwar Japan," *Journal of the American Academy of Religion* (December 1999): 769–796; Bardwell Smith, "Buddhism and Abortion in Contemporary Japan: *Mizuko Kuyō* and the Confrontation with Death," *Japanese Journal of Religious Studies* (March 1988: 3–24; republished in *Buddhism, Sexuality, and Gender,* edited by Jose Ignacio Cabezon, 65–90 SUNY Press, 1992).

17. Robert Siegel, ed., *The NPR Interviews 1995* (Boston: Houghton Mifflin Company, 1995), 172–173.

18. William R. LaFleur, *Liquid Life: Abortion and Buddhism in Japan* (Princeton, NJ: Princeton University Press, 1992), 216–217.

19. The use of such loaded terms as "Christian," "feminist," "pro-choice," and "pro-life" is inevitably spurious because these distinctions are far from mutually exclusive. Many Christians are feminists and vice versa; polls suggest that most Americans hold a mixture of views that simultaneously seek to limit abortion and to keep it legal. Thus we encounter an article by Anne Maloney, a pro-life feminist Catholic, titled "You Say You Want a Revolution? Pro-Life Philosophy and Feminism" in the Fall 1995 issue of *Studies in Pro-Life Feminism,* which uses *mizuko kuyō* to critique pro-choice feminists. For the sake of clarity, I have most often chosen in this chapter to follow the lead of each author in how she chooses to present herself, unless there is a compelling reason to do otherwise. Thus when an author positions herself as first and foremost a feminist, I refer to her as such, and don't usually seek to interrogate her denominational affiliation unless it has some particular significance. If an author presents herself as a Christian voice on an issue, then that is the label by which I most readily refer to her.

20. Richard John Neuhaus, "Never Again?" *First Things* (August/September 1994): 45. Other examples of pro-life (generally Christian) periodicals carrying *mizuko kuyō*-related articles include Joan Frawley Desmond's "Apologizing to the Babies" in the Winter 1997

issue of *Human Life Review* (itself a reprint of an article on *mizuko kuyō* in *First Things* the previous October, pp. 13–15), and Mormon scholar Camille S. Williams's at times caustically sarcastic "Feminism and Imaging the Unborn" in the pro-life anthology *The Silent Subject: Reflections on the Unborn in American Culture* (1996).

21. Eve Kushner, *Experiencing Abortion: A Weaving of Women's Words* (New York: Harrington Park Press, 1997), 76. Additional examples of left-leaning or specifically pro-choice venues that have discussed *mizuko kuyō* include Pro-Choice Connection's Web site; Naomi Wolf's "Our Bodies, Our Souls," in the 16 October 1995 issue of the *New Republic* (pp. 26–35); and Dayna Macy's "Unspeakable Losses," in the 15 April 1998 edition of *Salon*.

22. Anonymous, "He Who Frames the Question, Wins the Argument!" (flier), Elizabeth, NJ, Gateway Pregnancy Centers (1999?), 1. Gateway Pregnancy Centers are evangelical Christian operations that essentially function as "stealth" antiabortion centers: they purport to provide nonjudgmental information and services for pregnant women, but in practice hold to a strict pro-life agenda and steer callers and visitors away from facilities that include abortion among their treatment options. Gateway is only one example of this flourishing American phenomenon, which typically has a conservative Christian connection.

23. Linda Layne, *Motherhood Lost: A Feminist Account of Pregnancy Loss in America* (New York: Routledge, 2003), 9. These pregnancy-loss support Web sites are yet another major channel through which non-Buddhist Americans learn about *mizuko kuyō*. They receive extensive exploration in chapter 6.

24. Ibid., 13–19.

25. Again, these two poles of "conservative Christian" and "secular feminist" are somewhat ideal types, and they do not exhaust the variety of participants in this phenomenon. For example, *Return to Spirit*, a set of "independent study guidebooks for spiritual development" that draw mainly on New Age materials and sentiments (including elements of Hinduism, Transpersonal Psychology, and Buddhism), give step-by-step instructions in how to perform a private *mizuko kuyō* as part of one's post-abortion healing. See Barbara Stone, *Return to Spirit, Book II: Emptiness to Form, Soul Loss* (Lee, MA: House of Spirit, 1997).

26. Candace De Puy and Dana Dovitch, *The Healing Choice: Your Guide to Emotional Recovery after Abortion* (New York: Fireside, 1997: 150, 200–201).

27. Exhale, "After Abortion Resources," available at www.4exhale.org/resources.php.

28. Wakō Shannon Hickey (priest, Kojin-an Zendo, of Oakland), interview by author, 21 May 2005, at Café Driade, Chapel Hill, NC.

29. Kim Kluger-Bell, *Unspeakable Losses: Healing from Miscarriage, Abortion, and Other Pregnancy Losses* (New York: W. W. Norton, 1998), 119.

30. This claim is based on the prevalence of references to Bays's *Jizo Bodhisattva* in the works of non-Buddhists. For just one example, see Mark Hill, *Reaching Tokyo*, 19 February 2006, at www.reachingtokyo.com. Bays is one of the American Zen teachers who has placed articles or invitations to water baby ceremonies in non-Buddhist post–pregnancy loss support forums, such as *Brief Encounters* and *Loss Journal*.

31. Thomas A. Tweed and Stephen Prothero, eds., *Asian Religions in America: A Documentary History* (Oxford: Oxford University Press, 1999).

32. Wendy MacLeod, *The Water Children* (New York: Dramatists Play Service, 1999).

33. Anne Harris, *Inventing Memory* (New York: Tor Books, 2004). Similarly, the gift of a *mizuko* Jizō brings postmiscarriage healing to a character in Heather Swain's 2004 novel, *Luscious Lemon*.

34. Emily Raboteau, *The Professor's Daughter: A Novel* (New York: Henry Holt, 2005). Another example of *mizuko kuyō* in American fiction is Poul Anderson's short story "The Shrine for Lost Children" in the October–November 1999 issue of *Fantasy and Science Fiction Magazine*.

35. Arthur Golden, *Memoirs of a Geisha* (New York: Arthur A. Knopf, 1997), 320.

36. Holland Cotter, art review, "Yoke Inoue," *New York Times*, 9 May 2003, E2:39.

37. Rachel Ray-Hamaie and Ruth Reese, "Mizuko Shrine," Washington University Tyson Research Center, 2002, www.biology.wustl.edu/tyson/projectsray.html.

38. Kevin Short, "Studying in the Cemetery," *FuneralWire*, 13 March 2002.

39. I intentionally employ the term "rhetorical" in this and the following sections because of its multiple associations. Rhetorical can mean "related to the use of language": the appropriations I study here are purely in the realm of discussion, not action. Rhetorical language is often specifically intended to be *persuasive: mizuko kuyō* is appropriated to further arguments. And rhetorical in the vernacular often means that no reply is expected because the answer is obvious: many of the people here are preaching to the choir (sometimes literally) while using *mizuko kuyō* to bolster their arguments.

40. John MacArthur Jr., "The Biblical View on Abortion, Part 1," sermon delivered 1992, transcription April 1, 2003. Details taken from Grace to You, e-mail message to author from Grace to You ministries, 17 July 2006.

41. Ibid.; italics added. Interestingly, this sermon is substantially the same as one titled "Forever Life" that was delivered by Rev. Jon McNeff at the nondenominational North Creek Church in Walnut Creek, CA, on January 28, 2001. There seem to be two possible explanations. Either McNeff's sermon is based on MacArthur's widely circulated (through audiotapes, and, more recently, online transcriptions) sermon, or both McNeff and MacArthur are drawing on a common source that is circulating in evangelical pro-life communities (the dating of MacArthur's sermon—1992—suggests that he may have learned about it from William LaFleur's *Liquid Life*, or, less directly, from reviews or reactions to the book published shortly after it was released). Both possibilities point to the networks along which information about Buddhism travels in America well outside of contact with any actual Buddhists—presumably neither preacher learned about the practice of *mizuko kuyō* from a Buddhist, and certainly their congregations remained completely isolated from interaction with *mizuko kuyō*. Yet after hearing these sermons, the listeners would find their understanding of the possibilities within religion expanded by rhetorical encounter with foreign Buddhist practices at church.

42. These labels and configurations can be considerably nuanced—not all secularists are progressives, not all evangelicals are conservative—but are generally faithful to the overall culture war battle lines.

43. James Davison Hunter, *Culture Wars: The Struggle to Define America* (New York: Basic Books, 1991), 42–43.

44. Ibid., 122.

45. Ibid., 122–126.

46. John MacArthur Jr., *Why One Way? Defending an Exclusive Claim in an Inclusive World* (Nashville, W Publishing Group, 2002); John MacArthur Jr., *Fool's Gold: Discerning Truth in an Age of Error* (Wheaton, IL: Crossway Books, 2005). As an aside, *Why One Way?* features a prominently placed Buddha on its cover below a praying Muslim—both are trumped by the crucified Jesus who, in a nimbus of heavenly light pushing back the darkness, hangs at the very top and center of the cover.

47. This concept is also alternatively labeled "post-abortion stress syndrome."

48. See charismatic Jesuits Dennis Linn and Matthew Linn's *Healing the Greatest Hurt* (with Sheila Fabricant; New York: Paulist Press, 1985) for accounts of postmortem healing rituals designed to move traumatized fetuses on to heaven.

49. Jack Wilke and Barbara Wilke, *Why Can't We Love Them Both?: Questions and Answers about Abortion* (Cincinnati: Hayes, 1997).

50. Reardon's medical, psychiatric, and bioethical credentials are a subject of dispute. He apparently received a Ph.D. in philosophy of business administration through online work with Pacific Western University. In select forums, he represents himself as a confessional Christian but tends to elide his denominational affiliation; reasoning from attention to the specific forums where he most often appears and the persons and organizations with which he is most associated suggests that he is a Catholic. See Emily Bazelton, "Is There a Post-Abortion Syndrome?" *New York Times Magazine*, 21 January 2007.

51. David Reardon, "The Complexity and Distortions of Post-Abortion Research," Project Rachel, 2000. Project Rachel, originally organized as a Catholic outreach program, is the largest post-abortion counseling and support organization.

52. This should not suggest that God is fully absent from these considerations. In these worldviews, after all, it is God who set things up such that an abortion would lead to psychological trauma. But it is nonetheless remarkable how rarely God is pointed to as the actual direct cause of post-abortion stress sufferers' distress. Some of these same commentators are prepared to acknowledge God's wrathful hand in tornados, hurricanes, and other natural disasters, but shy from—at least explicitly—implicating God in the suffering of women who have had abortions.

53. Joan Frawley Desmond, "Apologizing to the Babies," *First Things* 66 (October 1996). Emphasis added.

54. Anthony Zimmerman, "Grieving the Unborn in Japan," *Catholic World Report*, February 1996.

55. Reardon, "Complexity and Distortions." "Jizu" is the spelling used by Reardon.

56. Marvin Olasky, "From Denial to Tears," *World Magazine*, 18 January 2003. A nearly identical version of this article was posted the same week at TownHall.com, one of the most prominent right-wing American political Web sites at the time.

57. Paul deBarrie, "Stilling the Cries of Grief," *Life Advocate Magazine*, April 1996. Emphasis added. The article that deBarrie quotes is Sheryl WuDunn's *New York Times* article "In Japan, a Ritual of Mourning for Abortions."

58. Vince Ackeret, "Spiritual Leaders, Politicians, and Abortion," *Superior Catholic Herald;* June 2003. Emphasis added.

59. Cynthia L. Cooper, "Abortion Under Attack," *Ms.*, August/September 2001.

60. Peg Johnston, *Pregnant? Need Help? Pregnancy Options Workbook* (Binghamton, NY: Ferre Institute, 1998), 72. Johnston takes her ideas about religion and abortion even further in the 2003 publication *Viable Utopian Ideas*, wherein she envisions a better future where women will be able to pay for many different boutique abortion services. One suggestion she offers is a spiritual retreat abortion package in which women can meet with a spiritual guide, do rituals from various traditions (Eastern philosophy is specifically mentioned and apparently refers to *mizuko kuyo*, since the other options are the same ones given in her workbook), have an abortion, and come back a year later for a follow-up consultation. Hypothetical price: $5,000. See Arthur B. Shostak, ed., *Viable Utopian Ideas: Shaping a Better World* (Armonk, NY: M.E. Sharpe, 2003).

61. Daniel C. Maguire, *Sacred Choices: The Right to Contraception and Abortion in Ten World Religions* (Minneapolis: Fortress Press, 2001), 67.

62. Ibid., 68–69. Emphasis in the original.

63. Ibid., 70.

64. Daniel Maguire, *Sacred Rights: The Case for Contraception and Abortion in World Religions* (Oxford: Oxford University Press, 2003), 285–287.

65. See http://www.prochoiceconnection.com/psco5.html. This page refers the reader to LaFleur's *Liquid Life* as "a good resource" for additional reference.

66. Dorothy C. Wertz, "The Cult of Jizo," *The Gene Letter,* 1 February 2000. LaFleur's book was in fact included in a review article in *Second Opinion,* another major bioethics forum, in 1993. As a side note, Kathleen Nolan, the author of the review, has been personally involved in Zen Buddhist practice in the United States.

67. Michael J. Meyer and Lawrence J. Nelson, "Respecting What We Destroy: Reflections on Human Embryo Research," *Hastings Center Report* 31, 1 (January–February 2001): 16–23.

68. Ibid., 20. The authors draw mainly on Hardacre for their discussion of *mizuko kuyō*. It is worth noting that the article is illustrated with a photo of a particularly plaintive and infantile-looking *mizuko* Jizō. *Tikkun* is a Jewish concept that roughly means "to mend the world."

69. Daniel Callahan. Letter to the editor, *Hastings Center Report* (July-August 2001): 4. Meyer and Nelson's rather acerbic reply: "We no more 'root around in anthropology files to find cultures that do what we want to do' than we think Callahan usually roots around in a dictionary to find definitions that support what he wants to do." Michael J. Meyer and Lawrence J. Nelson. Letter to the editor, *Hastings Center Report* (July-August 2001): 5.

70. Cynthia B. Cohen, "Human Embryo Research: Respecting What We Destroy?" letter to the editor, *Hastings Center Report* 31, 4 (July/August): 5. The debate over *mizuko kuyō's* level of support for human embryo destruction and experimentation has continued since this exchange. See, for instance, William Fitzpatrick. "Surplus Embryos, Nonreproductive Cloning, and the Intend/Foresee Distinction," *Hastings Center Report* 33, 3 (May–June 2003); and Michael Brannigan, "Fixations on the Moral Status of the

Embryo," *Biomedical Ethics Reviews: Stem Cell Research,* ed. James Humber and Robert Almeder (Totowa, NJ: Humana Press, 2004).

71. "MHE 497 Final Project Proposal," *Academia as an Extreme Sport,* 16 February 2005.

72. Tweed, "Night-Stand Buddhists," 84. Emphasis in original.

73. Peter Kreeft, *How to Win the Culture War: A Christian Battle Plan for a Society in Crisis* (Downer's Grove, IL: InterVarsity Press, 2002), 16.

74. LaFleur, *Liquid Life,* xv.

75. Ibid., 216. Although he devotes less space to the subject, LaFleur also speculates that *mizuko kuyō* could have the additional benefit of ministering to abortive American mothers' distress. This second concern of LaFleur's is discussed in depth in chapter 6.

CHAPTER 6

1. Gloria Swanson, *Swanson on Swanson* (New York: Random House, 1980), 519. The epigraph is taken from page 3 of Silko's book *Ceremony* (New York: Penguin, 1986).

2. I intentionally employ the term "therapeutic" because of its multiple associations. In its most basic definition, therapeutic means something that is healing or has the power to heal: healing societies and healing persons are the appropriations we examine in this chapter. In common parlance, therapeutic has the tendency to become associated with psychotherapy in particular: as we will see, the religious aspect of *mizuko kuyō* appropriation becomes entangled with clinical and popular notions of psychotherapy and ministering to emotional distress.

3. Gary Chamberlain, "Learning from the Japanese," *America* 171, 7 (17 September 1994). Emphasis added.

4. Anthony Zimmerman, "Memorial Services for Aborted Children in Japan," *All About Issues,* April 1989. Emphasis added.

5. Brian Clowes, *Pro-Life Activist's Encyclopedia,* American Life League, 1998. Emphasis added.

6. Lynn Wardle, "'Crying Stones': A Comparison of Abortion in Japan and the United States," *New York Law School Journal of International and Comparative Law,* 1993: 14. Because of their belief in the premortal spirit world, Mormons might potentially respond more favorably than other Christians to the basic concept of *mizuko.* In Mormon cosmology, prior to mortal birth, spirits already exist in a premortal life conceptually similar in some ways to the undefined spirit existence of future babies in Japanese religion. Though I am unaware of any Mormons who feel that abortion returns fetuses to the premortal life (most, it seems, believe that they progress on to the postmortal world), it seems plausible to imagine that such a belief could arise in the future as a way of dealing with the theological and emotional difficulties of abortion.

7. Wardle, "'Crying Stones,'" 239–240. Emphasis added.

8. Wren Farris, "Honoring the Unborn," *Vision Magazine,* September 2005: 14–15. Emphasis added.

9. Zachery Braverman. "Stone and Moss," [Translator's Note:] (www.biocomjp. com/ee), 3/15/03. Emphasis added.

10. Beyond the United States as savior/Antichrist trope (and given the gender implications of abortion), one might point to the virgin/whore trope common in American Christianity as another applicable analogy. The chaste and faithful woman is potentially the most exalted of all Christian types, whereas the promiscuous or unfaithful woman is excoriated as the wickedest of sinners. Similarly, many fundamentalist Christians and conservative Catholics put America on a pedestal, but when the United States fails to toe their preferred line on social issues, their disappointed wrath is proportional to their feeling of just how far the country has fallen.

11. Morris P. Fiorina, *Culture War? The Myth of a Polarized America* (New York: Pearson Longman, 2005), 63–66.

12. Naomi Wolf, "Our Bodies, Our Souls," *New Republic*, 16 October 1985, 35.

13. Elaine J. Ramshaw, "Ritual for Stillbirth: Exploring the Issues," *Worship* 62, 6 (November 1988): 537. Ramshaw is a Methodist pastor.

14. Many other post–pregnancy loss manuals by non-Buddhists that do not carry explicit information about *mizuko kuyō* nonetheless draw on other elements of Buddhism to provide comfort and healing practices. Examples include *Peace after Abortion*, by Ava Torre-Bueno, and *Miscarriage: Women Sharing from the Heart*, by Marie Allen and Shelly Marks.

15. The Internet addresses for these sites are as follows: Post Abortion Stress Abortion Syndrome (www.afterabortion.com), Pro-Choice Connection (www.prochoicecon nection.com), Exhale (www.4exhale.org), Life After Abortion (afterabortion.blogspot. com), Earth Island Angels (www.earthislandangels.com).

16. The Internet addresses for these sites are: MotheringDotCommune (www. mothering.com) and BabyCenter (www.babycenter.com). Both of these sites have grief forums where women have exchanged information about *mizuko kuyō* with one another.

17. Joan Snider, "Jizo Ceremony for Aborted and Miscarried Children," in *Keys to the Open Gate: A Woman's Spirituality Sourcebook*, ed. Melody Ermachild (Berkeley, CA: Conari Press, 2004); Barbara Stone, *Return to Spirit, Book II: Emptiness to Form, Soul Loss* (Lee, MA: House of Spirit, 1997).

18. Patti Hartigan, "The Kindness of Strangers," *Boston Globe Magazine*, 8 April 2002.

19. Sociologist of religion Lorne Dawson has observed how the semi-anonymous nature of online communication actually makes it an excellent medium for expressions and feelings that otherwise have no formal outlet in society: "Suppressed, maybe even truly repressed, feelings may be expressed—from anger to love. People simply will say things they would not say otherwise. Rather virulent expressions of ridicule or hatred, for example, are commonly encountered on the Internet. So are statements that would probably be too embarrassing for most of us to say in other kinds of public forums. Ironically, under conditions of technical anonymity, the sociality of the Internet offers an unparalleled opportunity for greater self-disclosure and exploration." Lorne Dawson, "Researching Religion in Cyberspace: Issues and Strategies," in *Religion on the Internet: Research Prospects and Promises*, eds. Jeffrey K. Hadden and Douglas E. Cowan (New York: Elsevier Science, 2000), 34.

20. Christopher Helland, "Online Religion/Religion-Online and Virtual Communities," in *Religion on the Internet: Prospects and Promises,* eds. Jeffrey K. Hadden and Douglas E. Cowan, 205–224 (New York: Elsevier Science, 2000).

21. Miss Zoot (www.misszoot.com), "Thank You GetupGrrl for Giving Me My Mizuko" thread, 6–8 August 2004. Miss Zoot alleges to live in Alabama and claims to "Hate/Abhor/Loathe" organized religion. Note that there are numerous grammatical and spelling errors in the online messages in this chapter, but I have elected not to include "[*sic*]" because it would quickly become too distracting. Also, it is the nature of online communication that shorthand and symbols are frequently employed, such that the offline rules of proper writing are less applicable to e-mail and Web messages.

22. Chez Miscarriage (chezmiscarriage.blogs.com), "Mizuko" thread, 5 August 2004. GetupGrrl is the pseudonym of the proprietor of Chez Miscarriage. "Grrl" is a common alternate spelling of "girl," intended to convey a sense of female power (note how it sounds like a fierce animal growling). Online pseudonyms frequently carry important meaning about how a person sees herself or wishes to be seen. "GetupGrrl," for instance, suggests a woman who has been knocked around by life but refuses to be beaten, as in "Don't just lie there, get up, girl!"

23. Chez Miscarriage (chezmiscarriage.blogs.com), "Mizuko" thread, various contributors, 5–13 August 2004. These are only a small sampling of the messages left in this one thread.

24. Pope John Paul II, *The Gospel of Life* (Washington, DC: Georgetown University Press, 1995). There are a number of loopholes—for example, the woman must have been aware that abortion is wrong and cannot have been coerced into it.

25. Linda Layne, *Motherhood Lost: A Feminist Account of Pregnancy Loss in America* (New York: Routledge, 2003), 74–75.

26. Eva Moskowitz, *In Therapy We Trust: America's Obsession with Self-Fulfillment* (Baltimore: Johns Hopkins University Press, 2001).

27. Sukie Miller with Doris Ober, *Finding Hope When a Child Dies: What Other Cultures Can Teach Us* (New York: Fireside, 2002), 19–21.

28. Ibid., 24.

29. Ibid., 100; 105. Emphasis in original.

30. For an overview of Sapir and Whorf's ideas, see Christine Jourdan and Kevin Tuite, *Language, Culture, and Society: Key Topics in Linguistic Anthropology* (Cambridge: Cambridge University Press, 2006).

31. Colleen McDannell, *Religions of the United States in Practice,* Vol. 2 (Princeton, NJ: Princeton University Press, 2001), 3.

32. As one woman who learned about *mizuko kuyō* online and then performed the ceremony during a visit to Japan declared: "The community we have online is my lifeline. and it is a hundred times more helpful to me than the support group we tried or even my therapist. what would we do without the internet?" lauralu, *Life is Sweet, Baby* (lifeisweetbaby.blogspot.com), 2 October 2005. This woman at first intended to do her own home *mizuko kuyō* based on Jan Bays's book, and invited her online friends to attend in person, but then canceled the ritual when it became clear that she and her partner would be going to Japan.

33. While *mizuko kuyō* is the thread I am tracing in this study, there are many other words, concepts, rituals, practices, artifacts, doctrines, and other elements of Buddhism that are or may be appropriated in all manner of situations. Just as an example, here is an appropriation of the notion of bodhisattvas from a post-miscarriage manual: "Marie gave me a note about a Buddhist belief in 'bodhisattvas'—souls that manifest for someone else's life and lessons rather than for their own spiritual growth. That made me feel so good. It helped explain the loving gift I have received from Jamie's life." See Marie Allen and Shelly Marks, *Miscarriage: Women Sharing from the Heart* (New York: Wiley 1993), 30.

34. Diane E. Papalia, Sally Wendkos Olds, and Ruth Duskin Feldman, *Human Development*, 9th ed. (New York: McGraw-Hill, 2004), 698.

35. Monica, *Deviant Woman* (monica.typepad.com), 22 January 2004. Emphasis added.

36. This process need not be conducted online: women I have spoken to have learned about *mizuko kuyō* through books or friends and then gone on to use this language to speak about their pain to others in real life, never involving the Internet. The Internet simply provides a particularly clear example to examine.

37. Instances of ritualization of pregnancy loss do appear in American history if one is diligent in searching for them. An example would be the baptism of stillborn and miscarried babies by Catholic hospitals, a once uncommon practice that seems to be on the rise. Nonetheless, this does seem to be an area of relative oversight or nonconcern, historically speaking, especially on the institutional level. One could point out that Japan too lacks a long history of such rituals, since *mizuko kuyō* as a formal and publicly acknowledged rite appears to date to the mid-twentieth century. The important point in this chapter is not whether pregnancy-loss rituals are wholly absent from American religious history, but the extremely widespread perception of such a lack on the part of women from all backgrounds.

38. Miller with Ober, *Finding Hope When a Child Dies*, 111–112, 117–118. Emphasis in original.

39. Ronald L. Grimes, *Deeply into the Bone: Re-Inventing Rites of Passage* (Berkeley: University of California Press, 2002), 315.

40. For information on how Caribbean religions such as Vodou have assimilated African, American Indian, Catholic, (and, now, Asian Indian) deities, see Karen McCarthy Brown, *Mama Lola: A Vodou Priestess in Brooklyn* (Berkeley, CA: University of California Press, 2001).

41. Kara Jones, "In Honor and Loving Memory of Our Children," *Kota Discussion Group*. Emphasis added. The Zen temple mentioned here is more commonly known as Great Vow Monastery.

42. This work focuses on Americans' involvement with *mizuko kuyō*, but it is worth noting in passing that some Christians in Japan have already been participating in the ritual when they could not or would not find solace in their own traditions. For examples, see Richard Fox Young, "Abortion, Grief, and Consolation: Prolegomena to a Christian Response to *Mizuko Kuyō*," *Japan Christian Quarterly* 55, 1 (Winter 1989): 31–39; Miura Domyo, *The Forgotten Child: An Ancient Eastern Answer to a Modern Problem*

(Henley-on-Thames, England: Aiden Ellis, 1983); and Michael Molloy, "The Healing of Mizuko Jizō," *Columban Mission Magazine*, May 2005: 16–18. In some cases, Christian clergy have actually sent grieving Christians in Japan to Buddhist temples to have their abortions memorialized.

43. The Web address for Flying Standby is flyingstandby.blogspot.com.

44. Such acts have longer history than one might think: prior to the legalization of abortion in America, Japan was a destination for the procedure, and sometimes women would perform *mizuko kuyō* there after the procedure was carried out. A 1973 article in *Josei* described a priest performing *mizuko kuyō* for women from Hawaii, but it is unclear whether these individuals were Buddhist. "Watakushi wa 300,000 no mizuko no sakebi-goe kiki, sono hahatachi no namida o mitekita," *Josei* 7 (16 May 1973): 191–193. Cited in Helen Hardacre, *Marketing the Menacing Fetus in Japan* (Berkeley: University of California Press, 1997), 79.

45. Mothering.com Pregnancy and Birth Loss Forum. "Ritual/Remembrance for miscarriage" thread, 27–28 December 2005. Sunnmama describes herself as an American former evangelical Christian, now a Unitarian Universalist; BCmamaof5 is apparently a Canadian.

46. See, for instance, Terra Wise, "Midwife for the Soul: Unbiased Post-Abortion Healing Support," *Vision Magazine*, June 2004; and Dayna Macy, "Unspeakable Losses," *Salon*, 15 April 1998.

47. Anonymous former member of Rochester Zen Center, interview by author, 2 November 2005, Starry Nite Café, Rochester, NY. Harper's body-oriented spiritual healing is called "somatics." Practices of this type fall somewhere within the broad range of New Age and Human Potential movements and can be considered alternative healing practices. The interviewee, who now lives in California, has practiced somatics with Harper. My attempts to contact Harper directly were unsuccessful.

48. Though not formally affiliated, many of these healers could be loosely identified as neopagans or New Age practitioners.

49. Robert Wuthnow and Wendy Cadge, "Buddhists and Buddhism in the United States: The Scope of Influence," *Journal for the Scientific Study of Religion* 43, 3 (September 2004): 369–371.

50. Less often, especially in the case of abortion, the father's potential grief is considered as well.

51. This is not meant to diminish the actual strong emotions expressed in these rituals and subsequent accounts.

52. Michel de Certeau, *The Practice of Everyday Life*, trans. Steven Rendall (Berkeley: University of California Press, 1984), 50.

53. The classic and still most influential text on this subject is Edward Said's *Orientalism* (New York: Pantheon Books, 1978).

54. Such a pessimistic assessment would assume that Americans will not become more open to fetus-as-life-in-process and reincarnation beliefs in the future. Naturally, it is possible that Americans could become more amenable to such beliefs, perhaps because of changes in American Christianity, greater popularity of Buddhist ideas, or

other unforeseen factors. It is not possible at this point to make clear predictions in this regard.

55. William LaFleur, *Liquid Life: Abortion and Buddhism in Japan* (Princeton, NJ: Princeton University Press, 1992), 217. The term *mizuko* is unitalicized in the original.

POSTSCRIPT

1. Bernard Faure, *Visions of Power: Imagining Medieval Japanese Buddhism* (Princeton, NJ: Princeton University Press, 1996), 71.

2. For an overview of this "performative turn" in Ritual Studies, see Catherine Bell, "Performance," *Critical Terms for Religious Studies,* ed. Mark Taylor, 205–224 (Chicago: University of Chicago Press, 1998).

3. Marilyn Ivy, "Modernity," *Critical Terms for the Study of Buddhism,* ed. Donald S. Lopez Jr. (Chicago: University of Chicago Press, 2005), 328.

References

PRIMARY SOURCES

Adashino Nembutsuji. *Adashino Nembutsuji.* Pamphlet, n.d. (collected 2006).
———. *Nembutsu–ji Temple at Adashino in Kyoto.* Pamphlet, n.d. (collected 2006).
Aitken, Robert. *The Mind of Clover: Essays in Zen Buddhist Ethics.* New York: North Point Press, 1984.
———. *The Practice of Perfection: The Paramitas from a Zen Buddhist Perspective.* Washington D.C.: Counterpoint Press, 1994.
———. *Taking the Path of Zen.* San Francisco: North Point Press, 1982.
Allen, Marie, and Shelly Marks. *Miscarriage: Women Sharing from the Heart.* New York: Wiley, 1993.
Anderson, Poul, "The Shrine for Lost Children," *Science Fiction and Fantasy Magazine,* October–November 1999, 198–213.
Anderson, Reb. *Being Upright: Zen Meditation and the Bodhisattva Precepts.* Berkeley, CA: Rodmell Press, 2001.
[Anonymous]. "Anti-Abortion/Pro-Choice." Letter to the editor. *Tricycle: The Buddhist Review,* vol. 7, no. 4 (Summer 1992): 6.
[Anonymous]. "Dispelling an Abortion's Bad Karma." *Harper's,* March 1993, 23.
Awashimadō Sōtokuji. *Awashimadō Sōtokuji.* Pamphlet, n.d. (collected 2006).
Bays, Jan Chozen. *Jizo Bodhisattva: Modern Healing and Traditional Buddhist Practice.* Boston: Tuttle, 2001.
———. "Jizo Bodhisattva: Protector of Women and Children." In *The Complete Guide to Buddhist America,* edited by Don Morreale, 187. Boston: Shambhala, 1998.
Benstenshū Meiōji. *Mizuko kuyō no Rei ni Yasuragi o.* Pamphlet, n.d. (collected 2006).

Blofeld, John. *Bodhisattva of Compassion: The Mystical Tradition of Kuan Yin*. Boston: Shambhala, 1988.

———. "Kuan Yin." *Tricycle: The Buddhist Review*, vol. 5, no. 3 (Spring 1996): 30–31.

Boucher, Sandy. *Discovering Kwan Yin, Buddhist Goddess of Compassion: A Woman's Book of Ruminations, Meditations, Prayers, and Chants*. Boston: Beacon Press, 1999.

———. *Opening the Lotus: A Woman's Guide to Buddhism*. Boston: Beacon Press, 1997.

Bradford, Hope, and Lena Lees. *The Living Word of Kuan Yin: The Teachings and Prophecies of the Goddess of Compassion and Mercy*. Charleston, SC: BookSurge, 2006.

Brannigan, Michael C. "Fixations on the Moral Status of the Embryo." In *Stem Cell Research*, edited by James M. Humber and Robert F. Almeder, 43–57. Totowa, NJ: Humana Press, 2004.

Burke, Theresa, with David C. Reardon (foreword by Laura Schlessinger). *Forbidden Grief: The Unspoken Pain of Abortion*. Springfield, IL: Acorn Books, 2002.

Chamberlain, Gary L. "Learning from the Japanese: Pro-Life Rituals in Buddhism and Shinto." *America*, vol. 171, no. 7 (17 July 1994): 14–16.

Chavis, Melody Ermachild. "A Ceremony for Aborted and Miscarried Children." *Turning Wheel: Journal of the Buddhist Peace Fellowship* (Summer 1990): 28–30.

Cohen, Cynthia B. "Human Embryo Research: Respecting What We Destroy?" Letter to the editor. *Hastings Center Report*, July–August 2001, 4–5

Collet, Richard A. "Anti-Abortion/Pro-Choice (Letter to the editor)." *Tricycle: The Buddhist Review* vol. 7, no. 4 (Summer 1992): 6.

Conroy, J. Patrick. "Cultural Differences...Or Honesty?" *Cincinnati Right to Life Education Foundation Newsletter*, vol. 33, no. 4 (April 2003): 2.

Davis, Deborah. *Empty Cradle, Broken Heart: Surviving the Death of Your Baby*. Golden, CO: Fulcrum, 1996.

De Puy, Candace, and Dana Dovitch. *The Healing Choice: Your Guide to Emotional Recovery after Abortion*. New York: Fireside, 1997.

Desmond, Joan Frawley. "Apologizing to the Babies." *First Things*, October 1996, 13–15.

Dharma Rain Zen Center. *Still Point* (newsletter), selected issues.

DharmaCrafts: The Catalog of Meditation Supplies, Spring 2006.

Dodd, Jan, and Simon Richmond. *The Rough Guide to Japan*. London: Rough Guides, 2001.

Dombrowski, Daniel A. *A Brief, Liberal, Catholic Defense of Abortion*. Urbana: University of Illinois Press, 2000.

Domyo, Miura. *The Forgotten Child: An Ancient Eastern Answer to a Modern Problem*. Henley–On–Thames, England: Aiden Ellis, 1983.

Drougge, Per. "Jizo Bodhisattva." *Zen Bow*, vol. 16, no. 3 (summer 1994): 30–31.

Ensōzan Jōtokuji. *Ensōzan Jōtokuji*. Pamphlet, n.d. (collected 2006).

Ermachild, Melody. "A Ceremony for Lost Children." *Yoga Journal*, November–December 1991, 120, 106–107.

Exhale. "After–Abortion Resources." *Freedom to Exhale*, no. 4 (Summer 2004), 2.

Fallows, Deborah. "Japanese Women." *National Geographic*, vol. 177, no. 4 (April 1990), 53–84.

Feldman, Christina. *Compassion: Listening to the Cries of the World*. Berkeley, CA: Rodmell Press, 2005.

Fernandez, Audrey. *American Zen Twenty Years*. Rochester, NY: Rochester Zen Center, 1986.

Fields, Rick. *How the Swans Came to the Lake: A Narrative History of Buddhism in America*. 3rd ed. Boston: Shambhala, 1992.

Fitzpatrick, William. "Surplus Embryos, Nonreproductive Cloning, and the Intend/ Foresee Distinction." *Hastings Center Report*, May–June 2003, 29–36.

Fleming, Jim. Program 02-01-27-A "I'm Sorry." *To the Best of Our Knowledge*, Madison: Wisconsin Public Radio, 2002.

Friedman, Lenore, and Susan Moon, eds. *Being Bodies: Buddhist Women on the Paradox of Embodiment*. Boston: Shambhala, 1997.

Gabrielson, Ruth. "A Prayer for the Water Children: Mizuko Kuyo in Japan." *Areopagus: A Living Encounter with Today's Religious World*, vol. 5, no. 5 (1992): 47–50.

Gateway Pregnancy Centers. "He Who Frames the Question, Wins the Argument!" Flier, n.d.

The General Convention of the Episcopal Church. *Summary of Actions of the 74th General Convention*. New York: Episcopal Church USA, 2003.

Genter, Penelope. *Returning Home: A Workbook for Following Your Path to Ascension— Channeled Lessons from Mother Mary, Merlin, and Quan Yin*. Cedar Crest, NM: MMB Publishing 2002.

Golden, Arthur. *Memoirs of a Geisha*. New York: Arthur A. Knopf, 1997.

Graef, Sunyana. "Water Baby Ceremony." *Walking Mountains*, August 2005, 5.

Green, Ronald M. *The Human Embryo Research Debates: Bioethics in the Vortex of Controversy*. Oxford: Oxford University Press, 2001.

Halifax, Joan. *A Buddhist Life in America: Simplicity in the Complex*. New York: Paulist Press, 1998.

Harris, Anne. *Inventing Memory*. New York: Tor Books, 2004.

Hongwanji International Center. *Jodo Shinshu: A Guide*. Kyoto: Hongwanji International Center, 2002.

Honolulu Diamond Sangha. *Honolulu Diamond Sangha* (newsletter), selected issues.

Hopkinson, Deborah, Michele Hill, and Eileen Kiera, eds. *Not Mixing Up Buddhism: Essays on Women and Buddhist Practice*. Fredonia, NY: White Pine Press, 1986.

Hōshuzan Daikannonji. *Hōshuzan Daikanoonji Goannai*. Pamphlet, n.d. (collected 2006).

Hua, Hsuan. *The Sutra of the Past Vows of Earth Store Bodhisattva*. New York: Buddhist Text Translation Society, 1974.

Hui, Pitt Chin, trans. *Bilingual Sutra on the Original Vows and Attainment of Merits of Kshitigarbha Bodhisattva*. World Fellowship of Buddhists, Singapore Regional Centre. Hong Kong Buddhist Book Distributor, 1976.

Imakumano Kannonji. *Saigoku Daijūgoban Reijō*. Pamphlet, n.d. (collected 2006).

Jenkins, Sara. *Buddha Facing the Wall: Interviews with American Zen Monks, from the Zen Monastery Practice Center under the Guidance of Cheri Huber*. Lake Junaluska, NC: Present Perfect Books, 1999.

Johnston, Peg. *Pregnant? Need Help? Pregnancy Options Workbook*. Binghamton, NY: Ferre Institute, 2002.

Kaizōzan Jishōan Hasedera. *Kamakura Hasedera (The Hase Kannon Temple)*. Pamphlet, n.d. (collected 2005).

Kapleau, Philip. *The Three Pillars of Zen: Teaching, Practice, Enlightenment*. Boston: Beacon Press, 1965.

———. *The Wheel of Life and Death: A Practical and Spiritual Guide*. New York: Doubleday, 1989.

Kazahaya, Katsuichi. *Koysasan Buddhist Temple, 1912–1962*. Los Angeles: Koyasan Beikoku Betsuin, 1974.

Kellenberger, James. *Moral Relativism, Moral Diversity, and Human Relationships*. University Park: Pennsylvania State University Press, 2001.

Kluger-Bell, Kim. *Unspeakable Losses: Healing from Miscarriage, Abortion, and Other Pregnancy Losses*. New York: W. W. Norton, 1998.

Kiriyama, Seiyu. *The Varieties of Karma*. Translated by Rande Brown. Tokyo: Agon Shu, 2000.

Kornfield, Jack. *After the Ecstasy, the Laundry: How the Heart Grows Wise on the Spiritual Path*. New York: Bantam Books, 2000.

Koyasan Buddhist Temple. "Bus-setsu Ma-ka Han-nya Ha-ra-mit-ta-shin-gyo." Flier, n.d. (collected 2007).

———. *Koyasan Jiho*. Newsletter, January 2004.

———. *Shingon Buddhist Service Book*. Los Angeles: Koyasan Shingon Mission, n.d.

Kreeft, Peter. *How to Win the Culture War: A Christian Battle Plan for a Society in Crisis*. Downer's Grove, IL: InterVarsity Press, 2002.

Kushner, Eve. *Experiencing Abortion: A Weaving of Women's Words*. New York: Harrington Park Press, 1997.

Kyōgaku Honbu, ed. "Shinshū no tachiba kara mita 'mizuko' mondai." *Nyōnin Ōjō Tsuite*. Kyoto: Honganji Shuppanbu, 1988.

Leighton, Daniel Taigen. *Bodhisattva Archetypes: Classic Buddhist Guides to Awakening and Their Modern Expression*. New York: Penguin Putnam, 1998.

Linn, Dennis, and Matthew Linn, with Sheila Fabricant. *Healing the Greatest Hurt*. New York: Paulist Press, 1985.

Los Angeles Nichiren Buddhist Temple. *Nichiren Shū Raihai Seiten*. Los Angeles: Nichiren Shu Beikoku Sangha Association, 2002.

MacArthur, John F., Jr. *The Biblical View on Abortion*. Parts 1 and 2. Sermon delivered at Grace Community Church, Sun Valley, CA, 1993. Transcript available at http://www.biblebb.com/files/MAC/ABORT.HTM.

———. *Fool's Gold: Discerning Truth in an Age of Error*. Wheaton, IL: Crossway Books, 2005.

———. *Why One Way? Defending an Exclusive Claim in an Inclusive World*. Nashville: W Publishing Group, 2002.

MacLeod, Wendy. *The Water Children*. New York: Dramatists Play Service, 1999.

Macy, Dayna. "Unspeakable Losses: Why Don't Americans Talk About Their Lost Pregnancies?" *Salon*, 15 April 1998.

Maezumi, Hakyu Taizan, and Bernard Tetsugen Glassman, eds. *On Zen Practice*. Los Angeles: Zen Center of Los Angeles, 1976.

———, eds. *On Zen Practice II*. Los Angeles: Zen Center of Los Angeles, 1977.

Maguire, Daniel C. *Sacred Choices: The Right to Contraception and Abortion in Ten World Religions*. Minneapolis: Fortress Press, 2001.

———. *Sacred Rights: The Case for Contraception and Abortion in World Religions*. Oxford: Oxford University Press, 2003.

Maloney, Anne. "You Say You Want a Revolution? Pro–Life Philosophy and Feminism." *Studies in Pro–Life Feminisim*, vol. 1, no. 4 (Fall 1995): 26–44.

McNeff, Jon. "Forever Life." Sermon delivered at NorthCreek Church, Walnut Creek, CA. 28 January 2001.

Megorugyōninzaka Matsubayashizan Daienji. *Megorugyōninzaka Daienji*. Pamphlet, n.d. (collected 2006).

Meyer, Michael J. and Lawrence J. Nelson. "Respecting What We Destroy: Reflections on Human Embryo Research." *Hastings Center Report*, January–February 2001, 16–23.

———. Letter to the editor. *Hastings Center Report* (July-August 2001): 5.

Miller, Sukie, with Doris Ober. *Finding Hope When a Child Dies: What Other Cultures Can Teach Us*. New York: Fireside, 2002.

Milliken, Margot Wallach. "On Abortion." In *Not Mixing Up Buddhism: Essays on Women and Buddhist Practice*, edited by Deborah Hopkinson, Michele Hill, and Eileen Kiera, 74–77.Fredonia, NY: White Pine Press, 1986.

Miyajimamisen Daihonzan Daishōin. *Miyajima Misen Daisyoin*. Pamphlet, n.d. (collected 2006).

Miyata, Taisen. "Koyasan Buddhist Temple of Los Angeles." Koyasan Buddhist Temple, Pamphlet, 20 October 2002.

Molloy, Michael. "The Healing of Mizuko Jizo." *Columban Mission Magazine*, May 2005: 16–18.

Nakao, Wendy Egyoku. "Journey to the Earth's Womb: A Healing Council on Abortion." *Water Wheel*, Zen Center of Los Angeles, 2000.

Nariai, John. "The Prolife Struggle in Japan." *New Oxford Review*, vol. 64, no. 2 (March 1997): 23–24, 29.

Natalie (Kittyonnails). "22 Weeks or 10 Months." *AdultFanFiction.Net: The Adult Fan Fiction Haven* (http://adultfan.nexcess.net/aff/).

Nathanson, Sue. *Soul Crisis: One Woman's Journey through Abortion to Renewal*. New York: New American Library, 1989.

National Memorial for the Unborn (http://www.memorialfortheunborn.org/).

Neuhaus, Richard John. "Never Again?." *First Things*, August–September 1994: 45.

Nichiren Shoshu Myohoji Temple of Los Angeles. "Application For Toba." Form, n.d. (collected 2007).

Nikken. "Earthly Desires Are in Themselves Enlightenment." Nichiren Shoshu Globalnet, 2003, http://www.nsglobalnet.jp/page/collected_sermons/32.htm.

Nolan, Kathleen. "What Makes an 'Other'? Diversity, Disability, and the Softening of Our Hearts." *Second Opinion*, vol. 19 (October 1993): 116–119.

Northrup, Christiane. *Life Touches Life: A Mother's Story of Stillbirth and Healing*. Troutdale, OR: New Sage Press, 2004.

Nyanasobhano, Bhikkhu. *A Buddhist View of Abortion*. Bodhi Leaves #117. Kandy, Sri Lanka: Buddhist Publication Society, 1989.

O'Connor, June. "Ritual Recognition of Abortion: Japanese Buddhist Practices and U.S. Jewish and Christian Proposals." In *Embodiment, Morality, and Medicine,* ed. Lisa Sowle Cahill and Margaret A. Farley, 93–111. Boston: Kluwer Academic, 1995.

O'Connor, Thomas P. "Consoling the Infants: For Whose Sake." *Japan Christian Quarterly,* vol. 50 (Fall 1984): 206–214.

Olasky, Marvin. "From Denial to Sadness." TownHall.com, March 2, 2003.

O'Neill, Jennifer. *You're Not Alone: Healing through God's Grace after Abortion.* Deerfield Beach, FL: Health Communications, 2005.

Oxenhandler, Noelle. *The Eros of Parenthood: Explorations in Light and Dark.* New York: Golden Books Adult Publishing, 2001.

Palmer, Martin, Jay Ramsay, and Man-Ho Kwok. *Kuan Yin: Myths and Revelations of the Chinese Goddess of Compassion.* London: Thorsons, 1995.

Ponte, Wendy. "Solitary Sadness: The Need to Grieve Miscarriage." *Mothering: The Magazine of Natural Family Living,* July–August 2002, 54–61.

Pope John Paul II. *The Gospel of Life.* Washington, D.C.: Georgetown University Press, 1995.

Post Abortion Stress Syndrome Web site (www.afterabortion.com).

PregnantPause.org (www.pregnantpause.org).

Pro-Choice Connection (prochoiceconnection.com/psco5.html). "Mizuko Kuyo." Retrieved April 24, 2003.

Quanyin (through Dan Klatt). *Experience Unconditional Love This Year.* Sedona, AZ: Cellular Publishing, 1999.

Raboteau, Emily. *The Professor's Daughter: A Novel.* New York: Henry Holt, 2005.

Padmakara Translation Group. *The Way of the Bodhisattva.* Boston: Shambhala, 1997.

Penang Nichiren Shu Buddhist Association. *Gongyō Seiten.* Penang, Malaysia: Penang Nichiren Shu Buddhist Association, n.d. (collected 2007).

Rabuzzi, Kathryn. *Motherself: A Mythic Analysis of Motherhood.* Bloomington: Indiana University Press, 1988.

Ramshaw, Elaine J. "Ritual for Stillbirth: Exploring the Issues." *Worship,* vol. 62, no. 6 (November 1988): 533–538.

Rand, Yvonne. "Abortion: A Respectful Meeting Ground." In *Buddhism through American Women's Eyes,* ed. Karma Lekshe Tsomo, 85–89. Ithaca, NY: Snow Lion, 1995.

———. "The Buddha's Way and Abortion: Loss, Grief, and Resolution." *Inquiring Mind,* Fall 1993, 21.

———. "A Ceremony for Children, Born and Unborn, Who Have Died." *God's Friends* 13, no 3 (November 2002): 7–8.

———. "Liquid Life: Abortion and Buddhism in Japan." *Tricycle: The Buddhist Review,* vol. 2, no. 3 (Spring 1993): 93–95.

Rapaport, Al. *Buddhism in America: Proceedings of the First Buddhism in America Conference.* Rutland, VT: Charles E. Tuttle, 1998.

Ratner, Herbert. "Gloria Swanson's Abortion." *Celebrate Life,* May–June 1994: 13–14.

Reardon, David C. "The Complexity and Distortions of Post-Abortion Research." Project Rachel, 2000. Available at www.hopeafterabortion.com/aftermath/index.cfm?page=reardon.

Reiber, Beth, and Janie Spencer. *Frommer's Japan*. Hoboken, NJ: Wiley, 2004.

Risshō Kōsei-kai. *Kyōden*. Tokyo: Risshō Kōsei-kai, 2001.

Risshō Kōsei-kai. *Kyōden Sutra Readings: Extracts from the Threefold Lotus Sutra*. Tokyo: Risshō Kōsei-kai, 2003.

Rissho Kosei-kai Buddhist Church of Los Angeles. "Buddhism for Today." Pamphlet, n.d. (late 2006 or early 2007, collected 2007).

Rome, David I. "Anti-Abortion/Pro-Choice." Letter to the editor. *Tricycle: The Buddhist Review*, vol. 7, no. 4 (Summer 1992): 6.

Rosenblatt, Roger. *Life Itself: Abortion in the American Mind*. New York: Random House, 1992.

Rowthorn, Chris, and Ray Bartlett. *Lonely Planet Japan*. Oakland, CA: Lonely Planet Publishing, 2005.

Rutherford, Scott. *Insight Guide: Japan*. London: Insight Guides, 2003.

Seery, John. "Moral Perfectionism and Abortion Politics." *Polity*, vol. 33, no. 3 (Spring 2001): 345–364.

Seligsen, Fred Jeremy. *Queen Jin's Hand Book of Pregnancy*. Berkeley, CA: North Atlantic Books, 2001.

Sherman, Aliza. Babyfruit Miscarriage and Pregnancy Blog. (http://babyfruit.typepad.com/baby).

Shokai, Kanai. "Abortion and a Memorial Service for the Unborn Babies." *The Bridge*, Autumn 2000, 1.

Shostak, Arthur B., ed. *Viable Utopian Ideas: Shaping a Better World*. Armonk, NY: M.E. Sharpe, 2003.

Shunryū Suzuki. *Branching Streams Flow in the Darkness: Zen Talks on the Sandokai*. Berkeley: University of California Press, 2001.

———. *Zen Mind, Beginner's Mind*. New York: Weatherhill, 1970.

Siegel, Robert, ed. *The NPR Interviews, 1995*. Boston: Houghton Mifflin, 1995.

Snow, Kimberly. *In Buddha's Kitchen: Cooking, Being Cooked, and Other Adventures in a Meditation Center*. Boston: Shambhala, 2003.

Sōhonzan Enmanin Monzeki. *Mizuko Sō Kuyō Daihōyō Goansei*. Pamphlet, n.d. (collected 2006).

———. *Shūha o towanai, Anjin no Okunaibochi! Nōkotsu Gobutsudan no Goaisei*. Pamphlet, n.d. (collected 2006).

Sōtōshū Shūmucho. *Soto School Scriptures for Daily Services and Practice*. Tokyo: Sōtōshū Shūmucho, 2001.

———. *Sōtōshū Nikka Gongyō*. Tokyo: Sōtōshū Shūmucho, 2000.

Stetson, Brad, ed. *The Silent Subject: Reflections on the Unborn in American Culture*. Westport, CT: Praeger, 1996.

Stone, Barbara. *Return to Spirit, Book II: Emptiness to Form, Soul Loss*. Lee, MA: House of Spirit, 1997.

Stotland, Nada L. "Abortion and Psychiatric Practice." *Journal of Psychiatric Practice*, vol. 9, no. 2 (March 2003): 139–149.

Swain, Heather. *Luscious Lemon*. New York: Downtown Press, 2004.

Swanson, Gloria. *Swanson on Swanson*. New York: Random House, 1980.

Tanukidanizan Fudōin. *Gokuyō.* Form, n.d. (collected 2006).

Tisdale, Sallie. "We Do Abortions Here: A Nurse's Story." *Harper's,* October 1987: 66–70.

Torre-Bueno, Ava. *Peace after Abortion.* San Diego, CA: Pimpernel Press, 1997.

Tōeizan Jōmyōin. *Hachimanyonsentai Jizō.* Pamphlet, n.d. (collected 2006).

Tuesday Women's Group. "Anti-Abortion/Pro-Choice." Letter to the editor. *Tricycle: The Buddhist Review,* vol. 8, no. 1 (Fall 1992): 6.

Tworkov, Helen. "Anti-Abortion/Pro-Choice: Taking Both Sides." *Tricycle: The Buddhist Review,* vol. 1, no. 3 (Spring 1992): 60–69.

———. *Zen in America: Five Teachers and the Search for an American Buddhism.* New York: Kodansha International, 1994.

Veatch, Robert M. *Cross-Cultural Perspectives in Medical Ethics.* Sudbury, MA: Jones and Bartlett, 2001.

Vermont Zen Center. *Walking Mountains.* Newsletter, 2006–present.

von Sturmer, Richard, and Jospeh Sorrentino. *Images From the Center: Daily Life at an American Zen Center.* Rochester, NY: Rochester Zen Center, 1998.

Wardle, Lynn D. "'Crying Stones': A Comparison of Abortion in Japan and the United States." *New York Law School Journal of International and Comparative Law,* vol. 14 (1993): 183–259.

Waterman, Barbara. *Birth of an Adoptive, Foster, or Stepmother: Beyond Biological Mothering Attachments.* London: Jessica Kingsley, 2003.

Weil, Lise. "Taken to Task." Letter to the editor. *Tricycle: The Buddhist Review,* vol. 7, no. 4 (Summer 1992): 5.

Wertz, Dorothy C. "The Cult of Jizo." *Gene Letter,* 1 February 2000.

Weston, Anthony. *A Twenty-First Century Ethical Toolbox.* Oxford: Oxford University Press, 2000.

Wilke, Jack, and Barbara Wilke. *Why Can't We Love Them Both? Questions and Answers about Abortion.* Cincinnati: Hayes, 1997.

Wilkie, Laurie. *The Archaeology of Mothering: An African-American Midwife's Tale.* New York: Routledge, 2003.

Williams, Camille S. "Feminism and Imaging the Unborn." In *The Silent Subject: Reflections on the Unborn in American Culture,* edited by Brad Stetson, 61-90. Westport, CT: Praeger, 1996.

Wolf, Naomi. "Our Bodies, Our Souls." *New Republic,* 16 October 1985, 26–35.

Young, Richard Fox. "Abortion, Grief, and Consolation: Prolegomena to a Christian Response to Mizuko Muyo." *Japan Christian Quarterly,* vol. 55, no. 1 (Winter 1989): 31–39.

Yu, Chun-Fang. *Kuan-yin: The Chinese Transformation of Avalokitesvara.* New York: Columbia University Press, 2000.

Zen Mountain Monastery. "The Loss of a Child." Retreat schedule, 14 October 1994.

Zenith, S. Y. "Mizuko Kuyo: The Japanese Rite for the Unborn." Paganality.com, 8 May 2005.

Zimmerman, Anthony, S.V.D. "Aborted Women: A Japanese Perspective." *Pregnant Pause,* 9 September 2000. Available on line at www.pregnantpause.org/aborted/japview.htm

————. "Grieving the Unborn in Japan." *Catholic World Report,* February 1996. Available online at www.lifeissues.net/writers/zim/zim_70grievingunbornjapan.html

————. "The Historical Christ in World Religions." CatholicMind.com, 2000. Available online at http://lifeissues.net/writers/zim/zim_201worldreligions1.html

————. "Memorial Services for Aborted Children in Japan." *All About Issues,* April 1989. Available online at www.lifeissues.net/writers/zim/zim_101servicesaborted.html

Secondary Sources

Agostini, Giulio. "Buddhist Sources on Feticide as Distinct from Homicide." *Journal of the International Association for Buddhist Studies,* vol. 27, no. 1 (2004): 63–96.

Ahlstrom, Sydney. *A Religious History of the American People.* New Haven, CT: Yale University Press, 1972.

————, ed. *Theology in America: The Major Protestant Voices from Puritanism to Neo-Orthodoxy.* Indianapolis: Bobbs-Merrill, 1967.

Albanese, Catherine L. "Exchanging Selves, Exchanging Souls: Contact, Combination, and American Religious History." In *Retelling U.S. Religious History,* edited by Thomas A. Tweed, 200–226. Berkeley: University of California Press, 1997.

Anderson, Richard W., and Elaine Martin. "Rethinking the Practice of *Mizuko Kuyo* in Contemporary Japan: Interviews with Practitioners at a Buddhist Temple in Tokyo." *Japanese Journal of Religious Studies,* vol. 24, no. 1–2 (1997): 121–143.

Arai, Paula Kane Robinson. *Women Living Zen: Japanese Soto Buddhist Nuns.* New York: Oxford University Press, 1999.

Asai, Senryō, and Duncan Ryūken Williams. "Japanese American Zen Temples: Cultural Identity and Economics." In *American Buddhism: Methods and Findings in Recent Scholarship,* edited by Duncan Williams and Christopher Queen, 20–35. Richmond, UK: Curzon, 1999.

Balmer, Randall, and Lauren F. Winner. *Protestantism in America.* New York: Columbia University Press, 2002.

Bargen, Doris, G. "Ancestral to None: *Mizuko* in Kawabata." *Japanese Journal of Religious Studies,* vol. 19, no. 4 (1992): 337–377.

Barnhart, Michael G. "Buddhism and the Morality of Abortion." *Journal of Buddhist Ethics,* vol. 5 (26 June 1998).

Bell, Catherine M. "Performance." In *Critical Terms for Religious Studies,* edited by Mark C. Taylor, 205–224. Chicago: University of Chicago Press, 1998.

————. *Ritual: Perspectives and Dimensions.* New York: Oxford University Press, 1997.

Bodiford, William M. "The Enlightenment of Kami and Ghosts: Spirit Ordinations in Sōtō Zen." In *Chan Buddhism in Ritual Context,* edited by Bernard Faure. London: RoutledgeCurzon, 2003: 250–265.

————. *Sōtō Zen in Medieval Japan.* Honolulu: University of Hawaii Press, 1993.

————. "Zen and the Art of Religious Prejudice: Efforts to Reform a Tradition of Social Discrimination." *Japanese Journal of Religious Studies,* vol. 23, nos. 1–2 (1996): 1–27.

Braude, Ann. "Women's History *Is* American Religious History." In *Retelling U.S. Religious History*, edited by Thomas A. Tweed, 87–107. Berkeley: University of California Press, 1997.

Brooks, Anne Page. "'Mizuko Kuyo' and Japanese Buddhism." *Japanese Journal of Religious Studies*, vol. 8, nos. 3–4 (September–December 1981): 119–147.

Brown, Karen McCarthy, *Mama Lola: A Vodou Priestess in Brooklyn* (Berkeley, CA: University of California Press, 2001).

Busto, Rudiger V. "DisOrienting Subjects: Reclaiming Pacific Islander/Asian American Religions." In *Revealing the Sacred in Asian and Pacific America*, edited by Jame Naomi Iwamura and Paul Spickard, 9–28. New York: Routledge, 2003.

Cadge, Wendy. *Heartwood: The First Generation of Theravada Buddhism in America*. Chicago: University of Chicago Press, 2004.

Coakley, Sarah, ed. *Religion and the Body*. Cambridge: Cambridge University Press, 1997.

Coleman, James William. *The New Buddhism: The Western Transformation of an Ancient Tradition*. Oxford: Oxford University Press, 2001.

Cook, Elizabeth Adell, Ted. G. Jelen, and Clyde Wilcox. "Catholicism and Abortion Attitudes in the American States: A Contextual Analysis." *Journal for the Scientific Study of Religion*, vol. 32, no. 3 (September 1993): 223–230.

Csordas, Thomas. *Body/Meaning/Healing*. New York: Palgrave Macmillan, 2002.

Cuevas, Bryan J., and Jacqueline I. Stone, eds. *The Buddhist Dead: Practices, Discourses, Representations*. Honolulu: University of Hawaii Press, 2007.

Davis, Tom. *Sacred Work: Planned Parenthood and Its Clergy Alliances*. New Brunswick, NJ: Rutgers University Press, 2005.

Dawson, Lorne L., and Douglas E. Cowan, eds. *Religion Online: Finding Faith on the Internet*. New York: Routledge, 2004.

DeCaroli, Robert. *Haunting the Buddha: Indian Popular Religions and the Formation of Buddhism*. New York: Oxford University Press, 2004.

De Certeau, Michel. *The Practice of Everyday Life*. Translated by Steven Rendall. Berkeley: University of California Press, 1984.

Douglas, Thomas J. "The Cross and the Lotus: Changing Religious Practices among Cambodian Immigrants in Seattle." In *Revealing the Sacred in Asian and Pacific America*, edited by Jane Naomi Iwamura and Paul Spickard, 159–176. New York: Routledge, 2003.

Downing, Michael. *Shoes outside the Door: Desire, Devotion, and Excess at the San Francisco Zen Center*. Washington, D.C.: Counterpoint, 2001.

Duntley, Madeline. "Heritage, Ritual, and Translation: Seattle's Japanese Presbyterian Church." In *Gods of the City: Religion and the American Urban Landscape*, edited by Robert A Orsi, 289–309. Bloomington: Indiana University Press, 1999.

Dykstra, Yoshiko Kurata. "Jizo, the Most Merciful: Tales From *Jizo Bosatsu Reigenki*." *Monumenta Nipponica*, vol. 33, no. 2 (Summer 1978): 179–200.

Eiki, Hoshino, and Takeda Dosho. "Indebtedness and Comfort: The Undercurrents of *Mizuko Kuyo* in Contemporary Japan." *Japanese Journal of Religious Studies*, vol. 14, no. 4 (1987): 305–320.

———. "*Mizuko Kuyo* and Abortion in Contemporary Japan." In *Religion and Society in Modern Japan: Selected Readings*, edited by Mark Mullins, Shimazono

Susumu, and Paul Swanson, 171–190. Berkeley, CA: Asian Humanities Press, 1993.

Elgin, Suzette Haden. *The Language Imperative: The Power of Language to Enrich Your Life and Expand Your World*. New York: Perseus Books Groups, 2001.

Emerson, Michael O. "Through Tinted Glasses: Religion, Worldviews, and Abortion." *Journal for the Scientific Study of Religion*, vol. 35, no. 1 (March 1996): 41–55.

Faure, Bernard, ed. *Chan Buddhism in Ritual Context*. New York: RoutledgeCurzon, 2003.

———. *The Power of Denial: Buddhism, Purity, and Gender*. Princeton, NJ: Princeton University Press, 2003.

———. *The Red Thread: Buddhist Approaches to Sexuality*. Princeton, NJ: Princeton University Press, 1998.

———. *Visions of Power: Imagining Medieval Japanese Buddhism*. Princeton, NJ: Princeton University Press, 1996.

Finke, Roger, and Rodney Stark. *The Churching of America, 1776–1990: Winners and Losers in our Religious Economy*. New Brunswick, N.J.: Rutgers University Press, 1992.

Finney, Henry C. "American Zen's 'Japan Connection': A Critical Case Study of Zen Buddhism's Diffusion to the West." *Sociological Analysis*, vol. 52, no. 4 (Fall 1991): 279–396.

Fiorina, Morris P. *Culture War? The Myth of a Polarized America*. New York: Pearson Longman, 2005.

Foulk, T. Griffith. "About Soto Zen Liturgy." *Soto School Scriptures for Daily Services and Practice*. Tokyo: Sōtōshū Shūmucho, 2001.

———, "Ritual in Japanese Zen Buddhism," in *Zen Ritual*, ed. Steven Heine and Dale Wright, 21–82 (Oxford: Oxford University Press, 2008).

Frankiel, Tamar. "Ritual Sites in the Narrative of American Religion." In *Retelling U.S. Religious History*, edited by Thomas A. Tweed, 57–86. Berkeley: University of California Press, 1997.

Fujii, Masao. "Buddhism and Bioethics." *Theological Developments in Bioethics*, eds. Andrew B. Lustig, Baruch A Brody, H. Tristram Englehardt, and Laurence B. McCullough, 61–68. Dordrecht, Netherlands: Kluwer, 1991.

Green, Ronald M. "The *Mizuko Kuyo* Debate: An Ethical Assessment." *Journal of the American Academy of Religion*, vol. 67, no. 4 (1999): 809–824.

———. "Rejoinder: One More Time: Comparative Ethics and Mizuko Kuyo." *Journal of the American Academy of Religion*, vol. 69, no. 2 (June 2001): 471–474.

Gregory, Peter. "Describing the Elephant: Buddhism in America." *Religion and American Culture*, vol. 11, no. 2 (Summer 2001): 233–263.

Gregory, Peter, and Suzanne Mrozik, eds. *Women Practicing Buddhism: American Experiences*. Boston: Wisdon Publications, 2008.

Griffith, R. Marie. *Born Again Bodies: Flesh and Spirit in American Christianity*. Berkeley: University of California Press, 2004.

Grimes, Ronald L. *Deeply Into the Bone: Re-Inventing Rites of Passage*. Berkeley: University of California Press, 2002.

Hack, Sheryl N. "Collective Identity and Sacred Space: A Study of Seven Zen Communities in Northern California." MA thesis. University of Delaware, 1989.

Hadden, Jeffrey K., and Douglas E. Cowan, eds. *Religion on the Internet: Research Prospects and Promises*. New York: Elsevier Science, 2000.

Hall, David D. *Lived Religion in America: Toward a History of Practice*. Princeton, NJ: Princeton University Press, 1997.

Hammond, Phillip, and David Machacek. *Soka Gakkai in America: Accommodation and Conversion*. Oxford: Oxford University Press, 1999.

Hardacre, Helen. *Marketing the Menacing Fetus in Japan*. Berkeley: University of California Press, 1997.

Harrison, Elizabeth.Z. "*Mizuko kuyo*: The Re-production of the Dead in Contemporary Japan." In *Religion in Japan: Arrows to Heaven and Earth*, edited by P. F. Kornicki and I. J. McMullen, 250–266. Cambridge: Cambridge University Press, 1996.

———. "Strands of Complexity: The Emergence of *Mizuko Kuyo* in Postwar Japan." *Journal of the American Academy of Religion*, vol. 67, no. 4 (December 1999): 769–796.

———. "Women's Responses to Child Loss in Japan: The Case of Mizuko Kuyo." *Journal of Feminist Studies in Religion*, vol. 11, no. 2 (Fall 1995): 67–94.

Harvey, Greg, *Grieving for Dummies*. Hoboken, NJ: Wiley, 2007.

Harvey, Peter. *An Introduction to Buddhist Ethics*. Cambridge: Cambridge University Press, 2000.

Heine, Steven, and Charles Prebish, eds. *Buddhism in the Modern World: Adaptations of an Ancient Tradition*. Oxford: Oxford University Press, 2003.

Heine, Steven, and Dale S. Wright, eds. *Zen Ritual: Studies of Zen Buddhist Theory in Practice*. Oxford: Oxford University Press, 2008.

Hori, G. Victor Sōgen. "Japanese Zen in America: Americanizing the Face in the Mirror." In *The Faces of Buddhism in America*, edited by Charles S. Prebish and Kenneth K. Tanaka, 49–78. Berkeley: University of California Press, 1998.

Hubbard, Jamie. "Embarrassing Superstition, Doctrine, and the Study of New Religious Movements." *Journal of the American Academy of Religion*, vol. 66, no. 1 (1998): 59–92.

Hunter, James Davison. *Culture Wars: The Struggle to Define America*. New York: Basic Books, 1991.

Ivy, Marilyn. "Modernity." In *Critical Terms for the Study of Buddhism*, edited by Donald S. Lopez Jr., 311–331. Chicago: University of Chicago Press, 2005.

Jolivet, Muriel. *Japan: The Childless Society?* London: Routledge, 1997.

Jones, Rachel K., Mia R. S. Zolna, Stanley K. Henshaw, and Lawrence B. Finer. "Abortion in the United States: Incidence and Access to Services, 2005." *Perspective on Sexual and Reproductive Health*, vol. 40, no. 1 (March 2008): 6–16.

Jourdan, Christine, and Kevin Tuite. *Language, Culture, and Society: Key Topics in Linguistic Anthropology*. Cambridge: Cambridge University Press, 2006.

Joyce, Patrick William. "Experience of Place at the Zen Center of Los Angeles." MA thesis. California State University, Fullerton, 1998.

Kantor, Deborah. *Ritual Healing in Suburban America*. New Brunswick, NJ: Rutgers University Press, 1988.

Keown, Damien, ed. *Buddhist and Abortion*. Honolulu: University of Hawaii Press, 1999.

———. "Comparative Ethics and *Mizuko Kuyo*: A Response to Ronald M. Green."*Journal of the American Academy of Religion*, vol. 69, no. 2 (June 2001): 465–469.

Keown, Damien, et. al., eds. *"Journal of Buddhist Ethics* Conference on Human Rights archive." October 1–14, 1995. Available online at www.buddhistethics.org/confer2. html

Kieschnick, John. *The Impact of Buddhism on Chinese Material Culture.* Princeton, NJ: Princeton University Press, 2003.

King, Richard. *Orientalism and Religion: Postcolonial Theory, India, and 'The Mystic East.'* London: Routledge, 1999.

Klass, Dennis. "Continuing Bonds in the Resolution of Grief in Japan and North America." *American Behavioral Scientist* 44 (2001): 742–763.

Klass, Dennis, and Amy Olwen Heath. "Grief and Abortion: Mizuko Kuyo, the Japanese Ritual Resolution." *Omega: Journal of Death and Dying;* no. 34 (1997): 1–14.

Komatsu Kayoka. "Mizuko Kuyo and New Age Concepts of Reincarnation." *Japanese Journal of Religious Studies* 30, nos. 3–4 (Fall 2003): 259–278.

LaFleur, William R. "Abortion, Ambiguity, and Exorcism." *Journal of the American Academy of Religion,* vol. 67, no. 4 (1999): 797–808.

———. "Buddhism and Abortion: The Way to Memorialize One's Mizuko." In *Religions of Japan in Practice,* edited by George J. Tanabe Jr., 193–198.Princeton, NJ: Princeton University Press, 1999.

———. "Contestation and Confrontation: The Morality of Abortion in Japan." *Philosophy East and West,* vol. 40, no. 4 (October 1990): 529–542.

———. "The Cult of Jizo: Abortion Practices in Japan and What They Can Teach the West." *Tricycle: The Buddhist Review,* vol. 4, no. 3 (Spring 1995): 40–44.

———. *Liquid Life: Abortion and Buddhism in Japan.* Princeton, NJ: Princeton University Press, 1992.

———. "Silences and Censures: Abortion, History, and Buddhism in Japan, A Rejoinder to George Tanabe." *Japanese Journal of Religious Studies,* vol. 22, nos. 1–2 (1995): 185–196.

Landres, J. Shawn. "Symbolic Subject, Subjected Symbol: Mizuko Kuyo, Gender, and the Social Order in Japan." *Journal of Contemporary Religion,* vol. 11, no. 1 (January 1996): 57–68.

Layman, Emma McCloy. *Buddhism in America.* Chicago: Nelson-Hall, 1976.

Layne, Linda. *Motherhood Lost: A Feminist Account of Pregnancy Loss in America.* New York: Routledge, 2003.

Lecso, Phillip A. "A Buddhist View of Abortion." *Journal of Religion and Health,* vol. 26, no. 3 (Fall 1987): 214–218.

Lee, Susan J., Henry J. Peter Ralston, Eleanor A. Drey, John Colin Partridge, and Mark A. Rosen. "Fetal Pain: A Systematic Multidisciplinary Review of the Evidence." *Journal of the American Medical Association,* vol. 294 (24 August 2005): 947–954.

Lock, Margaret M. *Twice Dead: Organ Transplants and the Reinvention of Death.* Vol. 1 of *California Series in Public Anthropology.* Berkeley: University of California Press, 2002.

Lopez, Donald S., Jr., ed. *Critical Terms for the Study of Buddhism.* Chicago: University of Chicago Press, 2005.

———, ed. *Curators of the Buddha: The Study of Buddhism under Colonialism.* Chicago: University of Chicago Press, 1995.

———. *Elaborations on Emptiness: Uses of the Heart Sutra*. Princeton, NJ: Princeton University Press, 1996.

———, ed. *A Modern Buddhist Bible*. Boston: Beacon Press, 2002.

Machacek, David, and Kerry Mitchell. "Immigrant Buddhists in America." In *Global Citizens: The Soka Gakkai Buddhist Movement in the World*, edited by David Machacek and Bryan Wilson, 259–279. Oxford: Oxford University Press, 2001.

Maffly-Kipp, Laurie. "Eastward Ho! American Religion from the Perspective of the Pacific Rim." *Retelling U.S. Religious History*. Edited by Thomas A. Tweed, 127–148. Berkeley: University of California Press, 1997.

Manning, Christel J. "Women in a Divided Church: Liberal and Conservative Catholic Women Negotiate Changing Gender Roles." *Sociology of Religion*, vol. 58, no. 4 (Winter 1997): 375–390.

Maxwell, Carol J. C. *Pro-Life Activists in America: Meaning, Motivation, and Direct Action*. Cambridge: Cambridge University Press, 2002.

McCauley, Robert N., and Thomas E. Lawson. *Bringing Ritual to Mind: Psychological Foundations of Cultural Forms*. Cambridge: Cambridge University Press, 2002.

McCloud, Sean. *Making the American Religious Fringe: Exotics, Subversives, and Journalists, 1955–1993*. Chapel Hill: University of North Carolina Press, 2004.

McDannell, Colleen. *Material Christianity: Religion and Popular Culture in America*. New Haven, CT: Yale University Press, 1995.

Midori, Igeta. "A Response to 'Women's Responses to Child Loss in Japan: The Case of Mizuko Kuyo.'" *Journal of Feminist Studies in Religion*, vol. 11, no. 2 (Fall 1995): 95–100.

Morgan, David, and Sally M. Promey, eds. *The Visual Culture of American Religions*. Berkeley: University of California Press, 2001.

Moskowitz, Eva. *In Therapy We Trust: America's Obsession with Self-Fulfillment*. Baltimore: Johns Hopkins University Press, 2001.

Moskowitz, Marc L. *The Haunting Fetus: Abortion, Sexuality, and the Spirit World in Taiwan*. Honolulu: University of Hawaii Press, 2001.

Mullins, Mark, Susumu Shimazono, and Paul Loren Swanson. *Religion and Society in Modern Japan: Selected Readings*. Nanzan Studies in Asian Religions. Berkeley, CA: Asian Humanities Press, 1993.

Nakamasa, Hirochika. "Jizō no Kataru Hawaii Nikkei Imin no Rekishi." *Minzokugaku*, vol. 4, no. 2 (1980): 98–105.

Nattier, Jan. "Who Is a Buddhist? Charting the Landscape of Buddhist America." In *The Faces of Buddhism in America*, edited by Charles S. Prebish and Kenneth K. Tanaka, 183–195. Berkeley: University of California Press, 1998.

Ng, Zhiru. "The Formation and Development of the Dizang Cult in Medieval China." Ph.D. diss. University of Arizona, 2000.

Numrich, Paul David. *Old Wisdom in the New World: Americanization in Two Immigrant Theravada Buddhist Temples*. Knoxville: University of Tennessee Press, 1996.

———. "Two Buddhisms Further Reconsidered." *Contemporary Buddhism*, vol. 4, no. 1 (2003): 55–78.

Oaks, Laury. "Fetal Spirithood and Fetal Personhood—The Cultural Construction of Abortion in Japan." *Women's Studies International Quarterly*, vol. 17, no. 5 (September–October 1994): 511–523.

Orsi, Robert A. *Between Heaven and Earth: The Religious Worlds People Make and the Scholars Who Study Them.* Princeton, NJ: Princeton University Press, 2005.

———. *Thank You, St. Jude: Women's Devotion to the Patron Saint of Hopeless Causes.* New Haven, NJ: Yale University Press, 1996.

Papalia, Diane E., Sally Wendkos Olds, and Ruth Duskin Feldman. *Human Development.* 9th ed. New York: McGraw-Hill, 2004.

Payne, Richard. "Hiding in Plain Sight: The Invisibility of the Shingon Mission to the United States." In *Buddhist Missionaries in the Era of Globalization,* edited by Linda Learman, 101–122. Honolulu: University of Hawaii Press, 2005.

Perrett, Roy W. "Buddhism, Abortion, and the Middle Way." *Asian Philosophy,* vol. 10 no. 2 (July 2000): 101–114.

Picone, M. "Infanticide, the Spirits of Aborted Fetuses, and the Making of Motherhood in Japan." In *Small Wars: The Cultural Politics of Childhood,* edited by N. Scheper-Hughes and C. Sargent, 37–57. Berkeley: University of California Press, 1998.

Pike, Sarah M. *New Age and Neopagan Religions in America.* New York: Columbia University Press, 2004.

Plutschow, H. E. "The Fear of Evil Spirits in Japanese Culture." *Transactions of the Asiatic Society of Japan,* 3rd ser., vol. 18 (1983): 133–151.

Prebish, Charles S. *Luminous Passage: The Practice and Study of Buddhism in America.* Berkeley: University of California Press, 1999.

———. "Two Buddhisms Reconsidered." *Buddhist Studies Review,* vol. 10, no. 2 (1993): 187–206.

Prebish, Charles S., and Martin Baumann, eds. *Westward Dharma: Buddhism beyond Asia.* Berkeley: University of California Press, 2002.

Prebish, Charles S., and Kenneth K. Tanaka, eds. *The Faces of Buddhism in America.* Berkeley: University of California Press, 1998.

Rappaport, Roy A. *Ecology, Meaning, and Religion.* Richmond, California: North Atlantic Books, 1979.

Reader, Ian. *Religion in Contemporary Japan.* Honolulu: University of Hawaii Press, 1991.

Reader, Ian, and George Tanabe. *Practically Religious: Worldly Benefits and the Common Religion of Japan.* Honolulu: University of Hawaii Press, 1998.

Riggs, Diane. "*Fukudenkai*: Sewing the Buddha's Robe in Contemporary Japanese Buddhist Practice." *Japanese Journal of Religious Studies,* vol. 31, no. 2 (2004): 311–356.

Ruben, Eva R., ed. *The Abortion Controversy: A Documentary History.* Westport, CT: Greenwood, 1994.

Said, Edward. *Orientalism.* New York: Pantheon Books, 1978.

Scharf, Robert H. "Buddhist Modernism and the Rhetoric of Meditative Experience." *Numen,* vol. 42 (1995): 228–281.

———. "Sanbōkyōdan: Zen and the Way of the New Religions." *Japanese Journal of Religious Studies,* vol. 22, nos. 3–4 (1995): 417–458.

———. "The Zen of Japanese Nationalism." *Curators of the Buddha: The Study of Buddhism under Colonialism.* edited by Donald S. Lopez, Jr., 107–160. Chicago: University of Chicago Press, 1995.

Seager, Richard Hughes. *Buddhism in America.* New York: Columbia University Press, 1999.

———. *The World's Parliament of Religions: The East/West Encounter, Chicago, 1893.* Bloomington: Indiana University Press, 1995.

Senauke, Hozan Alan. "A Long and Winding Road: Sōtō Zen Training in America." *Teaching Theology and Religion*, vol. 9, no. 2 (2006): 127–132.

Smith, Bardwell. "Buddhism and Abortion in Contemporary Japan: *Mizuko Kuyo* and the Confrontation with Death." *Japanese Journal of Religious Studies*, vol. 15, no. 1 (1988): 3–24.

———. "Buddhism and Abortion in Contemporary Japan: Mizuko Kuyo and the Confrontation with Death." In *Buddhism, Sexuality, and Gender,* edited by Jose Ignacio Cabezon, 65–90. Albany: State University of New York Press, 1992.

———. "The Social Contexts of Healing: Research on Abortion and Grieving in Japan." In *Innovations in Religious Traditions: Essays on the Interpretation of Religious Change,* edited by Michael A. Williams, Collett Cox, and Martin S. Jaffee, 285–318. Berlin: Mouton de Gruyter, 1992.

Smith, Christian. *American Evangelicalism: Embattled and Thriving.* Chicago: University of Chicago Press, 1998.

Smith, Jonathan Z. *To Take Place: Toward Theory in Ritual.* Chicago: University of Chicago Press, 1987.

Snodgrass, Judith. *Presenting Japanese Buddhism to the West: Orientalism, Occidentalism, and the Columbian Exposition.* Chapel Hill: University of North Carolina Press, 2003.

Steffen, Lloyd, ed. *Abortion: A Reader.* Cleveland, OH: Pilgrim Press, 1994.

Steinhoff, Patricia G. "Reply to William LaFleur's Rejoinder to My Review of Helen Hardacre, *Marketing the Menacing Fetus in Japan.*" *Japanese Journal of Religious Studies*, vol. 25, no 2 (Summer 1999): 496–497.

Straus, Lilo T., et. al. *Abortion Surveillance—United States, 2004.* Atlanta: Centers for Disease Control and Prevention, 2007. Available online at www.cdc.gov/mmwr/preview/mmwrhtml/ss5609a1.htm.

Sullins, D. Paul. "Catholic/Protestant Trends on Abortion: Convergence and Polity." *Journal for the Scientific Study of Religion*, vol. 38, no. 3 (September 1999): 354–369.

Takemi, Momoko. "'Menstruation Sutra' Belief in Japan." *Japanese Journal of Religious Studies*, vol. 10 (June–September 1983): 229–246.

Tanabe, George J., Jr. "Helen Hardacre, *Marketing the Menacing Fetus in Japan.*" *Japanese Journal of Religious Studies*, vol. 25, nos. 3–4 (1998): 377–380.

———. "Sounds and Silences: A Counterresponse." *Japanese Journal of Religious Studies*, vol. 22, nos. 1–2 (1995): 197–200.

———. "William R. LaFleur, *Liquid Life: Abortion and Buddhism in Japan.*" *Japanese Journal of Religious Studies*, vol. 21, no. 4 (1994): 437–440.

Tentler, Leslie. *Catholics and Contraception: An American History.* Ithaca, NY: Cornell University Press, 2004.

Toshio, Kuroda. "The World of Spirit Pacification: Issues of State and Religion." *Japanese Journal of Religious Studies*, vol. 23, nos. 3–4 (1996): 321–351.

Tribe, Laurence H. *Abortion: The Clash of Absolutes.* New York: W. W. Norton, 1992.

Tuan, Yi-Fu. *Space and Place: The Perspective of Experience.* Minneapolis: University of Minnesota Press, 1977.

Turner, Victor. *The Ritual Process: Structure and Anti-Structure*. London: Routledge and Kegan Paul, 1970.

Tweed, Thomas A. *The American Encounter with Buddhism, 1844–1912: Victorian Culture and the Limits of Dissent*. Chapel Hill: University of North Carolina Press, 2000.

———. *Crossing and Dwelling: A Theory of Religion*. Cambridge, MA: Harvard University Press, 2006.

———. "Narrating U.S. Religious History." Introduction to *Retelling U.S. Religious History*, edited by Thomas A. Tweed, 1–26. Berkeley: University of California Press, 1997.

———. "Night-Stand Buddhists and Other Creatures: Sympathizers, Adherents, and the Study of Religion." In *American Buddhism: Methods and Findings in Recent Scholarship*, edited by Duncan Ryuken Williams and Christopher S. Queen, 71–90. Richmond, UK: Curzon, 1999.

———. *Our Lady of the Exile: Diasporic Religion at a Cuban Catholic Shrine in Miami*. Oxford: Oxford University Press, 1997.

Tweed, Thomas A., and Stephen Prothero, eds. *Asian Religions in America: A Documentary History*. Oxford: Oxford University Press, 1999.

Tyson, Ruel, James L. Peacock, and Daniel Patterson. *Diversities of Gifts: Field Studies in Southern Religion*. Urbana: University of Illinois Press, 1988.

Underwood, Meredith. "Strategies of Survival: Women, Abortion, and Popular Religion in Contemporary Japan." *Journal of the American Academy of Religion*, vol. 67, no. 4 (1999): 738–768.

Vryheid, Robert Edward. "An American Buddhist Monastery: Sociocultural Aspects of Soto Zen Training." Ph.D. dissertation. University of Oregon, 1981.

Werblowsky, R. J. Zwi. "Family Planning, Abortion, and the Buddhist Cult of Jizoh." *Asiatic Society of Japan Bulletin*, nos. 1–2 (1995). Available online at http://www.tiu.ac.jp/~bduell/ASJ/12-94_spec_lect_summary.html.

———. "*Mizuko Kuyo*: Notulae on the Most Important 'New Religion' of Japan." *Japanese Journal of Religious Studies*, vol. 18, no. 4 (1991): 295–354.

Whitehouse, Harvey. *Arguments and Icons: Divergent Modes of Religiosity*. Oxford: Oxford University Press, 2000.

———. *Modes of Religiosity: A Cognitive Theory of Religious Transformation*. Walnut Creek, CA: AltaMira Press, 2004.

Williams, Duncan Ryūken. "Asian-American Buddhism Bibliography." Cambridge, MA: Pluralism Project, 2004. Available online at www.pluralism.org/resources/biblio/as-am_buddhism.php.

———. *The Other Side of Zen: A Social History of Soto Zen Buddhism in Tokugawa Japan*. Princeton, NJ: Princeton University Press, 2005.

Williams, Duncan Ryūken, and Christopher S. Queen, eds. *American Buddhism: Methods and Findings in Recent Scholarship*. Richmond, UK: Curzon, 1999.

Wilson, Jeff. "Aesthetics of American Zen: Tradition, Adaptation, and Innovation in the Rochester Zen Center Garden." *Japan Studies Review*, vol. 9 (2005): 101–114.

———. "'There's No Such Thing as Not My Buddhism': Cross-Sectarian Buddhist Hybridity in the American South." Presentation to the Asian North American

Religion, Culture, and Society Group, American Academy of Religion annual meeting, San Antonio, TX, 21 November 2004.

Wuthnow, Robert. *After Heaven: Spirituality in America since the 1950s.* Berkeley: University of California Press, 1998.

———. *The Restructuring of American Religion: Society and Faith since World War II.* Princeton, NJ: Princeton University Press, 1988.

Wuthnow, Robert, and Wendy Cadge. "Buddhists and Buddhism in the United States: The Scope of Influence." *Journal for the Scientific Study of Religion,* vol. 43, no. 3 (September 2004): 363–380.

Yamada, Patricia. "A Friend in Need: The Bodhisattva Jizo." *Japanese Religions,* vol. 16 (1991): 76–92.

———. "The Worship of Jizo." *Kyoto Journal,* vol. 2 (Spring 1987): 22–26.

Yu, Chun-fang. *Kuan-yin: The Chinese Transformation of Avalokitesvara.* New York: Columbia University Press, 2000.

Yuko, Nakano. "Women and Buddhism—Blood Impurity and Motherhood." In *Women and Religion in Japan,* edited by Akiko Okuda and Haruko Okano, translated by Alison Watts. 65–85. Weisbaden, Germany: Harrassowitz Verlag, 1998.

Index

abortion
    in America, 13–17, 68, 214–215
        n.48
    Buddhist attitudes towards,
        46–47, 62, 99
    in Japan, 6–7, 8,10, 11, 12, 13
Aitken, Robert, 59, 60, 68, 212–213
        nn.16–19, 214 n.40
altars, 24–25, 31–32, 35, 36, 41, 44,
        50–51, 73, 81, 84, 92, 186,
        216 n.59
Althouse, Robert, 104
American Civil Liberties Union, 167
American Life League, 166
American Zen Teachers
        Association, 66
Americanization in Buddhism,
        24–25, 50–54, 67, 104–105,
        117–127, 131, 165, 188, 192–195
Amida Buddha, statues of, 35, 40, 44
Avalokiteshvara. *See* Kuan-yin

Bays, Hogen, 65, 84
Bays, Jan Chozen, 70, 74–75
    and connections to other Zen
        priests, 65
    religious background of, 69

as source of water baby
    ceremony information,
    55–56, 62–64, 66, 67, 69,
    70, 73, 75, 139, 226 n.30
as water baby ceremony
    officiant, 57, 61, 82–88, 96
as water baby ceremony
    participant, 61, 74
Berkeley Buddhist Monastery
    (Berkeley, CA), 57, 211
bibs, 3, 7, 83–84, 92, 94, 108, 114,
    118–119, 139, 185. *See also* Jizō,
    offerings to; *mizuko kuyō*,
    offerings in ceremonies of;
    and water baby ceremonies,
    offerings in ceremonies of
Bodhidharma, statues of in Jizō
    garden, 87
bodhisattva movements in convert
    Buddhism, 70–73
Boissevain, Angie, 62, 66
Boucher, Sandy, 72, 73, 74, 75
Buddhism in America
    historiography of, 3, 48, 51, 107,
        131–132, 194–197
    involvement of non-Buddhists
        in, 121, 138–139, 184–185, 187

Buddhism in Canada, 77
Buddhism in Costa Rica, 77
Buddhism in Japan, 6–13, 22, 44
Buddhism in New Zealand, 77
Buddhism in Poland, 77
Buddhist Churches of America, 21
Buddhist magazines, 60, 73, 116, 139
Buddhist Peace Fellowship, 60, 75–76
Buddhist vendors, 25–26, 76
butsudans, 98, 208. See also gohozens

Cadge, Wendy, 115
Cambridge Insight Meditation Center
    (Cambridge, MA), 73, 115
Casa Zen (Santo Domingo de Heredia,
    Costa Rica), 77
Chamberlain, Gary, 165–166, 168, 171
Chicago Zen Center (Evanston, IL), 57,
    63, 65, 77, 119
Chingodō (Tokyo, Japan), 9
Christian Science, 13
Clouds in Water Zen Center (St. Paul,
    MN), 62, 217 n.6
columbaria, 28–29, 43, 121–122, 194,
    209 n.49
culture war, 143–145, 157, 160, 166,
    169–170, 190, 191, 227 n.42

Dainichi Nyorai, statues of, 36, 44
Daishōin (Miyajima, Japan), 10
De Puy, Candace, 138
Dharma Communications, 76
DharmaCrafts, 76
Dharma Rain Zen Center (Portland, OR), 57
Diamond Sangha (Honolulu, HI), 59
Dōgen, statues of, 25
Dovitch, Dana, 138

Earth Island Angels, 173, 231
Elliot Institute, 145
emas. See tablets, votive or wooden
Empty Hand Zen Center (New Rochelle,
    NY), 60, 213 n.24
Enmanin (Ōtsu, Japan), 8
Enmei Juko Kannon Gyō, 86, 96, 212 n.8
Exhale (organization), 138, 173

Floating Zendo (San Jose, CA), 62, 66
Fugen (Samantabhadra), images of, 25

Gateway Pregnancy Centers, 137, 226 n.22
Gennō, Shinshō, 193, 197
Goat-in-the-Road Zendo (Muir Beach,
    CA), 60, 64, 138
gohozens, 208 n.47. See also butsudans
Golden, Arthur, 140
Golden Chain, 33, 52
gomas, 37
Grace Community Church (Panorama
    City, CA), 142
Graef, Sunyana, 61, 62, 77
Great Vow Monastery (Clatskanie, OR),
    17, 57, 74, 79–88, 96, 120–121,
    220 n.42
Green Gulch Farm Zen Center (Muir
    Beach, CA), 57, 60, 61, 82
Grimes, Ronald, 184

halls, worship
    layouts of, 24–25, 31–32, 35, 36,
        40–41, 50–51, 194, 211 n.59
    as location of ceremonies, 7, 33,
        42–43, 91, 118
Hannya Rishu Kyō, 36
Hardacre, Helen, 65, 136, 137
Harper, Sarah, 186, 234 n.47
Harris, Wendy, 140
Harrison, Elizabeth, 136
Hasedera Kannondō (Kamakura,
    Japan), 132, 134, 135
Heart Sutra, The, 26, 36, 44, 66, 86,
    95–96, 108, 212 n.8
Higashi Honganji, 22
Higashi Honganji Buddhist Temple (Los
    Angeles, CA), 34, 39
Hilo Hooganji Mission (Hilo, HI), 209 n.51
Hilo Nichiren Mission (Hilo, HI),
    209 n.49, 209 n.51
hondōs. See halls, worship
Honpa Hongwanji Mission of Hawaii,
    21–22, 52
hōzas, 41–42, 43, 44, 52, 208 n.45
human cloning, 154–156

ihais. *See* plaques, memorial
immigration, 13, 39, 45, 46, 49–50, 51,
   53–54, 104, 109, 131, 211 n.58
infertility, 173, 175
Inoue, Yoko, 140
Insight Meditation. *See* Vipassana

Jizō
   gardens, 56, 61, 62, 74, 84, 117–118,
      120, 121, 184
   mantra, 27, 44, 86, 96, 108,
      206 n.36, 212 n.8
   movement, 70, 71, 73–76, 116, 215 n.51
   and non-Buddhists, 130–131
   offerings to, 28–29, 56, 83–85,
      87, 91, 94, 118–119, 139 (*see also*
      bibs; *mizuko kuyō*, offerings
      in ceremonies of; *and* water
      baby ceremonies, offerings in
      ceremonies of)
   veneration of, 6, 113
Jizō Bosatsu Hongan Kyō (*Sutra of the*
     Bodhisattva Jizō's Vows), 26, 51
Jizōs for Peace, 76
Jōdo Shinshū, 21–22, 23, 34, 45, 49, 50,
   53, 211 n.58
Jōdo Shū, 23, 30, 34, 47, 53
Jodo Shu North America Buddhist
     Mission, 34–35, 44, 45, 46, 50
Johnston, Peg, 151, 229 n.60
jukkai, 92–94, 113, 218 n.21
Jung, Carl, 103

*kaimyō*s, 40, 41, 44, 206 n.29, 217 n.4
Kanai, Shokai, 19, 32, 46, 47, 52, 210 n.54
Kanjo, 32
Kannon. *See* Kuan-yin
Kapleau, Philip, 65, 67, 112
Kasai, Jōshin, 93, 94
Keizan, statues of, 25
Kennedy Institute for Ethics
     (Washington, D.C.), 155
Kiyomizudera (Kyoto, Japan), 224 n.10
Kjolhede, Bodhin, 65, 68
Kjolhede, Sunya, 57, 62, 65
Kluger-Bell, Kim, 138, 184

Kobun, Chino, 66, 213 n.35
Koganji Jizoin (Honolulu, HI),
   207 n.40, 208 n.48
Kohala Koboji Mission (Kapa'au, HI),
   211 n.59
Kojima, Shūmyō
   as *mizuko kuyō* officiant, 23–28,
      51–52, 66
   and understanding of *mizuko kuyō*
      ritual, 25, 26, 28, 47
Koyasan Buddhist Temple (Los Angeles,
     CA), 21, 36–37, 38, 41, 44, 45, 46,
     50, 53, 206 n.30, 206 nn.35–37,
     207 n.38, 209 nn.50–51
Kreeft, Peter, 158–159
Kshitigarbha. *See* Jizō
Kuan-yin
   mizuko, 7, 50, 96
   movement, 70–74, 76, 185,
      215–216 nn.55–56
   veneration of, 26, 96, 113
   statues of, 132
Kubler-Ross, Elizabeth, 137
Kushner, Eve, 137
Kwan Um School of Zen (Cumberland,
     RI), 116

LaFleur, William, 63, 65, 69, 136, 139, 152,
   154, 155, 159–161
Larch Mountain Zen Center (Corbett,
     OR), 61
Larger Pure Land Sutra, 35, 44
Leighton, Taigen Dan, 70
Life after Abortion (Web site), 173
Linn, Dennis, 187, 228 n.48
Linn, Matthew, 187, 228 n.48
Lord Buddha's Children, 33, 52
Los Angeles Nichiren Buddhist Temple
     (Los Angeles, CA)
   mizuko kuyō ceremonies at,
      19, 32–34, 43–44, 45–46, 52,
      209 n.51
   objects of worship at, 43–44
   in relation to other temples, 39,
Lotus Sutra, The, 22, 31, 32–33, 44, 208,
     216 n.56

MacArthur, John, Jr., 142–143, 144–145,
    148, 150, 157, 158, 159
MacLeod, Wendy, 139, 157
Madison Zen Center (Madison, WI), 57
Maezumi, Taizan, 60, 61, 64, 65, 69, 109,
    214 n.41
Maguire, Daniel, 151–153, 157
Manjushri, 70, 71, 81
Mary, Virgin, statues of in Jizō gardens,
    87, 120–121
meditation. See zazen
Miller, Sukie, 178–179, 181, 183–184
Minnesota Zen Center
    (Minneapolis, MN), 116
miscarriage, 32, 42, 45, 59, 61, 62, 83, 98,
    102, 138–139, 172–173, 177, 179,
    182, 185–186
Miyata, Taisen, 37
Mizutani, Shōkō, 39, 47, 52,
    208 nn.42–44
mizuko jizōdōs, 7, 50, 209 n.49
mizuko kuyō
    acculturation, religious, of, 48–52,
        104–105
    Catholics and, 134–136, 137, 138, 145,
        147–148, 150, 158, 165–167, 187
    evangelicals and, 129–130, 137,
        142–145, 148–151, 194
    fees paid for, 7, 11, 12, 45–46, 136,
        143, 217 n.6
    in Japan, 6–13, 204 n.6
    in Japanese-American Buddhist
        temples, 20–54
    Jews and, 168, 171, 185
    Mormons and, 131, 167, 230 n.6
    Neopagans and, 191
    offerings in ceremonies of, 7, 32,
        34–35, 40, 43, 44, 136 (see also
        bibs; Jizō, offerings to; and water
        baby ceremonies, offerings in
        ceremonies of)
    pro-choice appropriations of, 151–154
    pro-life appropriations of, 142–151
    scientific community's
        appropriations of, 154–156
    Unitarian-Universalists and, 131,
        167, 234 n.45

MotheringDotCommune (Web site),
    173, 231
Monju (Manjushri), statues of, 25
mudras, 58, 212 n.12

naijins. See altars
Nakao, Wendy Egyoku, 57, 63, 68,
    100, 101
National Organization for Women, 167
National Public Radio, 136
National Right to Life (organization), 145
nembutsu, 35
Neuhaus, Richard John, 137, 157
New Religions of Japan, 11
New Thought, 13
Nichiren, statues of, 32, 44
Nichiren Shū, 19, 23, 29–30, 31, 32, 34,
    53, 59, 206 nn.29–31
Nichiren Shūshō, 22, 29–30, 31–32, 39,
    53, 59, 206 n.27
Nichiren Shoshu Myohoji Temple of Los
    Angeles, 31, 32, 44, 45, 46, 50
nightstand Buddhists, 132, 139, 156–157
Nishi Honganji, 21
nōkotsudō. See columbaria
North Creek Church (Walnut Creek, CA),
    227 n.41

Okunoin (Kōyasan, Japan), 204 n.6
Okuribi, 37, 207 n.39
Olasky, Marvin, 148, 150
omamori, 54
omikuji, 54
O'Connor, Thomas P., 134–135
O'Neill, Jennifer, 129–130, 132, 135, 138, 157
Operation Rescue, 16
Ordination names, posthumous.
    See kaimyōs
Orenstein, Peggy, 175–176, 185
ōryōki, 66, 113

Packer, Toni, 196
plaques, memorial, 7, 22, 25–26, 44, 46,
    50, 56, 95, 108, 194, 205 n.26,
    206 n.33, 206 n.35
Post Abortion Stress Syndrome (Web
    site), 173

post-Buddhism, 196–197
post-pregnancy loss manuals, 138, 173,
    180, 182, 183–184, 231 n.14
    post-abortion manuals, 129–131,
        138, 173
    post-miscarriage manuals, 138, 173,
        233 n.33
post-abortion syndrome, 145–149, 151,
Postal, Susan Jion, 60
Pro-Choice Connection, 153, 173
Project Rachel, 228 n.51
psychotherapy in American Zen thought,
    102–104
Purple Cloud Temple (Shiun-zan Jizō-ji,
    Chichibu, Japan), 165–166

Raboteau, Emily, 140
Rachel's Vineyard (organization), 17
Ragir, Judith, 62
rakusus, 92–94
Rand, Yvonne
    as source of water baby ceremony
        information, 61, 63, 73, 82
    as water baby ceremony officiant, 57,
        58–60, 61, 62, 64, 68, 74, 89,
        211 n.6, 213 n.23
Ray-Hamaie, Rachel, 141
Reardon, David, 145, 148, 157, 228 n.50
Reconstructionist Zen, 114, 222 n.15
Reese, Ruth, 141
Reiyūkai, 208 n.45
Ringu (film), 210 n.53
Rinzai Zen, 57, 60, 61
Risshō Kōsei-kai, 25, 38–39, 41, 53, 109
Rissho Kosei-kai Buddhist Church of
    Los Angeles (Los Angeles, CA),
        39–42, 43, 44, 45, 46, 52, 54,
        108–109, 208 n.44
Ritual, 201 n.3
    Zen and, 110–117
Rochester Zen Center (Rochester, NY)
    history of other ceremonies at, 111
    Jizō-based children's celebration at, 74
    as training center, 61, 63, 65, 116,
    and water baby ceremonies, 3, 17, 57,
        62, 63, 65, 68, 76, 97, 118, 119, 124,
        220 n.42

Roe v. Wade, 14, 15, 17, 137, 142, 148
Rose, Jikyu, 207 n.40, 208.48, 210 n.50
Ross, Sevan, 57, 63, 77

San Francisco Zen Center (San Francisco,
    CA), 60, 93, 116, 223 n.18
Sanbōkyōdan, 57, 61
Sanbujō, 35
Sanjūsangendō (Kyoto, Japan), 224 n.10
Sankiraimon (Three Refuges Prayer), 26
Santa Cruz Zen Center (CA), 64
Segaki, 113, 222
sexual behavior, religious judgment of,
    11–12, 14, 98, 203 n.21
Shakyamuni Buddha (Shaka Nyorai),
    statues of, 25, 32, 40, 43, 195. See
    also Siddhartha Gautama
Shambhala International (Vajradhatu), 116
Shasta Abbey Buddhist Monastery
    (Mount Shasta, California), 66
Shin Buddhism. See Jōdo Shinshū
Shin Isseis, 45, 49–50, 54, 208 n.41
Shingon Shū, 23, 30, 35–36, 53, 59, 204 n.6
Shiseige, 35
Siddhartha Gautama, 70. See also
    Shakyamuni Buddha
Smith, Bardwell, 136
Sobutsuge, 35
Sōjiji (Tsurumi, Japan), 66
Sōka Gakkai, 21, 30, 31, 34, 39, 53, 110,
    206 n.31
Sōtō Shū (Sōtō Zen), 23, 25, 53, 57, 61, 68,
    70, 98, 110
Sōtōkuji (Kyoto, Japan), 11
Southern Tier Women's Services clinic
    (Binghamton, New York), 151
spirit attacks. See tatari
stem cells, 155–156
Stuart, Maureen, 60
Sutra of Innumerable Meanings, The
    (Muryōgi Kyō), 208 n.44
Sutra of Meditation on the Bodhisattva
    Samantabhadra, The (Kanfugen
    Kyō), 208 n.44
Sutra of the Past Vows of Earth Store
    Bodhisattva, The, 6
Suzuki Daisetsu (D.T. Suzuki), 112

Suzuki, Shunryū, 58, 64, 70, 109
Swanson, Gloria, 163–165

tablets, votive or wooden, 7, 10, 22, 32, 35, 36, 37, 44, 54, 92, 95, 194. See also *tōba*
Tanaka, Kōdō, 34, 47, 210 n.53
Tassajara Zen Center (Carmel Valley, CA), 58
tatari, 8, 10, 47–48, 65, 96–97, 146, 188, 210 nn.52–53
Tendai Shū, 207 n.40
Tenrikyō, 70
tikkun, 155, 158, 171
Thanas, Katherine, 64
Theravada, 72, 73, 115
Tibetan Buddhism, 73
tōba, 31, 46, 50, 95, 205 n.26, 206 n.33, 206 n.35. See also tablets, votive or wooden
Toronto Zen Center (Toronto, ON), 77
Trejner, Stamen, 77
Tworkov, Helen, 139

Vermont Zen Center (Shelburne, VT), 61, 62, 65, 68, 77
Vipassana, 72–73

water baby ceremonies
    donations for, 88–89, 217 n.6
    earliest instances of, 59–60
    offerings in ceremonies of, 83–85, 87, 91, 118–119 (see also bibs; Jizō, offerings to; and *mizuko kuyō*, offerings in ceremonies of)
    prayer in, 91
    use of term, 58
Wilke, Barbara, 145
Wilke, John, 145, 147

Windhorse Zen Center (Asheville, NC), 57
Wolf, Naomi, 171, 172
Won Buddhism of Los Angeles (Los Angeles, CA), 51
Wrightson, Amala, 57, 62, 77, 213 n.34

Yamada, Kōun, 59, 214 n.40
Yokoji Zen Mountain Center (Mountain Center, CA), 212
Yokota, Myojo, 209 n.8

zazen, 25, 67, 90, 111–113, 207 n.40, 222 n.12
Zen Center of Los Angeles (Los Angeles, CA)
    in relation to other temples, 30, 60, 68, 116
    and water baby ceremonies, 17, 57, 63, 69, 101, 220 n.46
Zen Community of Oak Park (Oak Park, IL), 57, 104, 121
Zen Community of Oregon (Clatskanie, OR), 61
Zen Mountain Center (Mountain Center, CA), 57
Zen Mountain Monastery (Mt. Tremper, NY), 57
zendōs, 118, 125
Zenshuji Soto Mission (Los Angeles, CA)
    as compared to other temples, 31, 32, 34, 36, 41, 50, 68, 108, 122
    Jizō statues at, 205 n.20
    and *mizuko kuyō* ceremonies, 17, 23–30, 44, 45, 51, 66, 108
    object of worship at, 43
Zenworks, 75, 76
Zimmerman, Anthony, 147–148, 166, 224 n.13
Zōjōji (Tokyo, Japan), 92, 132, 133, 186